NewVegetarian Classics:
Soups

by
Mary F. Taylor

photographs by Diane Farris

The Crossing Press, Freedom, CA 95019

*To my mother, Carol Taylor, for her silent wisdom
and my father, Frank Taylor, for his love of the classics.*

Copyright © 1994 by Mary F. Taylor
Cover design by Amy Sibiga
Cover and interior photographs by Diane Farris
Text design by Sheryl Karas
Printed in Singapore

Library of Congress Cataloging-in-Publication Data

Taylor, Mary F.
    New vegetarian classics : soups / by Mary F. Taylor ; photographs
by Diane Farris.
        p. cm.
    Includes index.
    ISBN 0-89594-649-1.-- ISBN 0-89594-648-3 (pbk.)
    1.Soups. 2. Vegetarian cookery. I. Title.
TX757.T39 1994
641.8'13--dc20
                                                93-41697
                                                CIP

Acknowledgments

When cooking, it is the quality of the ingredients, as much as (if not more so than) the skill of the cook, that determines the outcome of a dish. So it was for me when writing this cookbook.

Without the support, enthusiasm and encouragement of many, I would never have been able to complete this task. First, I must thank Dennis Hayes for seeing what I was proposing to create in this book, and Elaine Gill for taking a chance with it. Also, I thank Karen Narita for her patience and tireless work in editing the manuscript, as well as other staff members at The Crossing Press for their help in bringing the book to this final form.

In addition, many friends and my family have helped tremendously by testing recipes, giving input on text, and keeping my spirits up during the writing process. To name just a few, many thanks to my parents, Carol and Frank Taylor, for everything; Anne and Richard Haimes for believing in the project; Barbara Bowerman for her critical eye; Alicia Rudnicki; Kimmer Macarus; Peter Mattisson, Jia Gottlieb and Eileen Martin; Heather Roberts; my assistant Desiree Sanchez; Doris Houghland and the staff of the Peppercorn for their generous use of props; and, of course, my friend and collaborator, Diane Farris, for her humor and exquisite photographs.

Finally I must thank my husband, Richard Freeman, and our son, Gabriel, for tasting more soups than many are called upon to taste in a lifetime, and for their generous gift of time as I spent endless hours working on the book.

Table of Contents

Introduction

It's soothing, restorative, and generally inexpensive to make. Served with crusty bread and salad, a steaming bowl of soup makes a revitalizing meal at the end of a tiring day, as easily as it can provide the start to an elaborate dinner. Once a staple at every meal including breakfast, as it still is throughout the Orient, soup has become more of a curiosity to the American table than standard fare. Perhaps this change is due in part to the fact that our ancestors ate so much soup, especially when finances were tight. By the time of the Renaissance in Europe, simple country fare, with a slow boiling cauldron for a trademark, was regarded with some disdain as a sign of poverty. Eventually, the traditional soup pot simmering on the back of the stove vanished from the average Western kitchen to be replaced by cabinets housing instant bouillon cubes, freeze dried powders and microwavable ramen.

In this age of convenience, when schedules are rushed, lack of time rather than status has kept the flame beneath the soup pot extinguished. What stand-up fast-food fanatic has time to sip spoon after spoonful of soup before rushing back to the office? For the cook, emerging from an age when canned and condensed soups were the order of the day, the image of slaving over a hot stove as the soup simmers holds little appeal. But times change and, as with any living art, our culinary tradition continues to evolve. Today, cooking is coming back into vogue and our eating style is eclectic. Creativity is at the core and there's fresh focus on economy, convenience and—above all—health.

Nothing could be more perfectly matched to these times than soup. Vegetarian soups are a particularly intriguing avenue to explore because the ingredients lend themselves to simple, fresh, healthy preparations. In addition, soups that are truly vegetarian—made without meat, poultry or fish stock—are uncommon in most classic cuisines so the creative possibilities are practically boundless.

I found the challenge irresistible and ten years ago began working on the recipes included in this book. At that time, I recognized that my taste preference and natural eating style were vegetarian. As a child I was not fond of meat, but I grew up as many Americans do, having no frame of reference for a diet that is not centered around meat. As my passion for working with food took shape, I pursued my interests by studying cooking in Paris. This gave me invaluable exposure to cooking as an art, but little first-hand experience with vegetarian cooking, for in classic French cuisine, even vegetable soups and side dishes are often made with meat-based stocks. Nonetheless, my preference for vegetarian foods persisted.

Eventually, I turned my full attention to vegetarian cooking with particular interest in how diet affects health. Despite years of culinary experience, I felt like a beginner as I encountered many unfamiliar ingredients and faced the baffling question of how to make recipes work without classic stocks and unlimited use of cream and butter. Soups were especially perplexing. How could one possibly prepare onion soup without a rich meat base or a vichyssoise without the velvety addition of cream? To develop healthy recipes for vegetarian soups, I studied classic soups more closely and analyzed what made them successful. Then I used these familiar models as springboards for my imagination in creating vegetarian soups.

It's important when extrapolating from the familiar in this way to keep an open mind, a lesson I learned while driving along the coast of Maine one afternoon. I was pondering vegetarian counterparts to some of the world's well known meat-based soups, when I came upon a tiny bait shop displaying a crudely painted sign which read "Newts worms creepers crawlers." I thought at once of the witches' brew found in Macbeth, perhaps one of the most famous soups on record. Even though the toil and trouble involved in maintaining a cauldron packed with newt's eyes, blind worm's sting and frog's toes were utterly out of the question, especially for a vegetarian, I couldn't pass up the opportunity to see what a newt actually looked like. Once inside, however, the tanks of murky water, crowded with squirming creatures, all looked alike to my uneducated eye. Eventually a gentle, elderly woman emerged from the back room and asked if she could help. When I told her I was looking for the newts she said, "Well, I'm Mrs. Newt and Mr. Newt's out back. What do you need?"

I relate this encounter to illustrate that when the mind is made up that something *is* a certain way, mistakes in thinking can easily occur. The power that this sort of preconception can have in regard to something relatively inconsequential, like vegetarian cooking, is remarkable. As a student and teacher I've seen that we often fall prey to conventional ideas about vegetarianism that stem from growing up in a traditionally non-vegetarian culture. For example, it's easy to be misled as to the nature of vegetarian soups. If we see them as chicken soup without the chicken, they are destined to pale in comparison. Problems will also arise if we conclude that, because vegetarian soups are often easy to make, they can be tossed together arbitrarily. There is some truth to the folk tale that, given water, a stone and whatever the community has to offer, you *will* have something to call soup, but a successful soup is well conceived from the start. By recognizing, and then focusing on the inherent quality of vegetarian ingredients, and by using classic cooking techniques it is possible to achieve a balance of tastes, textures and aromas that result in spectacular vegetarian soups.

In this soup volume of *New Vegetarian Classics* I offer you what I've learned about applying the fundamentals of classic cuisine to healthy vegetarian cooking. Concerning health, I believe it's necessary to concentrate first on integrating a healthy approach to food, cooking and eating into your daily routine. By this I mean savoring food, enjoying meals and taking time to select and prepare foods that are both nourishing and nurturing. The next step is to reduce consumption of fat and cholesterol, as well as refined and processed foods. While my recipes contain no meat, fish or fowl, some use dairy products which are the main source of fat and the only source of cholesterol in the recipes. Non-dairy alternatives are offered whenever possible.

I included a wide range of recipes that are quick and easy to prepare once you understand the basic procedures and principles of soup making. Each recipe lists preparation (prep) and cooking times as guidelines for your cooking practice. These may change given the circumstance. (Two years ago, when my son was born, I abruptly learned this shift in perspective as my kitchen prep time became a flexible part rather than a defined part of my schedule, and what had previously taken me twenty minutes to prepare, might now stretch out over the course of two days.) Finally, *New Vegetarian Classics: Soups* contains sections on ingredients, equipment and cooking techniques and special dietary needs.

I hope you find the recipes inviting to both your palate and your sense of innovation and that the book may trigger the creative cook in you, as I share with you the practicalities, passions and insights that are part of this vegetarian cook's tools.

À Votre Santé!

Mary Taylor

1 • The Soup Kitchen

Equipment

Why talk about equipment when you are just making soup? After all, what more do you need than a big pot, a knife, a cutting board and an able set of hands? Granted, not much, but cooking like any craft is simplified and is therefore more enjoyable (even when you're just making a straightforward broth), in a comfortable environment and when you have the right tools. So, take a look at your kitchen layout, organization and lighting to see that they are in order—counter tops a comfortable height, utensils within reach when you need them, and so on. Also consider what equipment will make it easier for you to prepare dishes you enjoy. Here are a few tips that may help in selecting the basic tools for making soup.

Knives. First and foremost you should consider investing in three or four high quality knives. I recommend having one or two all-purpose large knives for cutting, dicing, slicing and so forth. A 10- to 12-inch French Chef's knife and/or a 6- to 8-inch lightweight Japanese cleaver should serve you well. (Knife length is measured by the length of the blade, not including the handle.) In addition, you need a small 3- to 4-inch, straight-edged paring knife for peeling, paring, carving, and other fine work. Finally, an 8- to 10-inch wavy-edged bread knife is invaluable for cutting citrus, tomatoes and, of course, bread. There are many other types and sizes of knives available, but as a basic set, these should be adequate.

Look for knives of overall high quality construction with blades that are easy to sharpen. The best have durable handles, usually made of high quality wood or wood mixed with plastic. Whatever material is used, the knife handle should be extremely comfortable to your grip—not too big, not too small. (Knife handles with finger grips molded into them are unlikely to fit your hand.) The knife should feel balanced. This means that when you hold it in a loose grip and relax your wrist, the tip of the blade should not fall down and hit the counter, nor should the handle feel too heavy for the blade. Also, the tail of the knife (the continuation of the steel from the end of the blade) should run the entire length of the handle. This contributes to good balance in a knife, is an indication of overall quality, and guards against the handle detaching from the blade. Knives with full tails either have a visible band of steel all the way around the upper and lower perimeter of the handle, or you will see a dot of steel at the rounded end of the handle.

Of utmost importance when selecting a knife are the quality and type of steel used in the blade. Carbon steel is relatively soft; the blade takes a sharp edge and keeps it well, but it stains and discolors very easily. If it is not carefully washed and dried as the knife is in use, the blade will stain and may corrode over time. In fact, in some coastal areas carbon steel knives may actually pit and rust from the climate alone. Stainless steel, on the other hand, is hard and, as the name implies, does not discolor or stain easily. Though it always looks good, it is often difficult, if not impossible, to sharpen. The best choice in a blade, therefore, is a mix. Look for knives with high-carbon, stainless steel blades, giving you a sharper edge than plain stainless steel, on a blade that will not pit or rust.

Knives should be stored in a knife block or on a knife magnet, out of reach of children, but located convenient to the cutting area. Those stored in a drawer are likely to become dulled, bent or chipped from being knocked about. Knives should never be put in the dishwasher. Repeated exposure to high temperatures can disturb the molecular makeup of a blade, making it impossible to sharpen. In addition it is likely that the handle will eventually crack or break.

Knife Sharpener. Inseparable from a fine set of knives is a knife sharpener. No matter how good your knives, if you allow them to dull—as all knives do with use—cooking will lose its charm. The surface of a sharpening steel (or stone) must be harder than that of the knife, so that as the knife is drawn across the steel, the molecules along the edge of the blade of the knife will be re-aligned into a sharp formation. A hard steel, medium grained, 14-inch sharpening steel with a protected handle is a good, all purpose choice. If you prefer to use a stone, be sure that your knives are soft enough to respond to the stone's surface.

Whether you prefer a stone or a steel, the angle of the blade on the sharpener (20 degrees) is the most critical factor. Knife sharpening takes practice—getting to know your own knives and your sharpener. To sharpen a knife with a steel, begin by holding the knife as if you were going to cut something with it. Then, turn the knife point up and hold it in front of you so the side of the blade is facing you at about eye level and the cutting edge is at a 45 degree angle to the counter. Hold the steel in the opposite hand, even with the knife, tips touching. It helps to hold your elbows 8 to 10 inches from your sides. Move the tip of the steel so that it is touching the back side of the blade, just above the handle. Hold the knife with the sharp edge of the blade at a twenty degree angle to the steel. At this point, the sharp edge should be facing the sharpener's handle. Draw the cutting edge of the blade down to the bottom of the steel, so that the tip of the knife just falls off the steel. Use the same action to move the other side of the blade over the back side of the steel. The action is facilitated by keeping both arms still except the wrist of the hand holding the knife. Repeat this as many times as necessary to achieve a sharp edge. Always work gently. Pressing the blade too hard or at the wrong angle against the sharpening surface will not sharpen the edge and may possibly damage the knife. It is a good habit to sharpen your knives every time you cook.

Cutting Board. Finally, as a companion to good knives, you need a cutting board—one which minimizes dulling and provides a comfortable work space. I recommend a board that is no smaller than 12 by 18 inches, preferably larger. Allow yourself enough space on the board to cut up four or five onions, without feeling cramped. Wooden boards tend to dull knives less quickly than plastic boards, and bacteria does not grow as readily on wooden surfaces. The best wooden cutting boards are made of laminated hard wood such as maple, preferably the end grain. Whether you choose plastic or wood, all cutting boards should be thoroughly cleaned at least once a week. To do so, scrape off all food with a sturdy dough scraper or pancake turner, then rub the board with lemon juice and salt to remove stains. Rinse with water and dry immediately. Never wash wooden boards with soap. This will weaken the wood fibers. For very tough stains you may wash boards with a bleach solution (1 tablespoon of bleach to 1 quart of water), but be sure to clean the board extremely well after bleaching. Never soak a cutting board and never put it in the dishwasher.

Pots and Pans. Pots and pans are the obvious next concern. Choose those with heavy, flat (non-ribbed) bottoms. This will help prevent burning. They are best made of a material that conducts heat well. Copper and aluminum are excellent conductors, but they react with some foods, discoloring them. In addition, metal may be leached into the food, so unless they are lined with another material (usually stainless steel or tin), they should be avoided. An excellent all-purpose cookware is heavy gauged anodized aluminum with an interior stainless steel coating. For a less expensive alternative, enameled cast iron or double-layered, copper-lined stainless steel is good for most purposes.

Five or six basic pots and pans should be ample. You will need a large stock pot or Dutch oven for making stocks, cooking beans and making large quantities of soup. The volume of your largest pot will depend on whether you normally cook for two or ten, but a 4-quart capacity is minimum. All pots should have a lid that fits well enough to prevent steam from escaping. Though it is not essential, a pressure cooker is invaluable for preparing beans and accomplishing many other cooking tasks quickly. If you get one, a 6-quart capacity with a quick release valve is advisable. You will also need some smaller pots for cooking garnishes, sautéing small amounts of foods, and so forth. A 1-quart and a 3-quart heavy-bottomed sauce pan, and a 10- to 12-inch non-stick sauté or frying pan should do. In addition you will need a stainless steel steamer rack (collapsible) for preparing garnishes and a 12- to 14-inch wok for quick frying and simple soups.

Note: Many soups may be prepared in a pressure cooker in far less time than that listed in the recipes that follow—precise timing differences are varied, depending on the ingredients, but most can be ready in 10 to 20 minutes of cooking time. As a general rule, 1 to 3 cups less liquid are required and the texture is usually more homogeneous. In addition, certain flavors do not seem to develop as fully when cooked for a shorter period under steam. Though I endorse pressure cookers as convenient and usually effective, I do not elaborate on using them in the recipes that follow because they are less commonly found in many kitchens than traditional soup pots. For an excellent resource on using pressure cookers, I recommend *Cooking Under Pressure* by Lorna Sass.

Food Processor, Blender. A food processor, blender, and/or hand-held blender are the last essential pieces of soup-making equipment. If you get only one, I suggest a processor because it is so much more versatile than the others. Larger volumes of soup may be puréed in a processor in addition to the fact that it can be used for chopping, grating and slicing foods. (Hand-held blenders, however, have the advantage that you can purée foods in their cooking pot, eliminating some cleanup). When buying a processor, I recommend an 8-cup bowl unless you always cook for a crowd. A larger capacity bowl will not always work when chopping or beating small quantities. For smaller jobs and for certain ingredients such as nut milks, however, a blender is preferable to a processor. I recommend blenders with glass jars and as few control buttons as possible.

The following list is for additional equipment that will simplify your task as soup maker. Depending on how often you cook, what other foods you enjoy preparing and what your budget is, you may slowly build to this extent or expand far beyond it. Unless a piece of equipment requires special care or handling, I will not elaborate on that here.

Bowls. Assorted sizes of stainless steel and/or hard plastic mixing bowls in addition to several small bowls for pre-measuring ingredients as you cook. Serving bowls for soup should include various shapes, colors and sizes.

Citrus Juicer. A hand-held lemon juicer—a tear-drop shaped top on a handle—is available in wood or plastic. It works extremely well for juicing lemons and limes and small oranges. Alternatively, a plastic or glass counter top juicer that is made to fit all sizes of citrus is good.

Cooking Spoons. Assorted beech or boxwood spoons in various shapes and lengths. At least one flat-faced (rounded or squared end) spoon for scraping the bottom edge of a soup pot, and one "spaghetti" fork or plain wooden fork for removing pasta from cooking water. You may also find one or more stainless steel cooking spoons handy in addition to a stainless steel skimmer spoon for skimming foam from stocks and removing ingredients from soups as they cook.

Cutters. A set of tiny aspic cutters and cookie cutters in an assortment of shapes and sizes for cutting bread and other garnishes.

Dough Scraper. A rectangular stainless steel, sturdy-bladed dough scraper for clearing the work space, moving piles of prepared ingredients, and cleaning the cutting board.

Food Mill. A 9-inch (diameter at top) tinned or stainless steel food mill with three removable grinding plates. Not essential, but extremely useful for purée-ing soups containing ingredients with skins, seeds, or stringy membrane. The mill allows you to purée soup to an even consistency while removing unwanted texture. Clean plates with a sturdy scrubbing brush.

Garlic Press. Heavy gauged aluminum or stainless steel press. The best have small holes and are either designed to be self cleaning or are accompanied by a plastic-pronged cleaner.

Grater. An eight-sided stainless steel stand-up grater and/or a hand crank Mouli grater with replaceable grating disks.

Kitchen Apron and Towels. A store of at least 3 cotton aprons and 6 cotton kitchen towels is essential. Wearing one towel looped around your apron waist tie and having the towels hanging at various convenient points around the kitchen save time and promote neatness when cooking. The towels are also indispensable when drying vegetables, peeling nuts and so on.

Ladles. Ladles for serving and cooking in assorted sizes; one with a spout is particularly handy.

Measuring Equipment. One set of measuring spoons, pyrex liquid measuring cups in 1, 2 and 4 cup increments, and a set of stainless steel dry measuring cups. A reliable kitchen scale is very useful for measuring stock ingredients and large volumes of vegetables.

Pastry Brushes. A brush with 1-inch wide natural bristles and a wooden handle. Used for brushing melted butter or glazes. Wash by hand, rubbing bristles vigorously against the palm of your hand in hot, soapy water. Rinse well and dry thoroughly before storing.

Pepper and Nutmeg Mills. Both types of mills are critical to obtaining the optimal freshness in taste. A pepper mill should have adjustable coarseness for the grind, and both should have a stainless steel mechanism.

Rubber Spatula. Several sturdy, flexible rubber-bladed spatulas on wooden or plastic handles. For scraping clean bowls or pots and pans and for rubbing puréed food through a strainer. Do not use for cooking, the rubber blade can melt and warp.

Salad Spinner. A full-sized spinner. The best is a plastic bucket with a basket that fits inside and a top which is also the spinning handle. Leaf vegetables and fresh herbs may be rinsed in the bucket, drained, then spun.

Storage Containers. Glass and/or plastic storage containers in assorted sizes—from 1 cup to 3 quarts—all with tight-fitting lids. Used for freezing, refrigerating and storing crisped toppings at room temperature.

Strainers. One 12-inch, medium mesh wire strainer for straining stocks and quickly cooling cooked vegetables. One 8-inch fine mesh strainer for straining unwanted texture out of soups and one tea strainer for straining small amounts of liquid. Do not wash strainers in a dishwasher—clean the mesh with a semi-flexible cleaning brush.

Swivel-Edged Vegetable Peeler. A stainless steel rotating blade on a sturdy metal handle. The swivel action provides best control for peeling and garnishes.

Tea Kettle. An all-purpose tea kettle for adding water to soups as they cook.

Whisks. Two sauce whisks (not ballooned in shape) with tinned or stainless steel wires, one measuring 6 and the other 10 inches. Used for achieving smooth consistency in soups.

Ingredients

Using the right ingredients, those that are well selected, perfectly ripe and properly handled, is the key to good vegetarian soups. When each ingredient is prepared with care and understanding, so that its individual character is honored and balanced with others found in the soup, the taste will be right and the overall effect of the soup will be nurturing and nourishing. This may sound simple enough, until you run into recipes that call for ingredients such as miso, arame or soba. ("What does ripe arame look like?" you may wonder.) Even if you *are* familiar with all ingredients called for, you must know how to prepare them. A vichyssoise, for instance, made from improperly cleaned leeks would be disastrous. It takes time and experience to understand ingredients; to know how to choose and prepare them and to have a sense of the variety of tastes, aromas and textures an ingredient may contribute to a soup. In an attempt to expedite that process, below I offer general observations about common ingredients that are frequently used when preparing soups. For identifying information and cooking tips about less common ingredients used in the recipes that follow, refer to the Glossary of Ingredients (page 167).

Guidelines for Selecting Fruits and Vegetables

Fruits and vegetables should be plump and appropriately firm. A ripe plum, for instance, will feel like the ball of your thumb, whereas a good tomato feels more like the center of the pad on the heel of your foot. Every piece of produce is as unique in feel, as it is in taste, smell and other indicators of quality. Produce that is bruised, moldy, unpleasant-smelling, wilted or overly soft should be avoided. There are, of course, exceptions. For instance, a ripe persimmon is very soft and almost squishy. Slightly hard bananas with green tips bake well, but those that have even, brown spotting are better for raw purées. Ultimately, you must know your ingredients. Each time you use a particular kind of produce, pay close attention to what it looks, feels, smells and tastes like, and observe how the ingredient responds when cooked. In the recipes that follow, unless otherwise specified, all fruits and vegetables should be peeled.

Fruits

There are so many kinds and varieties of fruit that it is best to take time to get to know them individually. A general rule of thumb for storage, though, is to keep most at room temperature in a well-ventilated, non-sunny spot, until they are ripe (a basket or shallow bowl is best). You must keep a careful eye out for spoilage—one rotten apple (or anything else) will affect the bunch. Turn and rotate fruit regularly when stored at room temperature. This will prevent them from developing bruises due to their weight alone. Some fruit, like apples and grapes, are usually picked ripe, while others, pears and bananas for instance, are usually picked green and allowed to ripen. Those that are picked green will not ripen properly if refrigerated before they are ripe. Once ripe, however, most fruit may be refrigerated in a fruit or vegetable drawer, away from humidity, to retard spoilage. Bananas, of course, should never be refrigerated (though ripe bananas are fabulous if peeled and frozen in an airtight container, for use in a puréed soup, or sliced as a topping). Grapes, cherries and other soft-ripening fruit (strawberries, peaches, plums, etc.) last much longer—once they are ripe—if refrigerated. Citrus holds well in humid climates at room temperature, unless it is very hot, in which case it may spoil quickly. In very dry climates, however, citrus skins tend to harden and the fruit itself may dry out very quickly. So, when room permits, it is best to keep citrus refrigerated. It is always best to use all fruit at its peak of freshness.

When cooking, we often think of fruit in terms of the sweetness it may add. In soup making, fruit must also be considered for its thickening quality, such as the texture of bananas in a purée, or the viscous quality contributed by apples (due to a high pectin content) in a chilled broth. In addition, all fruits add some acid to a recipe. Usually this is not a problem, but in soups that contain milk, cream or other dairy products, fruit, especially citrus, may cause curdling. In the recipes that follow, the fruit that is called for should always be peeled unless otherwise specified in a recipe. When raw, most white-fleshed fruit discolors quickly. To minimize this, once it is cut up always add it immediately to whatever liquid it is to be cooked with. If the fruit is to be used as a garnish, covering it with water that has lemon juice added to it (acidulated water) will retard discoloring.

Dried Fruit. When using dried fruit, I strongly urge you to buy that which is organic whenever possible. 1/4 cup of raisins equals about 75 grapes. Imagine eating that many pieces of fresh fruit that have been heavily treated with pesticides (as many grapes have). In addition, sulfur is an additive that may be used on dried fruit to preserve color and texture. It causes severe reactions in some people, and for that reason I also recommend avoiding dried fruit which has been treated with it. Store dried fruit at room temperature in an airtight container. If they become very dry and hard, they may be plumped by soaking in fruit juice, water or liquor until soft.

Vegetables

The variety of vegetables available in most markets these days, like fruit, is vast. And, like fruit, when learning to select vegetables, it is best to take time to explore and get to know them individually. In terms of storage, onions, shallots, garlic, potatoes and gourds are best stored in a wire basket—optimally in a cool, dark place—with plenty of room to breathe. Tomatoes and avocados (which I consider vegetables in this text), should be stored at room temperature much like fruit. Most other vegetables maintain optimal freshness if refrigerated in a loosely folded plastic bag. If a bag is tied or twisted shut, or a vegetable is stored in an airtight container, humidity will accumulate inside the closed environment, promoting spoilage.

Most vegetables survive if they are peeled and cut up to 24 hours before proceeding with a recipe. Prepped carrots, potatoes, turnips, parsnips and other hard-root vegetables are best refrigerated in water. Most other vegetables remain relatively fresh when refrigerated in an airtight container. Porous vegetables, in particular mushrooms and summer squash, are best cut up just before use, and must be very dry—not moist from storage or washing—before being prepped (see "Mushrooms" on page 12). Greens, lettuce and fresh herbs hold well if washed and dried thoroughly in a salad spinner, then refrigerated in a loosely folded plastic bag which contains a clean cloth or paper towel in the bottom to absorb moisture. All vegetables begin to deteriorate and loose nutrients as soon as they are harvested. This process is accelerated if they are cut (as more surface area is exposed to air) and when stored in water, nutrients are leached into the water. Nonetheless, advanced preparation may be a necessary step if your schedule is full. In the recipes that follow, all vegetables are peeled unless otherwise specified. These general rules apply to most vegetables.

Greens. Spinach, kale, chard and other greens are instrumental to recipes throughout this book. They may usually be used interchangeably, but expect quite different effects in taste and cooking time. When choosing fresh greens, select those that are a vibrant color, with no yellowing or dryness at the tips of the leaves. The leaves should be plump and firm, as if they were still attached to a well watered plant. Cleaning greens is the trick to enjoying them. Hold the stem of the leaf in one hand. With your other hand, fold the leaf in half so that the back side, with the stem running along it, is exposed. Place the length of your thumb on one side of the leaf just at the rib of the stem, and your fingertips along the other side of the leaf, at the rib. Keep a tight grip as you pull the stem off, from the base of the leaf to the tip. Stems may be used in some dishes and stocks, but when a measured amount of greens is called for in the recipes that follow, the measurement should not contain stems. Place the leaves in the bucket of a salad spinner or a large bowl and cover them with cold water. Rinse well, then lift the leaves from the water into the spinner's basket or a strainer. Repeat this step until the water is completely clean. Do not pour the rinsing water and greens into the strainer, because dirt that rinses off the leaves and sinks to the bottom of the bucket or bowl will then be poured back over the leaves. Dry the greens in a salad spinner. They may be refrigerated for up to 5 days in a loosely folded plastic bag which contains a clean cloth or paper towel in the bottom to absorb moisture.

Mushrooms. In this text I refer to button mushrooms—the most common type—as "mushrooms." They should be plump, white—without discoloration—and the caps should tightly cup the stem. If the cap is open so that its underside is visible, the mushroom should be avoided. Most mushrooms require cleaning as they grow in dirt. The simplest method is to trim the stem even with the bottom of the cap. Save both cap and stem. Place them in a strainer over the sink and run a gentle stream of cold water over them, tossing and rubbing them to remove all dirt. Do not linger in this washing stage because the mushrooms will absorb the water rather than being cleaned by it. If you are cleaning more than a pound of mushrooms at a time, work in batches. Once all of the mushroom caps are clean (after about 1 minute of washing) turn them out immediately onto a dry counter, stem side down, onto a clean kitchen towel. Place the mushrooms at least 1/2 inch apart to allow room for the water to be absorbed by the towel. Arrange the stems separately alongside. Allow the mushrooms to rest at room temperature until completely dry, at least 30 minutes. If the towel becomes very wet within the first few minutes of draining, transfer the mushrooms to another dry towel. Once dry, the mushrooms may be refrigerated for up to 5 days in a loosely folded plastic bag which contains a clean cloth or paper towel in the bottom to absorb moisture. Mushrooms keep best if cleaned soon after purchase. Besides button mushrooms, there are many other types (see the Glossary of Ingredients for specific names).

Each type of mushroom has a distinctive taste and texture, making it the best choice when called for in a recipe. You may substitute one for another, but be aware that the recipe will be radically different. When selecting uncommon types of mushrooms, look for a clean, fresh smell—never musty! Most are flatter-headed than button mushrooms, so the cap does not curl to hold the stem tightly. The underside of the cap should be very clean and never moist. The mushroom itself should be plump, without dried edges, and it should never be slimy. Any dirt that clings to the mushroom is best brushed off gently with a pastry brush (or a mushroom brush). If the mushrooms are very dirty, they may be rinsed individually and dried like button mushrooms. They may be stored in a plastic bag in the same manner as button mushrooms.

Many mushrooms are available dried, in particular shiitake, porcini and tree ears. Their taste usually intensifies with drying and their texture is quite different, so if fresh are available, they are worth the investment. After soaking dried mushrooms, trim and discard tough stems. The soaking water is excellent added to stocks or soups (though it should be strained to be certain all sand is removed). Dried mushrooms may be refrigerated in an airtight container, in their soaking liquid, for up to 5 days.

Onions. Perhaps the most frequently used ingredient in this book, onions, common as they are, need some note in context of these recipes. Onions are used as a fundamental taste in most stocks. They are also frequently used, either sautéed to enhance sweetness, or simply added before simmering for depth to soups themselves. I call for a number of different varieties of onions and, though recipes are best prepared with that which is specified, the varieties may be used interchangeably with minimal change in effect. The most common type of onion is yellow-skinned. It is the most pungent, sometimes bordering on bitter, in taste. There are several large yellow-skinned varieties (most notably Vidalia and Maui), that have a mild, slightly sweet flavor. They are always tagged by name and, because of their intense sweetness, they are the least versatile type of onion. White-skinned onions have a well-rounded, smooth taste and, although they are usually more expensive than yellow, they are the best all-purpose choice. Red onions have a deep purple-red skin and the meat is a lighter version of the same color. Their taste is sharper than white onions, but sweeter as well. Pearl onions are available in yellow, white or red skin and make a nice garnish used whole in some soups. When peeling onions, be sure to remove the papery skin and all tough layers before cutting.

Peppers. Peppers have a vast and diverse role in virtually every cuisine that influences modern tastes, and therefore the soups in this book. Most peppers may be eaten raw, partially cooked, dried, smoked, simmered or broiled and peeled. Each treatment reveals a different character of the pepper. In soups, peppers contribute texture and taste and, in many cases, heat. For heat I generally call for either jalapeños or serranos when fresh, or dried red chili peppers when dried.

Fresh peppers should be firm and plump with unblemished skins and should be stored in a loosely folded plastic bag in the vegetable drawer of the refrigerator.

To roast and peel peppers, preheat the oven to 450° F., or preheat the broiler to high. Wash the peppers well. Place them on a baking sheet and bake in the hot oven or about 3 inches from a hot broiler, turning several times, until blistered on all sides. In an oven this will take about 20 minutes, under the broiler, about 10 minutes. The faster the peppers are blistered, the less of an effect on taste and texture the cooking will have on the pepper. Immediately place the pepper in a paper or plastic bag. Fold the bag shut to seal in the steam (which will help the skin of the pepper to detach itself). When the peppers are cool enough to handle, pull and scrape off the peel with the aid of a paring knife. Peeled peppers may be refrigerated in an airtight container for 2 to 3 days. If packed in oil they will last up to 10 days, or they may be frozen for several months.

Guidelines for Selecting Other Ingredients

Beans

Beans are the main protein source for most vegetarian diets, as well as a great source of complex carbohydrate and fiber. Beans come in a wide variety of shapes, sizes, colors, taste and textures. Like fruits and vegetables, it is best to experiment with beans to become familiar with the characteristics of different types. Most are usually available dried, though occasionally you may find them fresh. Once shelled, you can steam fresh beans and eat them with a sprinkling of salt and pepper (lemon juice and butter add a nice touch too), or add them to a simple soup broth. The light, juicy vegetable quality of beans—and their individual, inherent character suddenly become blatantly apparent when they are eaten fresh. So, if you do run across fresh beans, buy them.

Most often, though, you will probably rely on dried beans. They are widely available, may be bought in bulk at many markets, and, when stored in airtight containers in a cool, dark place, they keep indefinitely. (Though the longer they are stored, the dryer they become, so the longer they take to cook.) The following are general procedures for cooking all dried beans.

1. Before measuring, beans should be "picked over" to remove all rocks and debris. You should pour them out on a flat basket or cookie sheet. Tilt the basket at about a 30 degree angle. Allow the beans to roll down to the bottom edge of the basket, as you carefully search through for foreign matter. Most commercially produced beans are relatively free of rocks or debris, whereas some produced by smaller farms or supplied through international markets may contain a fair amount of foreign matter.

2. Once picked over, place the beans in a fine mesh strainer and rinse well in cold water. Split beans, lentils, peas and various forms of small "dal" (Indian-style beans) may stick together and clump when wet, so they should not be rinsed until just before being transferred to a soaking or cooking liquid.

3. After washing, beans may be placed in a large bowl and covered with cold water (4 cups water per cup of beans) then soaked overnight. This will speed up their cooking and aid in digestibility. As a time-saving device, they may be "quick soaked." To do this, place beans in a large pot of water (4 cups per cup of bean) and bring them to a boil. Cook them for 3 minutes, then cool in their liquid before proceeding with a recipe.

4. There are several methods for cooking beans. In the recipes that follow I usually recommend boiling them because it is the most simple method, requiring the least amount of equipment. To boil beans, for each cup of dried beans, add 4 cups of water and spices of your choosing to a large heavy-bottomed pot. (Diced onion, garlic, bay leaf and peppercorns are a versatile preliminary seasoning. Adding 2 teaspoons of oil per cup of beans may improve texture and reduce foaming. Do not add salt, miso, tamari, soy sauce or acidic foods such as lemon, tomato or vinegar, to the first cooking or the beans will be tough.) Bring the beans to a boil, skim and discard foam that rises to the surface, then reduce to a simmer and cook, covered until tender (usually 1 1/2 to 2 hours). Garbanzos, soy beans and canellini beans will take up to an hour longer. Black-eyed peas and anasazi beans cook more quickly and may be cooked without presoaking as may split peas and most dal.

There are other very good methods of cooking beans. The same cleaning and seasoning principles apply no matter what method is used: slow cookers—

4 to 1 ratio of water to beans, cooked on high for 1 hour, then 8 to 10 hours on low; oven baked—5 to 1 ratio of water to beans, brought to a boil on top of the stove for 20 minutes, then baked at 350° F. for 4 to 5 hours; pressure cookers—4 to 1 ratio of water to beans, brought to a boil and skimmed, then lid locked in place and beans cooked on medium heat for about 30 to 45 minutes, or on high heat for 8 to 35 minutes. (For an excellent resource on pressure cooking see *Cooking Under Pressure* by Lorna Sass.)

Whatever method of cooking you use, I advise cooking large quantities of beans as a time-saving device. You may then use a small amount for a recipe and freeze the rest for later use. There are also a number of high-quality organic canned beans available. Using pre-cooked beans will greatly reduce cooking time in most soups. If you use beans that are pre-cooked, you may wish to add seasonings that would have been cooked into the dried beans in preliminary stages of the recipe to the final cooking of the soup.

Notes:
1. For information about other soy-based foods, see Soy Products (page 174).
2. When first including beans in the diet, it is not uncommon to experience an increase in flatulence, primarily because it takes the body time to adjust to the volume of fiber they provide. A few simple steps when cooking the beans will usually eliminate or lessen the problem. First, soak or "quick soak" (boil and drain before cooking) dried beans before proceeding with a recipe. In addition, it may be helpful to add to the beans as they cook a small amount of epazote (page 168), bay leaf or kombu (page 170).

Fresh Herbs and Spices

Fresh and dried herbs as well as spices are essential to soup making. Though many herbs may be used dry, all are better fresh, except for rosemary which may taste bitter when fresh. A general rule for substituting dried herbs for fresh is to use 1/3 the volume, but because dried herbs lose flavor over time when stored, you must judge this substitution according to your own pantry. It is preferable to omit parsley, basil and cilantro from a recipe, rather than using them dried. Some fresh herbs such as oregano, thyme and sage are good cooked into soups and stocks from the start of cooking. Most other fresh herbs are best stirred in just at the end of cooking. To clean fresh herbs, large leaves (basil, mint, tarragon, etc.) should be removed from stems. The stems of softer-stemmed herbs, such as parsley and cilantro, may be chopped with the herb. Other stems are best used only as a flavoring that is removed before a soup is served. The leaves can be washed and dried in a salad spinner, then they may be refrigerated for up to 5 days in a loosely folded plastic bag which contains a clean cloth or paper towel in the bottom to absorb moisture. Fresh herbs may also be frozen (in small quantities, stored in plastic bags) for use in stocks. Once frozen, they are not appropriate as a garnish. Spices such as cinnamon, cardamom and cloves, as well as dried herbs, are readily available, sold in bulk, in most natural foods stores. Buy only enough to last 3 to 4 months. Store them in separate, airtight containers in a dark place, in order to maximize shelf life. Herbs and spices, like so many other ingredients, are so varied in flavor and effect that it is best to gradually experiment with them to discover which suit your taste. When recipes call for spices or seeds to be toasted or crushed, it is vitally important to do so as this matures and/or maximizes their flavor.

Of particular note in the recipes that follow are salt and pepper. When salt is used sensibly, with both moderation and discretion, it can transform dishes—uniting and optimizing their flavors. A soup should never taste particularly salty, but if it just tastes slightly flat a very small quantity of salt may be the missing ingredient. If a soup becomes too salty, soak a raw, peeled potato in the soup, off the heat, for 1 hour to absorb the salt. Remove the potato before continuing with the recipe. Whenever possible, use freshly ground black pepper to benefit from its subtle taste which disappears quickly in stored ground pepper.

Noodles

Many varieties of noodles are called for in the recipes that follow. For the most part, those recommended may have others substituted for them, depending on availability and your personal preference. A general note about noodles, though, is that the shape of the noodle will have a distinctive effect on a dish. In addition, noodles may be made from virtually any flour, with extremely different results. Traditional Italian noodles are usually made from wheat or semolina flour. They may or may not contain eggs—check the label if this is a concern. Those that do not contain eggs are usually labeled "cholesterol free." Noodles may be made from alternative flours—whole wheat, quinoa, rice, artichoke, etc. These may or may not be wheat-free, but again the label will have that information. Noodles made from flours other than wheat may not hold up well after cooking. Flavored noodles add an interesting visual effect, if not a change of taste.

Nuts

Nuts are best bought in small quantities and stored in the freezer when not in use. Because of their high fat content, most nuts will become rancid after shelling if stored at room temperature. Rancid nuts impart an unmistakable taste that permeates a dish. Toasting greatly improves the flavor of most nuts and unless they are used in a nut milk, I generally recommend toasting and, when applicable, skinning them. To do so, preheat the oven to 375° F. Lay the nuts on a dry baking sheet and toast, stirring once or twice, until brown to the core, about 10 to 12 minutes. Immediately transfer the nuts to a bowl or cool countertop, as they will continue to cook and will burn if left on the baking sheet. To remove the skins, turn the warm nuts onto a clean kitchen towel. Fold the towel over the nuts and rub them. If skins do not slip off easily (an indication that the nuts are not absolutely fresh), they may be placed in a strainer and rubbed against the metal mesh. They are slightly less attractive when skinned in this way, but if the nuts are to be ground, this is not a problem. I prefer buying raw nuts and roasting them myself (rancidity is easier to taste in the raw), but some high-quality roasted nuts are available commercially.

Oils

Various oils are called for in the recipes that follow. When first stocking your pantry, the most important to have on hand are a good olive oil, toasted sesame oil, and an all-purpose vegetable oil. After using, wipe the lip of the oil bottle with a clean paper towel to remove excess oil. This will retard spoilage. Oils should be stored in tightly capped jars, in a cool, dark cabinet. They may be refrigerated, but this is not necessary unless you use so little that they will not be used in about a year.

Sea Vegetables

When I first became interested in natural foods, I found it difficult to believe that anyone actually ate seaweed on purpose. To this day I fully understand why the nomenclature has it called sea vegetables, a much more appealing name for what I now add to many dishes—and eat—with great enthusiasm. There are many forms of eatable sea vegetables, most of which are available in natural foods stores and Asian markets. They are a key ingredient in Japanese cooking, and some lend themselves beautifully to more Western-style dishes. All are rich sources of protein, carbohydrate and minerals such as iron and iodine. Most should be rinsed to remove sand or dust, then briefly soaked before adding to a recipe. Dried sea vegetables will keep indefinitely if stored in an airtight container in a cool, dark place. For information about specific sea vegetables used in the recipes that follow, see the Glossary of Ingredients (page 167).

Sweeteners

In the recipes that follow, sweetness is derived from a number of sources. Often, ingredients cooked in the stock or soup, carrots, raisins or anasazi beans, for example, add sweetness. At other times, sweeteners are called for. When making soups, added sweeteners effect taste alone, rather than structure as they do in baked goods, so traditional sweeteners—sugar and honey—may be substituted. The benefits of using alternative sweeteners are that they are less refined and processed than table sugars, in addition to the fact that the impart different qualities of sweetness. All are readily available in most natural foods stores.

A Note About Organic Foods

Quality is judged by a combination of factors: taste, texture, aroma and appearance. Depending on an ingredient's role in a soup, the relative importance of these may vary; however, a top quality ingredient scores close to perfect in every way. As important as all of these obvious signs of quality is how the ingredient is grown and harvested. Until recently, in many consumers' minds, this took second fiddle to how readily available a food was and how pretty it looked on the shelf. Today, the use of chemicals and pesticides—those things that often give produce its long shelf life or the picture-perfect look—is being questioned in terms of how chemical residue may affect the environment and our health. Consequently, organic foods are gaining popularity. But when you first start questioning the use of chemicals and begin to notice organic foods, the notion may seem rather silly. After all, aren't all foods organic matter? And do the organic, sometimes blemished specimens of our favorite foods really deserve the higher price tag they may bear? In answering these and other questions about organic foods it is helpful to become familiar with the current agricultural definition of organic.

Organic farming employs methods that produce food without the use of any artificial chemicals, fertilizers, pesticides, herbicides or fungicides. Not only is the crop itself treated in this way, but the soil in which the crop is grown has been treated only with organic fertilizer for a minimum of three years. Sometimes foods grown under these "natural" conditions do not look picture-perfect—oranges may have a slightly mottled skin color or worms may be hiding in a bunch of broccoli—but the taste is almost always equal, if not superior, to commercially grown produce. An increasing number of farmers are electing to use organic growing methods so that the quality and availability of organic foods is on the rise. With this, prices are dropping so that locally produced organic foods are often as cheap as commercially produced counterparts. In addition many states now have organic certification regulations to assure the consumer of organic quality. In this light, considering "organic" as an indicator of quality makes sense. Organic foods are usually marked as such.

A Note About Low-Fat Soups

Using less fat when we cook is all the rage these days, and—for the most part—it is a good evolutionary path for our culinary tradition to be following. High-fat diets have been associated with all sorts of health problems from heart disease and cancer to the generally lower state of health that is associated with obesity.

The trend toward a low-fat diet is good—for the most part. I say this because if the primary focus of what and how we eat becomes a quest for low-fat everything at all costs, we will suffer severe consequences. In a gustatory and artistic sense, the discreet and well-thought-out use of high quality fat as we cook transforms the eating process from a barren experience to a highly sensual, nurturing part of our everyday life. First, foods change radically when cooked with a small amount of fat. Sautéing allows foods to sweeten and build individual character, while blending with other ingredients that are being cooked at the same time. In this way, fat may give a level of complexity to a dish that is unattainable without it. Second, as we eat, a small amount of fat coats the mouth, giving a full, satisfying quality to our sense of the food so that we may feel satiated more quickly and, therefore, eat less. Fat is not bad, but at the same time most foods need very little, if any, of it added to reach their optimal taste. Fat has its place—small though it should be—in the way we prepare our foods. As we cook, it becomes critical to recognize when fat is best eliminated from our cooking, and when it will give an added boost to a recipe.

There are many steps that may be taken to reduce fat in old-fashioned, high-fat soups. These are the principles on which all of the recipes in this book are based. The first basic step to lower fat in soups is to avoid sautéing ingredients—the first step in many soup recipes—or to include that step using a minimal amount of oil and to pour as much of the fat off as possible before adding liquid. Second, be certain that all fat is always removed from stocks before they are added to a soup. Third, use the highest quality, most flavorful fats possible. A tiny amount of high quality (full flavored) olive or toasted sesame oil permeates a dish quickly and fully whereas even a large quantity of a low quality oil will not satisfy the palate. The same principle applies to adding high fat ingredients such as cheese and nuts. A very small amount of top quality imported Italian Parmesan can transform a soup, whereas a low grade Parmesan type cheese simply adds a hint of flavor and the tendency is to keep adding more (to taste) which results in a much higher addition of fat. Finally, think before you add fat anywhere to your diet. If less can be added or it can be eliminated—do so. But if you have the desire for a high-quality, high-fat food, serve it in a menu that contains all other low- or non-fat foods. If you have a particularly high-fat menu, eat very low-fat menus for the next 3 or 4 meals. Allow your eating experience to be rich and full, but not gluttonous.

2 • Building Blocks

From a delicate consommé to a hearty bowl of chowder, all soups are unique combinations of a few simple components that tie together the primary ingredients of the soup. The components are the stock or base, the thickener, the enrichment, and the topping or garnish. Think of these components as the building blocks of soup and you'll see that even though variations and combinations of each go on ad infinitum, a basic understanding of how each is prepared and what function it serves will give you the primary tools needed to make any soup imaginable.

Stock: The Building Block of Taste

Good stocks are a cornerstone of most great cuisines, as they are in vegetarian cooking. But because most classic stocks are meat-based, and these are the predominant tastes that have shaped the current Western style of eating, stock made simply from vegetables may seem to be like comparing insipid dishwater to a fine French fumet or a Japanese dashi. A closer look reveals that this is not the case at all.

The classic method of making stock is a fine yet simple art, and when the same principles are applied to vegetarian ingredients the results can be superb. The two biggest differences between vegetarian and meat-based stocks are cooking time and complexity of flavor. When no bones are used, the cooking time is decreased dramatically because vegetables (unlike bones) break down and release flavor quickly. In terms of intensity, classic meat stocks have a complex layering of tastes and aromas with vegetables serving more as a backdrop than a primary focus. In addition, gelatin released from collagen contained in the bones gives the stock body and depth. In contrast, the characteristics of the vegetables themselves become the focal point in vegetarian stocks; and beans or grains may be added for body and depth. This results in stocks that are perfectly matched to the lighter, more delicate flavors that typify good vegetarian cooking. The process of making vegetarian stock is easy, and once you've prepared it a few times, you'll find that by cutting up a few extra vegetables as you cook you can always have homemade stock on hand.

While many ingredients may be added to it, stock is not simply a catch-all for trimmings, leftovers and whatever the dog refused. A good stock has a well-planned balance of flavors and aromas. It is in achieving this balance that the true art lies.

First, the ingredients selected must complement and accentuate each other and the soup for which the stock is intended. Some ingredients give taste and some lend texture, while the primary function of others is to penetrate and enhance the aroma. Next, the ingredients are simmered in a water bath until their essence is rendered to the broth. The ingredients must be considered individually, knowing when and how much of each to add so that none overcooks or becomes too dominant. (Overcooked ingredients may result in a bitter or otherwise bad-tasting stock.) As the stock comes to a boil, impurities rise and form foam that is skimmed off the surface and discarded before the stock is simmered. Depending on the ingredients used and the volume of stock being made, the cooking time may be anywhere from 20 minutes to several hours. Once cooked, the stock is strained and defatted if necessary. However, vegetarian stocks usually contain little fat unless ingredients are first browned in oil. Any residual fat may be skimmed from the surface of the stock after it chills. The stock is then ready to be used as is or it may be reduced and used as an enrichment.

Along with the recipes at the end of the chapter, the pointers that follow will serve as guidelines when you begin to dabble in the art of making vegetarian stocks. I include three basic stock recipes: light vegetable, hearty vegetable, and kombu (sea vegetable). Once familiar with these, you may wish to experiment with some of the suggested alternatives or create your own variations that take advantage of seasonal ingredients or complement the flavors of a particular soup. Most vegetables and some fruit may be added, though you must know how an ingredient responds to long cooking. For example, leafy greens tend to become bitter if overcooked and, with long cooking, members of the cabbage family break down to form compounds such as sulfides and ammonia. Their flavor can become very pronounced, so unless they are added at the very end of cooking, they are best not added to stocks. Consider the questions below when choosing which stock to use or how it might be modified.

Guidelines for Making Stock

• What are the underlying tastes and qualities of the soup for which the stock is intended? What ingredients will reflect or complement these basic characteristics? For example, a soup inspired by East Asian cooking would be likely to benefit from the addition of ginger to the stock, whereas you might stir a handful of grated coconut into a stock for an Indian-style soup. The key is to have a clear palatal sense of what you would like the finished soup to taste like. Then you can carefully think through the characteristics of the ingredients you plan to add to both the stock and the soup itself, balancing sweet with tart, adding an ingredient at the appropriate time to avoid unpleasant side effects from overcooking, and so on.

• Will the stock need body to stand on its own or will it be thickened or used in a soup that provides the needed texture and body? If body is needed, will the finished soup be enhanced, for example, by the meaty undertone of lentils or would it benefit more from the subtle addition of barley?

• Do the ingredients contained in the stock all respond well to the same methods and length of cooking or should some be treated differently than others?

• Does the stock seem, by all senses, to be balanced? You must take into account the tastes, aromas, textures and appearance of all of the ingredients and spices used. Ideally everything in the stock is harmonious and will maintain that balance when combined with the ingredients of the finished soup.

• Are all the ingredients of top quality? The stock is the sum of the ingredients used, so one "bad apple" can spoil the pot. Ingredients should be absolutely fresh and preferably at the peak of ripeness. This applies to herbs and spices as well. Leftovers, raw vegetable trimmings that have been frozen, or dried herbs are not necessarily ruled out, but unless all the ingredients are fresh enough to be served by themselves, they are likely to make the stock taste stale or flat.

• Is the stock to be used immediately or will it be refrigerated or frozen? If it is to be stored, be aware which flavors will intensify or diminish over time or from freezing. In general, when storing stock, use a mildly spiced basic recipe and add distinctive flavors just before it is used. In this way the stock's use is less limited.

• Is the stock salted appropriately? This will depend on what is in the finished soup as well as how the stock will be treated after being made. A stock that tastes appropriately salted on its own could result in an overly salty end product if used in a soup made with cheese, miso or other salty ingredients. Salting also depends on whether or not the stock will be reduced before it is used. When a stock is reduced, liquid evaporates, but the quantity of salt remains the same (the ratio of salt to liquid increases), so a "perfectly salted" stock is likely to be overly salty if reduced. When making stock with no immediate purpose in mind, add a minimum of salt.

• Is your pot or pan the right size for the volume of stock to be cooked or reduced? Stock prepared in a pot that is too large will cook too quickly and flavors of the ingredients might not have time to blossom. On the other hand, when a stock is being reduced it may burn if the pot is too big.

Alternatives to Homemade Stock

If you find yourself without homemade stock and don't have time to make a fresh batch, there are a number of ready-made alternatives available. Miso comes in many flavors and intensities (page 171) and may be added quickly at the end of cooking a soup for flavor and aroma. All miso, however, is very salty and has a characteristic fermented taste, so it does not work for every soup. Another good solution is to use an appropriate vegetable or fruit juice as part or all of the base flavoring. Several brands of vegetarian bouillon cubes are also available.

The simplest alternative to stock is pure water. When substituting water for stock, you may need to add additional ingredients to the soup itself. You might find that more salt or other seasonings and spices, in addition to base flavors such as onion, celery or garlic may be necessary to give some of the dimension that the stock would have provided.

On this note, and given that most vegetarian stocks cook quickly and seldom need fat removed, you may wonder, "Why not omit the step of making stock and simply add a few extra vegetables to the soup?" That's a good question and, in fact, when a soup is simple with only one primary flavor, such as a carrot or tomato, it is appropriate to use water and embellish the flavor of the soup as it is made. On the other hand, there are several arguments for making stock separately. First, having frozen or fresh stock on hand paves the way (if only in your mind) for making soup since the use of stock cuts down on prep and cooking time. More importantly, stock defines your starting point. When you use stock you begin with a known depth of flavor from which to build a more complex soup.

Thickeners: The Building Block of Texture

The initial palatal sense you have of a soup, before flavors burst forth, is a union of temperature and texture—a critical balance that must draw you in for more. Many soups are successful either cold or hot, though flavors may need minor adjustment to accommodate temperature change. A soup's texture, however, is not as adaptable. It is usually determined from the onset, depending on what ingredients the soup contains and how the soup is prepared. No matter what the cuisine, the texture of soups falls into one of two categories, either clear or thick.

Clear soups are just that—a plain soup base to which other ingredients are added, then simmered, to impart flavor. The soup may be served as is, or the cooked ingredients may be removed, leaving a flavorful broth. Clear soups may simply be called broth or bouillon in the West or "suimono" in Japan. But all are considered clear because they are not thickened. The most refined type of clear soup is called "consommé," a French word meaning clear. For a consommé, broth is clarified—a somewhat complicated process that renders liquid perfectly clean and crystal clear. The soup may then be served as is or with a garnish such as freshly minced herbs, shredded crepes or thinly sliced vegetables. Other clear soups are neither clarified nor thickened, but they still rely on a flavorful base to provide background for ingredients found in the soup. Many cuisines offer a variety of clear soups, most of which are known by individual names (such as chicken noodle or minestrone) rather than a genre of soup such as consommé. The most common exception to this is "bouillon" (French for boiled). Bouillons, which are often considered restorative, are simple stocks that have a distinctive or predominant flavor such as scallions, fresh herbs or shiitake mushrooms.

The majority of soups in most cuisines are thick. The definition of thick may range from a slightly cloudy soup made with miso to a robust bowl of black bean soup. The success of a thick soup relies on being held together to just the desired consistency so that it is never overly dominated in taste or texture by whatever the thickener may be.

Three methods for giving soups body are: to add a thickening agent at the beginning or end of cooking; to obtain thickness from starchy ingredients that are part of the main body of the soup; or to purée the cooked ingredients and rely on their volume for thickness. A soup may be thickened in one or a combination of these ways. A recipe containing a large proportion of a starchy ingredient that breaks down easily as it cooks—such as potatoes or lentils—may spontaneously thicken to a desired consistency. In contrast, puréed soups that do not contain a starchy ingredient—spinach soup, for example—may be thick but somewhat watery, a situation which can be remedied by the addition of a thickening agent. A soup's balance of taste is less likely to be upset by a thickening agent, such as flour, than by relying on a starchy vegetable for thickness.

Thickening Agents

Milled flours and powdered starches, the most common types of thickening agents, function similarly. Insoluble chains of glucose molecules, which make up the starch, bond with hydrogen in hot water. The granules absorb liquid, swell, and—just below the boiling point—intermingle totally with the water.

The liquid, which was initially cloudy from the uncooked addition of the thickening agent, suddenly clears. The soup increases in thickness briefly, until just past the boiling point and/or with continued cooking and stirring, at which point the thickener's capacity to thicken begins to diminish. For this reason, particular care should be taken when thickening agents are used in a soup that is prepared ahead of time because the increased stirring and boiling might cause the soup to thin. (This may be countered somewhat by evaporation as the soup cooks.) Starches derived from grains, such as wheat and corn, must be cooked after being added to eliminate the raw "cereal" taste. Root starches, including arrowroot and kuzu, do not have a raw taste, so do not need extensive cooking. They also tend to thicken more efficiently than grain starches, so less is needed per cup of liquid for an equivalent thickness.

Wheat flour is the most commonly used thickening agent in the West. It may be mixed to a smooth paste with cold liquid and added to the soup part way through cooking, but most often it is combined with fat and added in the form of a "roux," as one of the first steps in a recipe, or a "beurre mainé" which is blended into the soup towards the end of cooking. The degree of thickness achieved with or without fat is almost identical, but the addition of fat gives a fuller, creamier feel to the texture. To make a roux-based soup, ingredients are sautéed in oil or butter. Then enough flour to absorb all the fat is added and the roux is cooked to rid the flour of its raw taste before liquid is added. The roux for a light-colored soup may be cooked for only a minute. For a dark soup, it is allowed to brown slowly for up to 45 minutes so that it imparts a rich taste and dark color. More flour is needed to achieve an equal degree of thickening when the roux is cooked longer because, as the flour browns, its capacity to thicken diminishes. "Beurre mainé" means butter in the hand or kneaded butter. Equal amounts of flour and room temperature butter are combined to form a paste. The paste is whisked until smooth with a small amount of liquid from the soup, then the mixture is poured into the soup, heated to a boil, and cooked for only a few minutes before serving. The soup may be served as soon as the raw taste of flour disappears. In this way, a soup may be thickened at the last minute without having to contend with textural changes that may result from using powdered starches.

When using flour to thicken, whatever method is used, I prefer unbleached white flour to whole wheat. Their thickening capacity is about equal, but the bran left in whole wheat may cause problems. First, the bran browns and burns quickly when preparing a roux which will ruin the taste of the soup. Second, the bran settles out into the liquid as it cooks, resulting in a slight graininess. Finally, the hue of the soup is dulled by the bran contained in the whole wheat. All of these problems increase when coarse, stone ground whole wheat flour is used and when cooking large quantities of soup. Flours from grains other than wheat may be used, but none thicken as efficiently and many contain particles that, like the bran in whole wheat, have undesirable effects. In addition, most have very distinctive flavors and some contribute a dark, even muddy color. On the other hand, if you wish to limit wheat intake, a soup recipe can be designed to accommodate other flours.

Powdered starches are used to thicken as simple, last-minute additions. Cold liquid and starch are combined, two parts to one, to form a smooth paste (hot liquid forms lumps). A small amount of hot soup is stirred into the paste. This mixture is added to the soup which is then heated to a boil. Starches may also be added by mixing them into an enrichment such as egg, yogurt or cream, which can then be stirred into a soup towards the end of cooking. In this case, the soup should not be brought to a boil to avoid curdling the enrichment.

Cornstarch is widely used to thicken soups and sauces in China and other parts of East Asia. It has little flavor and adds a characteristic viscous texture that can become almost rubbery if too much is added. Arrowroot, which is also widely used throughout East Asia as well as in Europe, comes from the root of a West Indian tubular plant. It is similar in use and effect to cornstarch, yet it does not thicken as readily.

Another common starch is kuzu. Alongside highways in the South you are likely to see trees so covered with a lush green vine that they look like majestic creatures. This prolific vine is kudzu. Many Southerners consider it a menace, but starch extracted from its root is widely used in traditional Japanese cooking. For thickening, powdered kuzu is similar in effect to cornstarch but gives soups a more satiny, gently aromatic quality (again, too much turns rubbery). Kuzu should be crushed into a fine powder (lumps form when stored) and mixed with cold liquid before being used. It thickens at a lower temperature than cornstarch and has no cereal taste, so it is not necessary to bring the soup to a boil after the kuzu is added. This makes it an excellent choice for thickening miso-based soups because the digestive enzyme contained in miso is destroyed if boiled.

Other Methods for Obtaining Thickness

A soup may also be thickened by the inherent quality of ingredients it contains. Whole foods with a high starch content such as potatoes, some whole grains and bread (a thickener commonly used in the Middle Ages) break down as they cook and disperse throughout the liquid, resulting in a subtly thick soup. Hearty peasant-style soups with chunks of vegetables and a rich broth are often thickened in this simple way. This method of soup making has the inherent risk of producing a bland, unbalanced or tasteless soup, because with the addition of starchy ingredients, relatively little is needed to actually thicken, and most quickly flatten out other flavors in a soup. Proportions for thickening soups with potatoes, rice and other starches are elusive, depending on what end result is sought, the broth used and other ingredients contained in the soup. Nonetheless, the list of starchy ingredients that work well to thicken soups on page 163 will give you a starting point if you wish to experiment.

Puréeing

Another simple method for thickening soups is to "purée" or mash them. Ingredients that are not particularly porous even after long cooking, such as onion, radish or cauliflower, do not bind easily with liquid and, if used alone, result in a watery soup when puréed. This is true to a lesser extent for other vegetables and even most beans. It helps, therefore, to have a small amount of a starchy vegetable or grain as part of a puréed soup. Puréeing is a good method for elevating a peasant-style soup into the realm of elegance. The most famous example of this is a "vichyssoise" which in its unpuréed, hot form is known as a simple leek and potato soup called "soupe au parmentier."

A food processor is indispensable when making puréed soups. For best results, ingredients should be cooked until they are tender and can be easily mashed with the back of a fork. They should not be cooked so long that their character is distorted. Consequently, ingredients may need to be added at different times as a soup cooks. Spinach, for instance, becomes bitter or grassy when overcooked. Vibrant green vegetables take on an army green hue when overcooked or left covered and hot in a pan after cooking. Other ingredients, notably peppers, mushrooms, and curry, increase in intensity the longer they stay in a soup. Also keep in mind that dominant ingredients such as ginger (which has a very powerful flavor) or beans (which absorb other flavors) may become more dominant when puréed, so less is needed when making a puréed soup.

When using a processor to purée a soup, strain solid ingredients and reserve the liquids. Purée the solids, scraping down the sides of the bowl occasionally, until an even texture is obtained. For a slightly smoother texture add a small amount of the reserved liquid and purée for one minute more.

If you know that the ingredients could, by nature, have a smooth texture, but the soup simply does not reach the consistency you expect, it is likely that the ingredients are undercooked. Assuming the ingredients used are fresh and the soup tastes good, it would probably be best to serve the soup as is. If you feel you must have a smoother texture, transfer the soup solids to a bowl and steam or microwave them without adding more liquid (which will upset the soup's balance and make the vegetables impossible to purée) before puréeing again. Once the purée is complete, transfer it to a clean pot and whisk in the remaining soup broth before continuing with the recipe.

Soups may be puréed in a blender, though it is more work than with a processor because, given their volume, they must be puréed in several batches. If you use a blender, liquid must be added to the solids so the ingredients will purée evenly. A more labor-intensive method for puréeing, but one that may result in a superior soup, is to use a food mill (page 8). A good food mill has the advantage of having three puréeing plates with different sized holes, so that you can choose the consistency you want and obtain a very even texture. In addition, a food mill strains out skin, seeds, and other stringy bits of ingredients that get chopped up, but not truly puréed, in a processor or blender.

Enrichments: The Building Block of Harmony

In these low-fat, health-conscious days, enrichments are difficult to write about without tripping over myself offering explanations as to why and how they might be appropriate. They are, after all, luxury items, usually high in fat and/or cholesterol, that are mixed thoroughly into a soup to make the consistency richer. But rich is not necessarily a four-letter word. Whether or not you are watching fat and cholesterol, it is the indiscriminate use of rich ingredients that can cause health problems. With this in mind, enrichments can be incorporated in modest amounts to unite the subtle qualities of a soup by harmonizing ingredients or buffing tiny imperfections that might occur.

Creams

Cream is the first ingredient that comes to mind when the subject of enrichments arises. This is especially true when Western-style soups are the topic at hand. Cream of mushroom, tomato, asparagus, zucchini—you name it—we've creamed it and served it as soup. But creamed soups don't always contain cream.

Classically speaking, the category of French soups known as "crèmes" are those with cream added as a final liaison. They are always made with a roux (page 25) and differ from a related class of soups called "veloutes" only in the addition of cream at the end. These days "creamed" and "puréed" are sometimes used interchangeably. In addition, soups that are called creamed are not necessarily roux-based and may not contain cream.

In this book I do call for cream in some recipes. All, however, may be prepared without cream or with an alternative enrichment. Because cream—and other dairy products—are not included in many people's diet and because tastes have evolved towards lighter, less rich foods, cream is best used with deliberate caution. In the recipes that follow, when I list cream, do not hesitate to make a less fatty or non-dairy substitute. If you can eat cream, a small amount can have a delectable, transformative effect. Find the top-quality, best-tasting cream available and use it with discretion.

European cream is thick and fresh, pregnant with the sweet essence of grasses eaten by the cows that provided the milk from which it was made. In France, the cream most commonly used in cooking is called "crème fraîche" or fresh cream. It has a thicker consistency than the cream we are familiar with (somewhere between yogurt and sour cream) and its taste is a delicate balance of sweet and sour. Crème fraîche can also withstand higher cooking temperatures because it is higher in fat than American cream. Some commercial brands of crème fraîche are available here, or you can make your own quite simply (pages 34-35).

In the United States, cream is usually available in various thicknesses (most commonly called Half-and-Half, table cream, coffee cream, light cream, light whipping cream and heavy whipping cream), which differ from one another according to fat content. Half-and-Half typically has about 30% calories from fat and heavy cream may have as much as 90% fat calories. Most American cream is "ultra-pasteurized," which means that it was stabilized by being heated to 280°F. for one second. The primary goal of ultra-pasteurization is to produce cream that has a shelf life of three months. Unfortunately, the process also gives the cream a slightly peculiar, cooked flavor.

It is still possible in some parts of the country to find small dairies that produce non-ultra-pasteurized cream, but you are more likely to have to settle for that which has been ultra-pasteurized. Given the combination of fat content and somewhat odd taste of ultra-pasteurized cream, you may wish to experiment with alternatives such as good quality milk, yogurt, sour cream or soy milk when cream is called for in a recipe. If you choose to use a cream alternative, be aware that most have different cooking properties than cream. Because cream is so high in fat, it is more stable than most cream-like enrichments. Sour cream, yogurt, and soy milk, for example, will curdle and separate if heated to a boil. Most milk-based ingredients will curdle in the presence of acid such as lemon. Whole milk adds a hint of the creaminess contributed by cream, but skim milk functions more as a protein and calcium enrichment and should be thought of as such. Buttermilk makes an excellent enrichment because, in spite of its low fat content, it adds a creamy texture and its unique flavor merges well with a wide range of ingredients. At the end of this chapter you will also find recipes for crème fraîche as well as ricotta "cream" and tofu "cream."

The water inside a coconut and milk made from the meat (page 37), commonly used in many tropical cuisines and East Asian-style dishes, make delicious enrichments for soups. Because of coconut's high saturated fat content, and the fact that coconut and palm kernel oil have been used to excess in processed foods, the knee-jerk, "health-conscious" response is to run in fear at the mention of the word coconut. As a soup enrichment, however, relatively little is used and it lends a delicate flower-like aroma and taste. Further, the flavor of coconut combines beautifully with many flavors such as garlic, spinach, ginger, cauliflower, lentils, and chick peas.

Nuts, Fats, Eggs and Other Enrichments

Nut and seed butters can be used as high-protein enrichments for soups. They are particularly tasty mixed into puréed soups that have a high percentage of starchy ingredients such as winter squash, potato or rice. They can also work well when stirred into a simple broth. A small amount will permeate the soup and subtly unify tastes such as garlic, onion, radish or cabbage, that may otherwise overpower. Some nut and seed butters, such as tahini which is made from sesame seeds, have dominant flavors and must be used with discretion. To incorporate a nut or seed butter into a finished soup, a 1/4 cup of soup is whisked into every two tablespoons of the butter used to form a smooth paste. This mixture is then stirred back into the soup which is heated gently.

Milks made from nuts and seeds may also be used as a protein enrichment. The flavor of nut and seed milks is far less intense than butters made from the same nuts or seeds. The milks are also thin enough that they need not be diluted before being added. They may be used as either a last minute addition to the finished soup or as an enrichment to the stock. Commercially produced nut and seed butters and milks are available, but because of the fresh flavor homemade varieties give, I recommend making your own if time allows.

A small amount of unsalted butter or high quality olive oil may also be stirred into a soup as an enrichment that enhances texture and, to a lesser degree, taste. They may be used as they are or combined with herbs or spices before being added. I recommend enriching with such fats only on the rare occasion that a soup's taste dissipates almost immediately when it is first sipped. This may occur if the soup has been prepared with the addition of little, if any, fat or when it contains a light broth in combination with a bland or astringent ingredient.

Egg yolks may be used as an enrichment to give a velvety, rich consistency to soups. A small amount of hot liquid is beaten into the yolks. This is then stirred back into the soup which is warmed gently to produce the desired result. The soup must not be boiled after the eggs are added or the eggs will "curdle"—cooking and separating into grainy pieces in the liquid. Just below the boiling point the egg's optimal thickness is reached and there is no danger of salmonella poisoning because salmonella is killed well below that at about 140°F. One yolk per cup of liquid will result in a slightly thickened effect. As health-conscious tastes move towards lighter fare, and fear of eggs becomes more firmly rooted in our gastronomic unconscious, the luxurious effect that fat- and cholesterol-laden egg yolks can have on soups to thicken and enrich is often overlooked. However, eggs need not be taboo on a healthy vegetarian diet. As with all enrichments, their use is a matter of taste and discretion.

Grated or cubed cheese is another important ingredient that, when mixed into a soup, may be used to enrich. As always, moderation is essential. A delicate touch of Parmesan or a Parmesan paste such as pesto, for example, can enliven an otherwise ordinary soup. When adding cheese to a soup a few simple rules apply. First, most cheese is salty, so when seasoning the base, that should be kept in mind. Second, the protein in cheese separates and toughens when cooked, so it is usually best to add cheese at the end of cooking or when the soup is removed from the heat. Finally, the type of cheese added determines the effect, so you must be familiar with the characteristics of the cheese you select. Hard, well-ripened cheeses may be heated to higher temperatures. Higher fat cheeses or those containing more water blend more easily with soups.

You may also find it interesting to experiment with some cheese alternatives such as grated mochi or a soy "cheese." As with any alternative, choose them for their own properties rather than as substitutes that you expect to mimic the "real" ingredients.

Finally, stock glaze may serve as enrichments. A small amount stirred into a pot of soup will give a subtle, but intense, background flavor. Up to two teaspoons may also be stirred into individual bowls for a more pronounced effect. To prepare a glaze, defatted stock is simply boiled down slowly until it is thick and syrupy. (Typically, 8 cups of stock are reduced to about 1/2 cup.) To avoid burning, care should be taken to transfer the stock to increasingly smaller pots as it reduces in volume. A stock glaze may also be used as a sort of homemade bouillon cube—concentrated flavor that may be added to water for a soup's broth.

Toppings and Garnishes: The Building Block of Beauty

Toppings and garnishes are like gifts to the diner that add taste, texture, and visual appeal to a soup. The distinction I make between the two is that toppings always float and their primary function is to add texture and taste, while beauty is secondary. The texture or taste contributed by a garnish, while important, is secondary to its beauty. Garnishes may be mixed into the body of the soup, arranged on the surface as a visual highlight, or placed on the plate beside the soup bowl. Both toppings and garnishes should relate to and complement the ingredients already contained in the soup. Other than that restriction, virtually anything that is attractive and edible can be used as a topping or garnish. In the recipes that follow, toppings and garnishes are always optional. The soups are designed to taste complete and balance, and most are quite beautiful in their natural simplicity. But it is nice on occasion to liven up the service with an interesting topping or a handsome garnish. Either can elevate even the most modest broth to an elegant highlight within a meal. Below I have listed a number of alternatives for toppings and garnishes. The list is fluid—some recipes, but more ideas than specifics. In discussing toppings and garnishes in this way, I emphasize the playful element in cooking that keeps mealtime interesting for diner and cook. In addition, I hope to prime the wheels of your imagination so that you can use these particular toppings and garnishes on any soup, or create your own from the following ideas.

Baked Toppings. The recipes in this book call for several baked toppings and dumplings. This category is so broad, that I refer you to the recipe index and specific recipes for ideas. In general, however, anything like a pastry or filo cut-out, biscuit, or cracker may be used very successfully as a topping. For dessert soups, sweet versions and cookies are also delightful.

Bread. Soup and bread are age-old companions. In fact, part of the derivation of the word soup is integrally tied to bread—historically, bread was used to "sop" up the liquid from gruel. To this day—though most soups are no longer gruelish—bread remains the perfect match for a bowl of soup. Other than serving a crusty loaf of French bread alongside, there are numerous toppings and garnishes that are delightful.

First, of course, is croutons. The two recipes found in chapter 7 have different benefits—the higher fat version melts in your mouth, and the lower fat crouton retains its crispness exceedingly well, after it is in the soup. Both may be prepared plain, or with virtually any seasoning (or combination of flavors) mixed into the bread coating. In addition, they may be cut into interesting shapes before cooking and/or topped with grated Parmesan (or other cheese) during the last 10 minutes of baking. Croutons may be made ahead and stored in an airtight container at room temperature. They should be put on the soup just as the soup is brought to the table.

Another simple idea is to cut bread into 1 1/2-inch-thick slices. Brush it with oil or butter, then toast it in a waffle iron. Once cooked, cut or tear it into small squares or cut into other shapes. For a lower fat version, brush the bread with egg white that has been lightly beaten, to which you add 2 teaspoons of oil. Either coating may also be flavored with herbs or spices before being brushed. For variation, you may use 1-inch slices of bread, sandwiched together with cheese (or a combination of cheese and a vegetable, such as tomato). The sandwich can then be brushed and grilled. I suggest using these toasts on broths, such as Tarragon Bouillon, or purées, such as Leek Cardamom.

Similarly, you may sandwich chapatis or tortillas with cheese, then bake them and float strips in a light soup, as is called for in the recipe for Tortilla Soup.

Cheese. Cheese makes a fine topping or garnish for many soups. The one note of caution is that it will significantly raise the fat and salt content of the soup, so take that into account when planning the rest of the menu and preparing the soup. When you add cheese, select one with full flavor so that less is needed, and remember that most cheeses are salty, so the soup itself will not need to be as salty as it would without the cheese. Hard and semi-hard cheeses are best grated or shaved into thin pieces if they are to be floated on top. They may be broiled or baked to a light brown color or placed on top just before the soup is brought to the table (bread crumbs mixed with the cheese speeds up browning). Semi-hard and semi-soft cheeses (Gruyère and feta, for example) are tasty if cut or broken into tiny pieces, then stirred into the soup and allowed to melt at the table from the heat of the soup. Soft cheeses, in particular some goat cheeses, are quite nice sliced into rounds, brushed with oil, broiled, then floated in the soup.

Chocolate. For dessert soups, chocolate makes an irresistible garnish. Most fruit soups—except those made predominantly from apple, apricot or pineapple—combine nicely with chocolate, as do creamy-type, sweet soups. Cocoa may be made into a syrup (page 128) or dusted lightly over the top of a sweet soup. Bar chocolate may be grated (a small nutmeg grater works well), chopped, or made into "leaves" (page 160). When using bar chocolate, use a high quality bar (imported Swiss chocolate is good), as it will contain less sugar and have a more true chocolate flavor. A sprinkling of bittersweet may be nice on a very sweet soup, but otherwise semi-sweet, dark chocolate is usually the best choice. Chocolate-like garnishes may also be made with carob, substituting it powdered or in bar form 1 to 1 for chocolate.

Cream or Cream Alternatives. One of the most common—and beautiful—garnishes is á swirl or dollop of cream. The cream may be pulled out into the soup with a paring knife, to form a pattern, or a simple dollop may be garnished with a leaf of fresh herb. A cup of cream may also be frozen in a shallow 3-cup storage container which has been lined with wax paper. Once frozen, the block of cream may be lifted out, the paper peeled off and the cream may be cut with cutters or a sharp knife into attractive shapes. These shapes may be stored in the freezer until just before serving, at which time they may be floated in a soup.

Egg Roll Wrappers. Various simple garnishes may be made from ready-made egg roll wrappers. The most complex, Won Tons (page 154), may be filled with cheese, curried vegetables or virtually any semi-firm filling before being shaped and simmered. In addition, flat egg roll wrappers may be brushed with oil or butter, sprinkled with seasonings, cut into strips or other shapes, then baked in a 350°F. oven until crisp. Treated in this way, they become a sort of light, crispy crouton.

Eggs. Frequently used in French and Chinese soups, eggs make a good garnish as well as boost the protein in soup. Most simply, they may be added as in an Egg Drop Soup (page 56). Alternatively, you may make egg strips to add to consommés or other simple soups. To make strips, in a small bowl, beat a whole egg with 1/4 teaspoon of salt and 1 teaspoon of oil until frothy. Heat 2 teaspoons of oil in a small skillet or crepe pan until very hot but not smoking. Hold the pan off the flame and pour half of the egg mixture into the pan. Tilt the pan with a circular motion to spread the egg as thinly as possible into a round. Return the pan to the heat and cook for about 1 minute, or until it will lift off the pan. Transfer the egg sheet to a plate, then repeat with the remaining egg. Cut the egg sheets into fine shreds, stars or other shapes. They may be prepared up to 24 hours in advance if refrigerated in an airtight container.

Flowers. Flowers make a delicate garnish, either placed on the plate beside a bowl of soup, or floated on top. Small flowers, such as chives, violets and nasturtiums, are beautiful and add a bite of flavor. Larger flowers—roses or day lilies, for example—are best placed beside the bowl, if used whole, or separated into petals if you wish to float them on the soup. Whatever flowers you choose, be certain they are eatable. Rinse them just before placing them on the soup, and take care that they come from plants that have not been sprayed with harmful pesticides.

Fresh Herbs and Spices. Second to cream, fresh herbs are the most common garnish for most soups. A backyard or window sill herb garden makes this simple and inexpensive. Most leaves may be minced or placed on top of the soup whole. Whole leaves (especially chives) may also be used as a "tie" around a small bundle of enoke mushrooms or julienned vegetables. Spices, such as cinnamon or cracked black pepper, may be sprinkled over a smooth soup of contrasting color. Float leaves, such as basil or sorrel, may be shredded and added to a soup just before serving.

Mochi. Mochi (page 172) may be baked in strips until crisp before being floated in a soup. It is also very nice stuffed with cheese or a vegetable mixture after baking, or it may be sprinkled with grated cheese as it bakes. Slabs may be grated raw then used as a topping, like cheese, broiled on top of a bowl of soup, or cubes may be simmered—like dumplings—in a soup for 15 minutes before serving.

Nuts. Nuts add texture and color to soups when used as a garnish. They are best lightly toasted, whether used whole or cut into pieces. For a crispy or spiced nut, combine 1 egg white, 2 teaspoons of oil and spices (salt, cinnamon, cayenne or a spice mix). Beat the coating until frothy, then toss with 2 cups of nuts. Bake the nuts on a lightly oiled baking sheet at 275°F., stirring occasionally, until lightly browned, about 2 hours. Remove from the oven and cool, then store in an airtight container. A sprinkling of seeds, such as sesame, poppy, sunflower and so on, also may be used for a garnish.

Sea Vegetables. Nori (page 172) and dulse (page 168) make striking garnishes because of their dark color and delicate shape. They may be cut into strips, chopped, or nori may be used as a tie or wrapper for vegetables.

Vegetables and Fruit. Whatever vegetable or fruit is in a soup may become a garnish for it. Most vegetables are best lightly steamed to maximize color and retard spoilage. Most fruit are best raw, stored in acidulated water until time to use. The vegetable or fruit should be neatly trimmed or cut into an attractive shape. Some vegetables also work well raw, notably minced scallions, grated daikon, chopped tomatoes and cucumbers, or whole enoke mushrooms. Others, such as tomatoes or zucchini, may be sliced, topped with grated cheese, then broiled before being placed on top of a soup. Potatoes and some other vegetables are nice grated, then made into "patties," then brushed with oil and pan-fried or broiled (like hash browns) for a crispy topping. Potatoes and onions both make delightful garnishes if sliced very thin, tossed with a small amount of oil and baked in a moderate oven on an oiled baking sheet until crisp and brown. Virtually any vegetable and most firm fruit make striking and tasty garnishes if charred under the broiler or on top of the grill. In addition, remember that soup may be served in a container made from a vegetable or fruit. For example, hollowed-out red peppers, oranges, or tiny pumpkins make very nice serving vessels. (Remember to slice off a very thin layer from the bottom of the vegetable or fruit so that it will stand upright.) Some fruit, notably berries and bananas, may be frozen, then used as a whole berry or sliced fruit for a garnish. Many fruits and vegetables may also be carved to form various shapes. The simplest and perhaps most beautiful is a rose. Typically, tomatoes are used. With a sharp paring knife, peel the skin from the blossom end of a tomato in a 1-inch-wide strip. Make the strip as long as possible. Then curl the strip around itself, beginning at the blossom end, resting the rose on the counter for support. Other types of peel—orange or carrot, for example, can also be formed into roses. Flowers may also be formed by shaping a cone from a thin slice of cooked apple, pickled ginger or other thinly sliced vegetable, then layering additional slices around the cone as petals.

Almond Milk

Yield: 3 cups • Prep Time: 5 minutes

3/4 cup raw almonds
2 1/3 cups water
Pinch of salt (optional)

Nut and seed milks are similar to, but less intense in flavor, than nut butters. They can be used as part or all of a soup base, or may be added as a final touch to unite other flavors. I use water as the liquid in this recipe, but it can be replaced by milk, soy milk or rice milk with interesting results. You may also vary the amount of nuts used for a thicker nut "cream."

1. Place nuts and water in a blender and blend at medium speed until nuts are very finely ground, about 5 minutes. Scrape the blender beaker down as the nuts grind. The milk may be used as is or strained to produce a smooth-textured liquid with a slightly less intense flavor. Use the milk immediately or refrigerate in an airtight container for up to 3 days. Storage time varies depending on the freshness of the nuts used. If the milk has a slightly sour smell or taste it must be discarded. The milk may also be frozen in an airtight container for up to 3 months.

Crème Fraîche

Below I list three recipes for homemade versions of crème fraîche. The first is a standard concoction used by many cooks in this country to approximate the French original. Cultured buttermilk reacts with the cream to produce a thick, tangy, full-tasting cream that is very high in fat. The second recipe combines nonfat yogurt with cream. Again the mixture thickens after a number of hours, but the end result contains less fat and is more tangy and less stable when heated than the first. In addition, I use a spin-off idea, combining cream, nonfat yogurt, buttermilk and cheese, from Roy Andries de Groot's crème fraîche recipe in his book *Revolutionizing French Cooking*. Finally, I include a non-dairy cream substitute.

As with any enrichment, cream of any sort will increase the percentage of fat calories in a recipe, so use it with intention and discrimination. For all recipes, cream that is not ultra-pasteurized is recommended.

Crème Fraîche 1

Yield: 2 cups • Prep Time: 2 minutes • Resting Time: 24-36 hours

2 cups heavy whipping cream
2 tablespoons cultured buttermilk

While in India, I made a yogurt-based cream by letting it rest outdoors for about six hours. During the winter in Colorado, the same recipe sometimes takes two days. The resting time varies drastically depending on the culture mixed with the cream, in addition to the humidity and temperature of your kitchen.

1. Combine cream and buttermilk in a 6-cup glass jar and shake to combine. Screw the cap in place and set the jar aside in a warm (between 68° and 80°F.), draft-free place to ripen. A gas-lit oven or on top of the refrigerator often works well.

2. After 24 hours check the mixture. It should be slightly sour-smelling and it should have thickened so that you can scoop out a fingerful and a dent will remain in the cream. Refrigerate until ready to use. It will keep for up to 5 days.

Crème Fraîche 2

Yield: 1 3/4 cups • Prep Time: 2 minutes • Resting Time: 24 Hours

This is the least stable crème fraîche recipe I include. The yogurt may separate or curdle if stirred too much or if heated to a boil.

1/2 cup heavy cream
2 cups plain nonfat yogurt

1. Combine cream and yogurt in a 6-cup glass jar and whisk gently to combine. Screw the cap in place and set the jar aside in a warm (between 68° and 80°F.), draft-free place to ripen. A gas-lit oven or on top of the refrigerator often works well.

2. After 24 hours the cream should have thickened substantially. A layer of whey will have separated out from the solid cream. Line a large strainer with two layers of cheesecloth and place it over the sink. Transfer the cream mixture into the strainer, being careful to disturb it as little as possible. Allow the whey to drain off for at least 30 minutes. Place the cream in a clean jar. Screw the lid in place and refrigerate until ready to use. It will keep for about 5 days.

Crème Fraîche 3—Ricotta Cream

Yield: 2 cups • Prep Time: 10 minutes • Resting Time: 24 hours

This is the lowest fat crème fraîche variation I include. The taste has a delicate, nutty balance and the texture is light. Because of the cheese it is quite stable when heated, though be careful not to boil a soup vigorously once the cream has been added.

1/2 cup low-fat ricotta
1/4 cup cream
1/2 cup plain nonfat yogurt
2 tablespoons cultured buttermilk

1. Place the ricotta in a blender or food processor and purée until very smooth. Add the remaining ingredients and purée for 30 seconds more. Transfer to a 6-cup glass jar and cover tightly. Set the jar aside in a warm (between 68° and 80°F.), draft-free place to ripen. A gas-lit oven or on top of the refrigerator often works well.

2. After 24 hours the cream should have thickened substantially. A layer of whey will have separated out from the solid cream. Line a large strainer with two layers of cheesecloth and place it over the sink. Transfer the cream mixture into the strainer, being careful to disturb it as little as possible. Allow the whey to drain off for at 30 least minutes. Place the cream in a clean jar. Screw the lid in place and refrigerate until ready to use. It will keep for about 5 days.

Soy Cream

Yield: 1 cup • Prep Time: 5 minutes

10 ounces silken tofu, drained
1 3-inch piece kombu (page 170)
6 cups water
1/2 teaspoon salt
1 to 2 tablespoons tahini
   (page 175) or nut butter
   (optional)
1 tablespoon lemon juice

This non-dairy "cream" may be whisked into soups just before serving to add a creamy texture. It will not stand up to cooking.

1. Drain the tofu and rinse the kombu. Place the kombu in a 2-quart saucepan with 6 cups water. Bring this to a boil and add the tofu. Reduce to a simmer and cook for 5 minutes.

2. Drain the tofu and transfer it to a blender. Discard the kombu. Add the remaining ingredients to the blender and purée until very smooth, scraping the beaker as necessary. The cream may be prepared up to 2 days in advance if refrigerated in an airtight container.

Variation

1. If the soup is to be warmed with the cream in it, combine 2 tablespoons kuzu with 2 tablespoons cold water and add this to the tofu before blending. Do not boil the soup.

Hazelnut Butter

Yield: 1 cup • Prep Time: 15 minutes • Cooking Time: 15 minutes

1 1/3 cups (1/2 pound) hazelnuts

Most nuts and some seeds may be ground into "butter" and used as a delightful enrichment in soups.

1. Preheat the oven to 375°F. Arrange the nuts in one layer on a baking sheet. Bake in the center of the oven, stirring several times as they cook, until they are lightly brown to the core.

2. Immediately remove the nuts from the oven and turn them out onto a clean kitchen towel. Rub the nuts with the towel to remove the skins. Skins may be difficult to remove if the nuts are slightly stale. In this case, transfer the nuts to a strainer and rub them against the coarse mesh.

3. Separate nuts from the skin and transfer the nuts to the bowl of a food processor fitted with the metal chopping blade. Process until they turn into a smooth paste, scraping the corners of the bowl several times as the nuts are ground. Use the nut butter immediately or place it in an airtight container and store in the refrigerator for up to a month. If refrigerated, bring to room temperature before using.

Variation

1. Any nut may be ground into a "butter." Those with higher fat content (pecan, macadamia and cashew) are best ground to as smooth a consistency as possible so that the oil and meat remain as homogenous as possible.

Coconut Milk

Yield: 3 cups • Prep Time: 20 minutes • Cooking Time: 25 minutes

While working on an article about coconut with Bruce Healy, we cracked open and experimented with so many coconuts that I thought I might never utter the word again. Bruce, who was a practicing theoretical physicist before he turned his talents to French pastry (to author Mastering the Art of French Pastry), *was determined to simplify the task of working with what is notably one of the world's most difficult ingredients. I can't say that we actually simplified anything, but we got to know the coconut well. Milk extracted from the meat of a coconut can serve as either a base or an enrichment in soups. Making fresh coconut milk is rather labor-intensive given the fact that you must open a coconut and remove the meat from within. If you happen to live near an Asian market, you may find a one-armed coconut grater which attaches to the table and makes the job simple. Otherwise, the instructions below are the simplest we could devise. You may use good quality dried, unsweetened coconut in a pinch, but the results are not nearly as full-bodied. A third option is canned or frozen coconut milk, though you may wish to dilute the pre-made varieties (adding up to 1/4 their volume in water) as they are usually rather thick.*

1 large fresh coconut
5 cups water

1. Preheat the oven to 350°F. Rinse the outside of the coconut. Hold the coconut in one hand over a shallow baking dish. Smack the center horizontal axis of the coconut with the edge of the ball of a hammer. Repeat this, rotating the coconut so that you hit it on several spots of the axis, until it cracks open. Strain the water that spills into the baking pan and set it aside. (You may drink this water, or add it to a soup. It goes rancid very quickly—within 36 hours—so unless you plan to eat a soup immediately, do not add the water.) Place the coconut in the pan and bake until the meat begins to separate from the shell, about 24 minutes.

2. Remove the coconut to a counter. As soon as you can comfortably hold the coconut with a pot holder, pry the meat from the shell using a short-bladed, nonbendable knife such as an oyster knife. Chop the meat into 1-inch pieces and place it in a food processor fitted with the metal chopping blade. (Peeling is not necessary, but yields a whiter coconut milk.) Add the water and purée the mixture for 10 minutes.

3. Line a strainer with cheesecloth and place it over a mixing bowl. Pour the coconut in and drain by twisting the cheesecloth to extract as much milk as possible. Refrigerate the milk in an airtight container for up to 3 days, or freeze for up to 2 months.

Light Vegetable Stock

Yield: 10 cups • Prep Time: 15 minutes • Cooking Time: 1 1/2 hours

2 medium onions, quartered
2 large carrots, cut in 1-inch
  pieces
1 stalk celery, cut in 1-inch pieces
2 leeks, cleaned and chopped
1 small potato, cubed
1 parsnip, peeled and sliced
3 cloves garlic, sliced
12 cups water
2 sprigs fresh thyme or
  3/4 teaspoon dried
1 bay leaf
4 sprigs fresh parsley
4 fresh sage leaves or
  1/4 teaspoon dried
1/4 teaspoon dried marjoram,
  crushed
1 teaspoon salt
6 black peppercorns

This is the most versatile stock because it is so simple to prepare and though it has a complex depth of flavor, it is mild enough that it blends well with other flavors in any savory soup. You may simply wash the vegetables well, then add them to the stock pot skin and all—which will give the stock a darker color and more full flavor, or you may peel them for a more refined effect. As with all stocks, you may alter the vegetables and seasonings according to what you have on hand and the ingredients in the soup—adding asparagus for an asparagus soup or apples to complement a cabbage soup, and so on.

1. Combine the onion, carrots, celery, leeks, potato, parsnip and garlic in a large stock pot or Dutch oven. Add the water and bring to a boil, stirring occasionally. Skim and discard any scum that rises to the surface, then reduce to a simmer and stir in the thyme, bay leaf, parsley, sage, marjoram, salt and pepper. Cover and simmer, stirring occasionally, for 1 1/2 hours.

2. Remove the stock from the heat and cool to room temperature. Strain the broth into a large bowl, then return it to the cooking pot. Discard the cooked vegetables. Boil the broth for about 20 minutes, or until it is reduced to about 10 cups. Transfer it to a storage container and refrigerate, covered, until ready to use. The stock may be prepared up to 5 days in advance. It may also be frozen for up to 3 months.

Variations

1. For a mushroom stock, add 4 dried shiitake mushrooms and 1/2 pound button mushrooms to the original recipe. Increase the garlic to 6 cloves, the parsley to 10 sprigs and the salt to 1 1/2 teaspoons. You may also substitute 1 cup dry white wine for 1 cup of the water.

2. For a tomato stock, omit 1 cup of water from the original recipe. Increase the garlic to 4 cloves, and add 2 pounds chopped fresh tomatoes as well as 3 tablespoons maple sugar or rice syrup (page 172). In addition, you may add 1/4 cup fresh, chopped basil leaves, stirred in when the stock is first removed from the heat to cool, then allow the basil to steep in the stock before it is strained.

3. For a carrot stock, increase the carrots to 1 pound and add a total of 3 stalks of celery. A 1-inch cinnamon stick may also be added.

Hearty Vegetable Stock

Yield: About 10 cups • Prep Time: 15 minutes • Cooking Time: 2 hours

Lentils add depth and character to this recipe for an all-purpose hearty stock. You may vary the type of bean used and/or other ingredients and spices to suit the season, your taste and the soup for which the stock is intended. Hearty stock works especially well for consommés and other clear soups, as well as for soups with a unidimensional character, such as potato or onion.

1. Peel and quarter the onion and stud it with the cloves. Heat the oil in a heavy 6-quart stock pot over medium high heat until hot, but not smoking. Arrange the onion pieces, cut side down, in the bottom of the pot; they should sizzle briskly when first in contact with the oil. Cook, turning occasionally, for about 7 minutes to sear, then brown the onion. Reduce the heat to low and continue to cook, turning several times, for about 20 minutes or until the onion is evenly browned and soft. Put aside.

2. Trim the ends from the carrots and the turnip. Scrub the carrots, celery, turnip, and potato under cold running water, then cut each into 1 1/2 inch pieces. Quarter and core the apple. Remove about an inch of top, the root strands, and any discolored outer layers of stem from the leek. Beginning about 1 inch from the root end, cut through the leek, root to top, leaving the root end intact. Turn it 90 degrees and cut again in the same direction. Wash the leek thoroughly, inside and out, under cold running water to remove all sand and dirt, then chop into 1-inch pieces. Set the vegetables aside as the onion cooks.

3. Pick over the lentils, removing and discarding all stones and debris. Rinse the lentils and add them to the onion. Turn heat to medium and cook, stirring constantly for 5 minutes. Add the vegetables and stir to combine.

4. Turn the heat to high and pour the wine over the vegetables. Cook, stirring constantly, for about 1 minute, until all of the alcohol smell has cooked off. Add all of the remaining ingredients, cover and bring the stock to a boil. Reduce heat to low. Skim and discard any foam that has risen to the surface. Cover and simmer for 1 1/2 hours.

5. Remove the stock from the heat. It may be strained and used immediately or cooled and stored for later use. If you are not using the stock right away, cool it briefly at room temperature after removing from the heat, then place it in the refrigerator to cool completely. Cooling the stock in the refrigerator helps eliminate the possibility that the vegetables cook beyond their optimum point (and become bitter or grassy) and helps prevent bacteria from growing in the broth as it cools.

6. When the stock is completely cooled, strain it and discard the vegetables. Cool again and allow it to settle, then skim and discard all fat that remains on the surface. Refrigerate the stock and use it within 3 days, or freeze it in airtight containers for up to 6 months. Freezing some stock in 1 cup portions is convenient so that you can use it as an enrichment or added flavoring without having to thaw a larger quantity than may be required.

1 onion
4 whole cloves
2 tablespoons olive or sesame oil
2 carrots
1 turnip
2 stalks celery
1 red potato
1 Granny Smith apple
1 leek
1/2 cup brown lentils
1 cup dry white wine
12 cups water
1 teaspoon salt
10 black peppercorns
2 cloves garlic

BOUQUET GARNI:
8 springs parsley
4 sprigs thyme
  (2 teaspoons dried)
1 bay leaf
2 sprigs winter savory
  (1/2 teaspoon dried)

Kombu Vegetable Stock

Yield: 10 cups • Prep Time: 5 minutes • Cooking Time: 50 minutes

2 4-inch pieces kombu
(page 170)
1 carrot
1 sweet potato
1 stalk celery
1 onion
1 teaspoon salt
1 bay leaf
2 cloves garlic
6 peppercorns
12 cups water

When you first make stock with kombu you may be surprised at the strong ocean-like aroma it produces as it is being simmered. Once cooked and strained, however, the taste is gently aromatic, making it ideal for use in many soups. Kombu is widely used in Japan where it is highly regarded for its healing capacity. Kombu serves as the base for the most common form of Japanese stock, called "dashi." Stock made with kombu becomes cloudy after a day, so it is best used immediately.

1. Rinse kombu under cold water and place it in a 6-quart saucepan. Trim the ends from the carrot, sweet potato and celery, then scrub them well under cold water to remove all dirt. Cut each into 1-inch pieces and add them to the saucepan.

2. Peel the onion and quarter it. Add it with the remaining ingredients to the saucepan and bring to a boil. Reduce to a simmer, then skim and discard any foam that rises to the surface. Continue to cook, partially covered, for 45 minutes. Remove the stock from the heat and cool for at least 10 minutes before straining. Discard vegetables.

Variation

1. Add 8 slices of crushed ginger, 1 ounce burdock root and 1 small piece of daikon to the stock before simmering.

3 • Starters

Celery Root and Tomato Consommé

Yield: 8 servings • Prep Time: 30 minutes • Cooking Time: 50 minutes

Celery root has an intense celery flavor with none of the bite or bitterness that is sometimes found in branch celery. It gives a deep, smooth quality to this elegant consommé. Garnish the soup with Ricotta Pesto Won Tons (page 155), chopped tomatoes, or shredded egg sheets (page 32).

1. Sauté the sliced leeks, carrot, celery, and garlic in the butter over medium heat for about 10 minutes, until the leeks are wilted. Add the water. Cover, turn heat to high and bring the soup to a boil, then reduce to a simmer. Skim and discard any foam that rises to the surface. Cover and simmer for 10 minutes.

2. Peel and cube the celery root. Roughly chop the tomatoes. Add the celery root, tomatoes, celery seeds, salt, and peppercorns to the broth. Cover and simmer gently for 1 hour. Remove from the heat and strain. Taste and adjust the seasonings. Discard the vegetables and chill the broth overnight.

3. Skim and discard all fat that has risen to the surface of the broth. Pour the soup into a 2-quart saucepan, cover, and bring to a boil. Place the egg whites in a mixing bowl and beat with a fork until frothy. Add the chopped leeks and beat again. Remove the soup from the heat and immediately pour a thin stream of the egg white mixture into the soup. Use a wire whisk to gently agitate the broth as you pour. Return the soup to a very low heat and continue to agitate the broth gently until the egg mixture has risen to the surface and tiny bubbles begin to appear in the liquid. Stop whisking and leave the soup to clarify. After about 10 minutes, the broth visible beneath the egg whites should be crystal clear.

4. Remove the soup from the heat. Line a large strainer with several layers of cheesecloth and place it over a large bowl. With a skimmer or slotted spoon, gently remove and discard the thick layer of scum from the top of the soup, then carefully ladle the broth through the cheesecloth. It is imperative that you not agitate the soup too vigorously when whisking or pouring it through the strainer, or the clumps of egg white will break apart and the consommé will never become clear.

5. The consommé may be served immediately or prepared ahead and refrigerated in an airtight container for up to 4 days. It may also be frozen for up to 2 months. Before serving, warm the consommé until it is piping hot. Divide it among 8 serving bowls and garnish as desired.

1 pound leeks, cleaned and sliced
1 large carrot, diced
2 stalks celery, sliced
6 cloves garlic, sliced
2 tablespoons butter
12 cups water
2 pounds celery root
2 pounds tomatoes
1 teaspoon celery seeds
1 teaspoon salt
4 black peppercorns

FOR CLARIFICATION:
2 egg whites
2 leeks, roughly chopped, or substitute 1 cup parsley, packed

GARNISH:
Ricotta Pesto Won Tons (page 155) or 1/2 cup chopped tomatoes or 3 shredded egg sheets (page 32)

Beet and Fennel Consommé with Gorgonzola Won Tons

Yield: 8 servings • Prep Time: 30 minutes • Cooking Time: 50 minutes

This stunning soup has an extraordinary combination of flavors. The sweet taste of beet is complemented by a brisk bite of fennel to produce a well-balanced, deep rose-colored broth. Gorgonzola Won Tons add the finishing touch.

1 pound leeks, cleaned
    and thickly sliced
1 large carrot, diced
2 stalks celery, sliced
4 cloves garlic, sliced
2 tablespoons butter
12 cups water
3 pounds beet root
1 pound fennel root
1 teaspoon fennel seeds
1 teaspoon salt
4 black peppercorns

FOR CLARIFICATION:
2 egg whites
Trimmed tops chopped from
    leeks, above

GARNISH:
Gorgonzola Won Tons (page 154)

1. In a 6-quart saucepan, sauté the sliced leeks, carrot, celery and garlic in the butter over medium heat for about 10 minutes, until the leeks are wilted. Be careful not to let the leeks or the garlic get brown or they will add a bitter taste to the consommé. Add the water. Cover, turn the heat to high and bring the soup to a boil. Reduce to a simmer, then skim and discard any foam that rises to the surface. Cover and simmer for 10 minutes.

2. Peel and slice the beets. Remove any extremely tough or damaged outer layers of the fennel and trim 1 inch from the tops. Cut the fennel bulbs in half lengthwise, remove the cores, and slice each half thinly. Add the beets, fennel, fennel seeds, salt, and peppercorns to the broth. Cover and simmer gently for 1 hour. Remove from the heat and strain the soup, reserving the liquid. Taste and adjust the seasonings. (The broth will have a peppery quality that will disappear once the soup is clarified.) Discard the vegetables and chill the broth overnight.

3. Skim and discard all fat that has risen to the surface of the broth. Pour the soup into a 6-quart saucepan, cover, and bring to a boil. Place the egg whites in a mixing bowl and beat with a fork until frothy. Add the chopped leeks and beat again. Remove the soup from the heat and immediately pour a thin stream of the egg white mixture into the soup. Use a wire whisk to gently agitate the broth as you pour. Return the soup to a very low heat and continue to agitate the broth gently until the egg mixture has risen to the surface and tiny bubbles begin to appear in the liquid. Stop whisking and leave the soup to clarify. After about 10 minutes, the broth visible beneath the egg whites should be crystal clear.

4. Remove the soup from the heat. Line a large strainer with several layers of cheesecloth and place it over a large bowl. With a skimmer or slotted spoon, gently remove and discard the thick layer of scum from the top of the soup, then carefully ladle the broth through the cheesecloth. It is imperative that you not agitate the soup too vigorously when whisking or pouring it through the strainer, or the clumps of egg white will break apart and the consommé will never be clear.

5. The consommé may be served immediately or prepared ahead and refrigerated in an airtight container for up to 4 days. It may also be frozen for up to 2 months. Before serving, warm the consommé until it is piping hot. Divide it among 8 serving bowls. Place 4 cooked Gorgonzola won tons in each bowl and sprinkle feathery fennel fronds over the soup. Serve immediately. (The won tons gradually turn the consommé cloudy, so it is best to add them just as the soup is served.)

Butternut Squash Consommé with Curried Potato Won Tons

Yield: 8 servings • Prep Time: 30 minutes • Cooking Time: 60 minutes

The combination of apples, winter squash and curry has been hailed as a favorite for years. In this sophisticated broth the tastes are exquisitely blended. Serve it hot with Curried Potato Won Tons (page 155), or cold with Curried Chapati Chips (page 153).

1. Sauté the sliced onions, carrots, celery and garlic in the oil over medium heat for about 10 minutes, until the onions are wilted. Add the water. Cover, turn heat to high and bring the soup to a boil, then reduce to a simmer. Skim and discard any foam that rises to the surface. Cover and simmer for 10 minutes.

2. Halve and peel the squash. Scrape out and discard the seeds, then cube the meat. Quarter and core the apples. Add the squash, apples and remaining ingredients to the broth, then cover and simmer gently for 1 hour. Remove from the heat and strain. Taste and adjust the seasonings. Discard the vegetables and chill the broth overnight.

3. Skim and discard all fat that has risen to the surface of the broth. Pour the soup into a 3-quart saucepan, cover, and bring to a boil. Place the egg whites in a mixing bowl and beat with a fork until frothy. Chop the cilantro into large pieces and stir them into the eggs, then beat again. Remove the soup from the heat and immediately pour a thin stream of the egg white mixture into the soup. Use a wire whisk to gently agitate the broth as you pour. Return the soup to a very low heat and continue to agitate the broth gently until the egg mixture has risen to the surface and tiny bubbles begin to appear in the liquid. Stop whisking and leave the soup to clarify. After about 10 minutes, the broth visible beneath the egg whites should be crystal clear.

4. Remove the soup from the heat. Line a large strainer with several layers of cheesecloth and place it over a large bowl. With a skimmer or slotted spoon, gently remove and discard the thick layer of scum from the top of the soup, then carefully ladle the broth through the cheesecloth. It is imperative that you not agitate the soup too vigorously when whisking or pouring it through the strainer, or the clumps of egg white will break apart and pass through the cheesecloth and the consommé will not be clear.

5. The consommé may be served immediately or prepared ahead and refrigerated in an airtight container for up to 4 days. It may also be frozen for up to 2 months. Before serving, warm the consommé until it is piping hot. Divide it among 8 serving bowls and garnish as desired.

1 pound onions, sliced
1 1/2 cups diced carrots
2 stalks celery, sliced
6 cloves garlic, sliced
2 tablespoons peanut oil
12 cups water
4 pounds butternut squash
1 pound green apples
1 teaspoon coriander seeds
1 teaspoon salt
4 black peppercorns
1/2 teaspoon fennel seeds
1/8 teaspoon red chili flakes

FOR CLARIFICATION:
2 egg whites
1 cup cilantro, packed

GARNISH:
Curried Potato Won Tons
   (page 155) or
Chapati Chips (page 153)

Lotus Petal Soup

Yield: 8 servings • Prep Time: 15 minutes • Cooking Time: 1 1/2 hours

2 pounds carrots, sliced
4 leeks, cleaned and chopped
3 stalks celery, sliced
10 cups water
1 teaspoon salt
1 teaspoon celery seeds
1 teaspoon fennel seeds
1 teaspoon cumin seeds
8 black peppercorns
4 sprigs Italian parsley
1-inch ginger root, sliced
  and flattened

GARNISH:
16 nasturtium leaves (or Italian
  parsley, if nasturtium is
  unavailable)
1/4 cup pickled ginger
1/2 cup sliced carrot

Ginger, added in the final stage of cooking, lends fire to the delicately sweet taste of carrots in this simple bouillon. Garnish each bowl with whole nasturtium leaves, pickled ginger "flowers" and sliced carrots for a stunning presentation.

1. Combine all of the ingredients, except the ginger and garnishes, in a 4-quart saucepan. Bring to a boil, then reduce to a simmer and cook, covered and stirring occasionally for 1 1/4 hours. Add the ginger and continue to cook for 15 minutes.

2. Remove the soup from the heat. Lift out and discard the ginger, then allow the soup to cool with the ingredients in the liquid. Strain and serve hot or at room temperature, garnished with nasturtium leaves (or Italian parsley, if nasturtium is unavailable), pickled ginger and sliced carrot. The bouillon may be prepared up to 3 days in advance if refrigerated in an airtight container. It may also be frozen for up to 3 months.

Note: To make a flower shape from pickled ginger, select 5-7 small slices. Shape one into a cone and place it in the palm of your hand, cone pointing up. Wrap the remaining slices of ginger around the cone, overlapping them to form "petals."

Tarragon Bouillon

Yield: 8 servings • Prep Time: 15 minutes • Cooking Time: 1 1/2 hours

1 pound carrots, sliced
1 small red onion, quartered
2 leeks, cleaned and chopped
2 stalks celery, sliced
1 parsnip, sliced
1 large potato, cubed
1 small turnip, cubed
3 cloves garlic, sliced
10 4-inch stalks fresh tarragon
10 cups water
2 teaspoons salt
5 black peppercorns
4 sprigs parsley

GARNISH:
1 stalk fresh tarragon
1/4 cup diced red pepper

The refreshing taste of tarragon penetrates this simple broth for an uplifting start to a mid-summer's soup.

1. Combine all of the ingredients, except the garnish, in a 4-quart saucepan. Bring the soup to a boil, then reduce it to a simmer and cook, covered and stirring occasionally, for 1 1/2 hours.

2. Remove the soup from the heat and allow it to cool with the ingredients in the liquid. Strain the soup, discarding the solids. Taste and adjust the seasonings. Serve the broth warm or at room temperature, garnished with tarragon leaves and red pepper. The bouillon may be prepared up to 6 days in advance if refrigerated in an airtight container. It may be frozen for up to 4 months.

Variation

1. Combine 1 cup cooked garbanzo beans with 1 tablespoon balsamic vinegar, 1/4 teaspoon salt, 2 tablespoons chopped tarragon leaves and 1 tablespoon olive oil. Marinate overnight, refrigerated in an airtight container. Add the beans to the soup. Warm and serve with minced red bell pepper.

Porcini Bouillon

Yield: 8 servings • Prep Time: 20 minutes • Cooking Time: 1 1/2 hours

It is difficult to say whether the aroma or taste of this dark, rich broth is more appealing. No matter, the soup is sophisticated and elegant.

1. Drain the porcini mushrooms, saving their soaking liquid. Combine half of the porcini and the remaining ingredients, except the garnish, in a 3-quart saucepan. Bring to a boil. Stir in the reserved soaking liquid, then reduce to a simmer and cook, covered and stirring occasionally for 1 1/2 hours.

2. Remove the soup from the heat and allow it to cool with the ingredients in the liquid. Strain and stir the remaining porcini into the broth. Serve warm with fennel root in each bowl and sliced lemon on the side. The bouillon may be prepared up to 5 days in advance if refrigerated in an airtight container. It may be frozen for 3 months.

Variations

1. Serve topped with Sesame Parmesan Croutons (page 149).
2. Sauté 3/4 pound sliced mushrooms in 1/2 tablespoon olive oil until they are tender, about 10 minutes. Stir them into the finished broth along with 6 ounces fettucini (cooked), 1/4 cup chopped sun-dried tomatoes, and 2 tablespoons chopped fresh tarragon leaves.

2 ounces dried porcini
    mushrooms (page 172),
    softened in
    2 cups hot water
1/2 pound button mushrooms,
    sliced
2 carrots, peeled and sliced
1 small red onion, peeled
    and quartered
2 leeks, cleaned and chopped
1 stalk celery, sliced
3/4 cup sliced turnip
3 cloves garlic, sliced
1 small sprig thyme or
    1 teaspoon dried
1 bay leaf
2 teaspoons fennel seeds
8 cups water
2 1/4 teaspoons salt
5 black peppercorns
4 sprigs parsley
1 small fennel frond
    (1/4 cup chopped)

GARNISH:
3/4 cup sliced fennel root
Lemon wedges

Gazpacho Soup

Yield: 6 servings • Prep Time: 25 minutes

This recipe is a snap when using a food processor; otherwise, it is extremely labor-intensive. Fresh carrot juice serves as a fundamental flavor which is balanced with the bite of balsamic vinegar. Serve the Gazpacho very cold, topped with Sweet Onion Crisps (page 151) and Garlic Croutons (page 149).

1. Fit the food processor with the metal chopping blade. Turn the motor on and drop the garlic through feed tube to process finely. Cut the onion quarters crosswise in half. Place them in the processor bowl. Use an on-off pulse motion until the onion is minced. Cut the peppers into squares, add them to the processor bowl. Process finely. Transfer the mixture to a separate, large bowl. Stir in the jalapeño.

2. Cut the cucumber into 1-inch pieces and place it in the processor. With a pulse action, process it into small pieces. Add this to the onion mixture. Remove and discard the stem ends from the tomatoes. Chop the tomatoes and place them in the processor. Process until only small pieces remain. Add this to the onions along with remaining ingredients. Cover and chill overnight. Taste and adjust seasonings.

3 cloves garlic, peeled
1 small red onion, peeled
    and quartered
1 small green bell pepper,
    quartered, seeded, and
    white membrane removed
1 jalapeño pepper, minced
2 cucumbers, peeled and seeded
6 large ripe tomatoes
1/4 cup minced fresh parsley
1/4 cup minced fresh basil
3 cups fresh carrot juice
1 cup water
1 tablespoon olive oil
3 tablespoons balsamic vinegar
2 teaspoons ground cumin
1 teaspoon salt
1/2 cup jicama, finely grated

Cranberry Apple Gazpacho

Yield: 8 servings • Prep Time: 20 minutes

1 12-ounce package cranberries,
    frozen
3 cloves garlic, peeled
1 small red onion, peeled and
    quartered
1 small red pepper, seeded and
    roughly chopped
1 small cucumber, peeled and
    seeded and roughly chopped
2 to 3 tablespoons mellow white
    miso (page 171)
1 jalapeño pepper, seeded and
    minced
2 tablespoons rice syrup
    (page 172)
2 1/2 teaspoons ground cumin
1/2 cup orange juice
3 cups unfiltered apple juice
2 cups water
1/2 cup minced cilantro leaves

GARNISH:
Tiny dice of apple

At holiday time when novel ideas for entertaining are sometimes as scarce as fresh tomatoes, you can enchant your guests with this unusual "Gazpacho." The recipe calls for frozen cranberries, so stock up when they are available, then you can enjoy this soup year-round.

1. Pick over cranberries and discard any bits of stem that are attached to the berries and berries that are overly soft. Rinse well and place in an airtight container. Freeze completely.

2. Place the cranberries in a food processor fitted with the metal chopping blade and purée until fine and evenly ground. You may need to scrape the sides of the bowl down several times as you work. Transfer to a large bowl.

3. Replace the lid of the processor and start the motor with an empty bowl. Drop the garlic into the bowl with the motor running. When it is evenly chopped, stop the motor and place all of the onion in the bowl. Pulse the motor until the onion is chopped into about 1/2-inch pieces. Add the red pepper and then the cucumber, pulsing to chop after each addition.

4. In a small mixing bowl, combine the miso, jalapeño, rice syrup, and cumin. Whisk in the orange juice, add this mixture to the processor bowl and purée for 30 seconds to blend thoroughly. Add the onion mixture to the cranberries and stir to combine. Stir in the apple juice, water and cilantro. Serve chilled, topped with small pieces of apple if desired.

Peach and Pepper Gazpacho

Yield: 8 servings • Prep Time: 20 minutes • Resting Time: 24 hours

3 cloves garlic, peeled
1 small red onion, peeled and
    quartered
2 cups sliced peaches
1 red bell pepper, peeled,
    seeded and roughly chopped
1 green bell pepper, peeled,
    seeded and roughly chopped
1 cucumber, peeled, seeded
    and quartered
1/4 cup orange juice
3 tablespoons honey or sugar
2 teaspoons ground cinnamon
1 teaspoon salt
2 jalapeño peppers, seeded
    and minced
3 cups water
1/2 cup minced mint leaves

This unusual combination of flavors and textures is heavenly when served ice cold. It is an ideal soup to prepare well ahead, giving flavors a day or so to marry.

1. Fit the processor with the metal chopping blade and lock the lid in place. Start the motor and, with the motor running, drop the garlic through the feed tube into the bowl. When the garlic is evenly chopped, after about 10 seconds, stop the motor and place all of the onion in the bowl. Pulse the motor until the onion is chopped into about 1/2-inch pieces. Add the peaches, bell peppers and then the cucumber, pulsing to chop after each addition.

2. In a small mixing bowl, combine the orange juice, honey, cinnamon, salt and jalapeños. Add this mixture to the processor bowl and purée for 30 seconds to blend thoroughly. Stir in the water and mint, then transfer to a large bowl. Cover and chill for at least 24 hours. The soup may be prepared up to 6 days in advance if refrigerated in an airtight container. It does not freeze well. Serve chilled.

Potato Basil Soup

Yield: 6 servings • Prep Time: 25 minutes • Cooking Time: 1 1/2 hours

Basil and miso are blended to liven up a simple potato soup.

1. Place potatoes, garlic, onions and stock in a 3-quart saucepan. Cover and bring to a boil. Skim and discard foam that rises to the surface. Add the parsley, salt, pepper, nutmeg and cayenne. Reduce to a simmer and continue to cook until the potatoes are very tender, about 1 1/4 hours. Remove from heat and cool.

2. Strain the soup into a large bowl. Pour the soup broth into the soup pot (make sure no pieces of vegetable remain in the pot) and boil it until it has reduced to about 7 cups. Meanwhile, remove the parsley from the strainer, then purée the vegetables in a food processor or blender until very smooth. The soup may be prepared to this point up to 5 days in advance if refrigerated in an airtight container.

3. Crush the kuzu and combine it with 2 tablespoons of water. In a separate bowl, mix together the tahini, miso, and mustard. Stir the kuzu into the soup and cook until slightly thickened. Whisk 1/4 cup of soup into the miso mixture until smooth. Stir this back into the soup. Add the basil. Warm, but do not boil. Serve.

2 1/2 pounds Yellow Finn or other baking potatoes, peeled and cubed (8 cups)
12 cloves garlic, sliced
2 cups chopped yellow onion
9 cups water or light vegetable stock (page 38)
4 sprigs parsley
1/2 teaspoon salt
1/4 teaspoon pepper
1/4 teaspoon nutmeg
Pinch of cayenne
2 tablespoons kuzu (page 170)
3 tablespoons water
2 teaspoons tahini (page 172) (optional)
1/4 cup light miso (page 171)
1 teaspoon Dijon mustard
1/2 cup chopped basil

Carrot Saffron Soup

Yield: 6 servings • Prep Time: 20 minutes • Cooking Time: 1 1/4 hours

This simple soup is a gem! The combination of carrot and saffron echo and complement one another in color and taste for a very intriguing effect. The result is an elegant purée that serves well as a first course or a simple meal in itself.

1. Place the carrots, onion, celery, yam and water in a 4-quart saucepan. Cover and bring to a boil. Skim and discard foam that rises to the surface. Add the saffron, parsley, salt, pepper and cayenne. Reduce to a simmer and continue to cook until the carrots are very tender, about 1 1/4 hours. Remove from heat and cool.

2. Strain the soup into a large bowl. Pour the broth into the soup pot (make sure no pieces of vegetable remain in the pot) and boil it until it has reduced to about 6 cups. Meanwhile, remove the parsley from the strainer, then purée the vegetables in a mill or food processor until very smooth.

3. When the broth has reduced, whisk in the puréed vegetables and rice syrup. If you wish to have a slightly thicker consistency, mix the arrowroot with 3 tablespoons cold water, then stir this into the soup. Heat to a boil and serve immediately. The soup may be prepared in advance and refrigerated in an airtight container for up to 5 days. It may also be frozen for 2 months.

2 pounds carrots, cut in large rounds
1 1/2 cups chopped yellow onion
3 stalks celery, sliced
1 large yam, cubed
9 cups light vegetable stock (page 38) or water
2 teaspoons saffron threads, crushed
4 sprigs parsley
1 teaspoon salt
1/4 teaspoon pepper
Pinch of cayenne
2 tablespoons rice syrup (page 172)
2 tablespoons arrowroot (optional)

Variations

1. Stir 1/3 cup crème fraîche or soy cream into the finished soup and serve garnished with Garlic Croutons (page 149).

2. Float broiled goat cheese slices in each bowl.

Tomato Soup

Yield: 6 servings • Prep Time: 20 minutes • Cooking Time: 45 minutes

2 tablespoons olive oil
1 pound yellow onions, diced
4 cloves garlic, sliced
2 1/2 pounds vine ripe tomatoes
2 tablespoons flour
5 cups light vegetable stock
   (page 38)
2 sprigs parsley
1 sprig fresh thyme or
   1/2 teaspoon dried
1 bay leaf
1/2 teaspoon salt
1/8 teaspoon black pepper
1/4 cup minced basil or mint

GARNISH:
Garlic Croutons (page 149)
4 ounces freshly grated
   Jarlsberg cheese

A classic-tasting tomato soup that is best made in mid-summer when the crop is plentiful. Fresh herbs—in particular, basil or mint—stirred in just before serving add a refreshing touch. For a creamy version, 1/2 cup crème fraîche or soy cream may be stirred in as well. Serve the soup hot or cold, topped with Garlic Croutons (page 149).

1. In a 4-quart saucepan, heat the oil over medium heat until hot, but not smoking. Add the onions and cook, stirring constantly, until they are coated thoroughly with oil, about a minute. Reduce heat to medium low, add the garlic and continue to cook, stirring frequently, until the onions are soft and translucent, about 15 minutes.

2. Meanwhile, quarter each tomato. Trim the stem end from each wedge and cut the tomatoes into large chunks. Set them aside.

3. When the onions are very soft and translucent, turn the heat to high. Immediately sprinkle the flour over the onions and stir constantly. Cook until all of the vegetables are coated evenly with the flour, about 1 minute.

4. Gradually add the tomatoes to the onions. As you add them, stir the mixture so that the liquid from the tomatoes binds with the cooked flour and thickens evenly. When about half of the tomatoes are incorporated and the soup has begun to thin, you can stir in the remaining ingredients all at once except the minced basil and garnish. Cover and simmer, stirring often, until the onions are very soft, about 20 minutes.

5. Remove the thyme and bay leaf from the soup and purée it through the fine grade of the food mill. The soup may also be puréed in a food processor; however, seeds and skin from the tomatoes will remain. To obtain a fine texture, the soup will need to be forced through a fine mesh strainer.

6. When puréed, return the soup to a clean saucepan, stir in the minced basil, and warm. Taste and adjust the seasonings. The soup may be prepared up to 5 days in advance if refrigerated in an airtight container. It may also be frozen for up to 3 months. Ladle soup into bowls and top with garlic-flavored croutons or shavings of cheese.

Variation

1. Stir 2/3 cup chopped sun-dried tomatoes (drained) into the soup with the basil.

Mushroom Soup

Yield: 8 servings • Prep Time: 30 minutes • Cooking Time: 40 minutes

This full-flavored mushroom soup can become the main course when served topped with garlicky Spinach Dumplings (page 153).

1. Trim the stems from the mushrooms and place both caps and stems in a strainer over the sink. Quickly rinse them under cold, gently running water, tossing them with your hands to remove all dirt. Set them aside on a clean kitchen towel to dry as you prepare the rest of the ingredients for the soup. Heat the olive oil and butter in a heavy 4-quart saucepan over medium high heat. When the fat is hot, but not smoking, add the diced shallots. Sauté for 1 minute then turn the heat to low and cook slowly for about 15 minutes, stirring frequently, until the shallots are soft and translucent. Remove 1/4 of the shallots and set aside for use in the dumplings. Add the carrots, celery and walnuts. Continue to cook over low heat for several minutes as you prepare the mushrooms.

2. Chop 3/4 of the mushrooms into small dice and leave the remaining whole. Set aside.

3. Turn the heat under the saucepan to high and when the vegetables are hot, add the wine, which will sizzle and steam vigorously. Shake the pan until this activity dies down, then add the chopped mushrooms and 2 tablespoons of garlic. Sprinkle with lemon juice and mix well. Add the stock and spices, reduce the heat to low and simmer, half covered, until the carrots are soft when pressed between your fingers, about 30 minutes.

4. Remove the soup from the heat and strain the vegetables from the liquid, saving the broth. Discard the thyme sprigs and bay leaves, then purée the cooked vegetables until very fine and evenly ground. Meanwhile, return the reserved cooking liquid to the saucepan and boil it, uncovered, until it is reduced to about 8 cups.

5. Slice the reserved mushrooms and simmer them in the reduced broth until tender, about 10 minutes. (If you are serving the dumplings, cook them at this point.) Stir the puréed vegetables and the milk into the broth and mix well. Taste and adjust the seasonings. Serve immediately. The soup—without the dumplings—may be prepared to this point, up to 2 days ahead if refrigerated in an airtight container. It does not freeze well.

3 pounds mushrooms
4 teaspoons olive oil
4 teaspoons butter
1 1/2 cups finely diced shallots
1 cup finely diced carrot
3/4 cup finely diced celery
1/4 cup walnuts, toasted with
   skins removed (page 33)
1/2 cup dry white wine
3 tablespoons minced garlic
2 tablespoons lemon juice
10 cups mushroom stock
   (page 38)
4 sprigs fresh parsley
2 bay leaves
2 sprigs fresh thyme or
   1 teaspoon dried
1 teaspoon salt
1/4 teaspoon nutmeg
1/4 teaspoon black pepper
1/4 teaspoon cayenne pepper
1/4 teaspoon mace
1 cup soy milk or milk

Fresh Garlic Soup

Yield: 8 servings • Prep Time: 20 minutes • Cooking Time: 40 minutes

1 1/4 cups garlic cloves
2 tablespoons butter
1 tablespoon olive oil
1 1/2 cups diced onion
1 1/2 cups minced shallots
1/4 cup finely diced carrot
4 tablespoon flour
1 cup white wine
6 cups hearty vegetable stock
   (page 39)
3 extra cloves garlic, crushed
2 tablespoons minced parsley
Salt and black pepper
Pinch of nutmeg and cayenne
1/2 cup light cream or soy milk
   mixed with 2 tablespoons
   soy milk powder

GARNISH:
Pear Biscuits (page 147)

Don't be alarmed at the amount of garlic called for in this recipe. Garlic's taste mellows with long cooking, so this light soup is actually quite tame in flavor.

1. Smash the garlic cloves with the flat side of a large knife. Do not flatten the garlic, simply crack it open. Wet your hands and remove skins from the garlic. Slice each clove in half, then remove and discard the germinating center of each clove.

2. Melt the butter and olive oil in a 3-quart saucepan. Add the onions, shallots and carrots, then cook, stirring constantly, for 2 minutes. Add the garlic. Turn the heat to low and allow vegetables to cook, stirring occasionally, until the onions are glistening and translucent, about 20 minutes. Sprinkle flour over the vegetables. Cook, stirring constantly until the onions turn light brown, about 10 minutes.

3. Pour the wine into the pan and stir briskly, allowing the alcohol smell to cook off. Add the stock, whisking well to avoid having lumps form. Boil the soup, stirring, for 2 minutes, then reduce it to a simmer. Add the 3 crushed cloves of garlic, parsley, and seasonings. Allow the soup to simmer, half covered for 20 minutes.

4. Remove the soup from the heat and purée. Return it to the saucepan, add the cream and reheat. Taste and adjust seasonings. Serve warm with Pear Biscuits alongside.

Chanterelle Champagne Soup

Yield: 8 servings • Prep Time: 30 minutes • Cooking Time: 40 minutes

1 1/2 pounds chanterelle mushrooms (page 167) (may use
   hedgehog mushrooms)
2 pounds button mushrooms
4 teaspoons olive oil
4 teaspoons butter
1 cup finely diced carrot
1 cup finely diced onion
3/4 cup finely diced celery
1 cup dry champagne
2 tablespoons minced garlic
2 tablespoons lemon juice
10 cups mushroom stock
   (page 38)
4 sprigs parsley
2 bay leaves
2 sprigs fresh thyme
   (or 1 teaspoon dried)
1 1/2 teaspoon salt
1/4 teaspoon nutmeg

The elegant tastes of chanterelle mushrooms and champagne combine in exquisite harmony in this delicate soup.

1. Clean the mushrooms (page 49) and set them aside on a clean kitchen towel to dry, as you prepare the rest of the ingredients for the soup.

2. Heat the olive oil and butter in a heavy 3-quart saucepan over medium high heat. When the fat is hot, but not smoking, add the diced carrot, onion, and celery and sauté for 1 minute. Turn the heat to low and cook the vegetables slowly for about 15 minutes, stirring frequently, until the onion is soft and translucent.

3. Chop half of the chanterelles and all of the button mushrooms into small dice, then set aside. Turn the heat to high and, when the vegetables are hot, add the champagne, which will sizzle and steam vigorously. Shake the pan until this activity dies down, then add the diced mushrooms and the garlic, tossing them several times. Add the lemon juice and mix well. Stir in the stock and spices. Reduce the heat to low and simmer, half covered, until the carrots are soft when pressed between your fingers, about 25 minutes.

4. Remove the soup from the heat and strain the vegetables from the liquid, saving both. Discard the thyme and bay leaf, then purée the cooked vegetables in a food processor or blender until very fine and evenly ground. Meanwhile, return the reserved cooking liquid to the saucepan and boil it, uncovered, until it is reduced to about 8 cups.

5. Cut the reserved chanterelles into large pieces and simmer them in the reduced broth until tender. Stir the puréed soup base and the milk into the broth and mix well. Stir in the chervil, then taste and adjust the seasonings. Serve hot.

1/4 teaspoon black pepper
1/4 teaspoon ground mace
Pinch of cayenne pepper
1 cup milk or cream
1/4 cup minced chervil or
   2 tablespoons minced parsley

Variation

1. Replace the milk with 1 cup of cashew or almond milk (page 34) and replace the chervil with 3 tablespoons snipped chives.

Tree Oyster Bisque

Yield: 8 servings • Prep Time: 30 minutes • Cooking Time: 40 minutes

Tree oysters are slightly sweet-tasting mushrooms that got their name in part because their cooked texture and color are reminiscent of oysters. Delicate clumps of light brown to grey, petal-like tree oysters are available commercially cultivated in fine produce markets.

1. Clean the mushrooms and set them aside on a clean kitchen towel to dry, as you prepare the rest of the ingredients for the bisque. Cultivated tree oysters will probably only need to be brushed gently with a mushroom brush or dry paper towel.

2. Heat the olive oil and butter in a heavy 3-quart saucepan over medium high heat. When the fat is hot, but not smoking, add the diced carrot, onion, celery and red pepper. Sauté for 1 minute. Turn the heat to low and cook the vegetables slowly, stirring frequently, until the onion is soft and translucent, about 15 minutes.

3. Chop half of the mushrooms into small dice. Turn the heat to high and, when the vegetables are hot, add the cognac, which will sizzle and steam vigorously. Shake the pan until this activity dies down, then add the diced mushrooms and the garlic, tossing them with cooking juices. Squeeze in the lime juice and mix well. Add the stock and spices, reduce the heat to low and simmer, half covered, until the carrots are soft when pressed between your fingers, about 25 minutes.

4. Remove the bisque from the heat and strain the vegetables from the liquid, saving the broth. Discard the thyme and bay leaf, then purée the cooked vegetables until very fine and evenly ground. Meanwhile, return the reserved cooking liquid to the saucepan and boil it, uncovered, until it is reduced to about 8 cups.

5. Cut the reserved mushrooms into large pieces and simmer them in the reduced broth until tender. Stir the puréed soup base and the milk into the broth and mix well. Taste and adjust the seasonings, adding more salt, pepper and nutmeg if needed. Serve hot. The soup may be prepared ahead and refrigerated in an airtight container for up to 5 days. If you intend to prepare it ahead, wait to add the milk or cream until you are ready to reheat and serve the soup.

12 pounds tree oyster mushrooms
   (page 176) or part tree oysters,
   and part button mushrooms
4 teaspoons olive oil
4 teaspoons butter
1 cup finely diced carrot
1 cup finely diced onion
3/4 cup finely diced celery
1 1/2 cups diced red pepper
1/2 cup cognac
2 tablespoons minced garlic
2 tablespoons lime juice
10 cups mushroom stock
   (page 38)
4 sprigs fresh parsley
2 bay leaves
2 sprigs fresh thyme or
   1 teaspoon dried
1 teaspoon salt
1/4 teaspoon nutmeg
1/4 teaspoon black pepper
1/4 teaspoon cayenne pepper
1/4 teaspoon ground mace
1 cup milk, soy milk or cream

Borscht

Yield: 6 servings • Prep Time: 25 minutes • Cooking Time: 50 minutes

3 beets (1 1/4 pounds), peeled and grated
8 cups water
1 cup grated onion
2 tablespoons lime juice
1 1/2 teaspoons caraway seeds
1/3 cup dry red wine
1 teaspoon salt
1/2 teaspoon paprika
1/4 teaspoon black pepper
1 1/2 cups diced red potato
2 1/2 cups shredded savoy cabbage

GARNISH:
Lime wedges
1/3 cup nonfat yogurt or sour cream

Borscht, of Russian origin, has many variations—some with beets alone, some with cabbage and some with potatoes. The following combination is nice both for contrast in texture and visual appeal. Using the grating disk on a food processor saves a great deal of time in preparing the vegetables. Serve the soup cold as is or topped with yogurt.

1. In a 3-quart saucepan, combine the beets, water, onion, lime juice and caraway seeds. Bring to a boil, then cover and reduce to a simmer. Cook, stirring occasionally, for 10 minutes. Stir in the wine, salt, paprika and pepper and continue to cook for 25 minutes.

2. Stir the diced potato into the soup and continue to simmer, covered, until the potatoes are half tender, about 8 minutes. Add the cabbage and continue to cook, stirring often, until the cabbage is tender, but still a vibrant color, about 8 minutes. Taste and adjust the seasonings. Serve garnished with lime wedges and a dollop of yogurt.

Variation

1. Increase the beets to 2 pounds and replace the cabbage with 1 1/2 cups shredded spinach and 1 cup shredded sorrel. Prepare the recipe as directed above, but as soon as the greens are added, transfer the soup to a bowl and cool quickly in the refrigerator. Serve cold.

Butter Fruit Bisque with Chutney

Yield: 8 servings • Prep Time: 25 minutes • Cooking Time: 35 minutes

1/2 cup diced onion
1/4 cup diced celery
1/4 cup diced carrot
1 tablespoon minced garlic
2 tablespoons curry powder (or to taste)
3 tablespoons ghee (page 169) or peanut oil
4 cups light vegetable broth
3 cups coconut milk
5 ripe avocados
2 tablespoons lime juice
2 tablespoons minced mint
1/2 teaspoon salt
1/4 teaspoon pepper

GARNISH:
Apple Chutney (page 156)

In South India avocados are called butter fruit because of their buttery taste and velvety texture. You may serve this lightly curried soup with chutney as a condiment. The soup is rich, so plan to serve small portions.

1. Heat the ghee in a 3-quart saucepan until hot, but not smoking. Add the onion, celery, carrot, garlic, and curry powder. Cook over low heat, stirring often, until the onion is very soft, but not brown, about 15 minutes. Add the stock and coconut milk, then continue to cook until the carrots are tender, about 20 minutes. Drain the onion mixture, saving the broth.

2. Peel the avocados and remove their pits. Cut them into pieces and place them in a food processor or blender with the lime juice. Add the onion mixture and purée until smooth. Mix in the reserved soup broth and remaining seasonings. Blend for another minute and transfer to a mixing bowl. (A glass, plastic or stainless steel bowl is best, as the soup may discolor if left in bowls made of other metals or some ceramics.)

3. Place 2 of the avocado pits in the soup and cover the soup with a piece of plastic wrap touching its surface. (This will retard discoloring.) Chill for at least 2 hours. Serve in individual bowls with apple chutney for guests to add as desired. The soup may be prepared up to 8 hours in advance, if refrigerated. It does not freeze well.

Variation

1. For a less sweet soup, replace the coconut milk with soy milk or dairy milk.

Avocado Bisque

Yield: 8 servings • Prep Time: 25 minutes • Cooking Time: 15 minutes

In this simple cold soup, lime and garlic team up to highlight the subtle taste of avocado, and yogurt is stirred in for added smoothness. As avocado is naturally high in fat, plan to serve other low-fat menu items.

2 tablespoons butter
1/2 cup diced onion
1/4 cup diced celery
1 1/2 tablespoons minced garlic
5 ripe avocados
1/4 cup lime juice
4 cups carrot vegetable stock
   (page 38)
1/4 cup minced scallions
1/4 cup minced parsley
2 cups nonfat plain yogurt
1/2 teaspoon salt
1/4 teaspoon pepper

GARNISH:
2 tablespoons minced
   red pepper
Sweet Onion Crisps (page 151) or
   1/3 cup sliced black olives

1. Heat the butter in a 3-quart saucepan until hot, but not smoking. Add the onion, celery and garlic and sauté over low heat, stirring often, until the onion is very soft, but not brown, about 15 minutes.
2. Peel the avocados and remove their pits. Cut them into pieces and place them in a food processor or blender. Add the lime juice and cooked onions. Purée until smooth. Add the carrot stock and blend thoroughly. Mix in the scallions, parsley, and yogurt. Blend for another minute and transfer to a mixing bowl. (A glass, plastic or stainless steel bowl is best, as the soup may discolor if left in bowls made of other metals or some ceramics.)
3. Season the soup to taste with salt and pepper. Place 2 of the avocado pits in the center of the bowl and cover the soup with a piece of plastic wrap touching its surface. (This will retard discoloring.) Chill for at least 2 hours. The soup is best eaten within 8 hours and does not freeze well. To serve, ladle into chilled individual serving bowls and garnish with minced red pepper, Onion Crisps, or sliced olives.

Variations

1. For a dairy-free version, soy yogurt or 1 1/2 cups soy milk mixed until smooth with 2 tablespoons of soy milk powder, 2 teaspoons rice syrup (page 172) and 1 tablespoon tahini may be substituted for the yogurt.
2. Replace the parsley with cilantro and substitute 1 cup buttermilk for the yogurt.

Chunky Avocado Soup

Yield: 6 servings • Prep Time: 20 minutes

1/2 cup diced red onion
1 cucumber, peeled, seeded and diced
1 tablespoon minced garlic
1 small green pepper, peeled
1 to 2 jalapeño peppers, seeded and minced
2 large, ripe tomatoes
5 ripe avocados
1/3 cup minced cilantro
1 1/2 cups orange juice
3 cups light vegetable broth
3 teaspoons ground cumin
3/4 teaspoon salt
1/4 teaspoon pepper

The character of this soup is somewhere between a gazpacho and a guacamole. It is lighter than most avocado soups and makes an excellent accompaniment to a light summer meal. Serve it with Toasted Corn Tortillas (page 152) and chili sauce (page 157).

1. Place the onions in a food processor and, with a pulse action, chop roughly. Add the cucumber, garlic, bell pepper and jalapeño. Process until finely chopped, about 30 seconds. Core the tomatoes and chop them, then add them to the processor and process until blended, about 10 seconds.

2. Peel the avocados and remove their pits. Chop them into small dice and add them to the food processor with the cilantro. Add about 1/4 cup of orange juice and purée just to combine. Transfer the soup to a large bowl and stir in the remaining juice, broth, cumin, salt and pepper. Place 2 of the avocado pits in the soup and cover it with a piece of plastic wrap touching its surface. (This will retard discoloring.) Chill the soup for at least 2 hours. Serve in individual bowls with Toasted Corn Tortillas. The soup is best eaten within 8 hours and does not freeze well.

Celery Apple Soup

Yield: 8 servings • Prep Time: 25 minutes • Cooking Time: 15 minutes

2 pounds celery, sliced
2 Granny Smith apples, peeled, cored and chopped
2 Winesap apples, peeled, cored and chopped
1 onion, quartered
1 cup sliced carrot
1 cup diced russet potato
1 small parsnip, sliced
1/4 cup rye berries
2 tablespoons minced garlic
2 teaspoons celery seeds
1 1/4 teaspoons salt
1 teaspoon anise seeds, crushed
6 black peppercorns
1 small sprig fresh thyme or 1 teaspoon dried
7 cups hearty vegetable stock (page 39)

GARNISH:
4 stalks celery, sliced thin
1 red-skinned apple, cored and sliced thin

The delicate sweetness of apple rounds out celery's sharp edge. Serve this soup hot or cold.

1. Combine all ingredients, except the garnish, in a 6-quart saucepan. Cover and bring to a boil. Reduce the heat to a simmer and cook, stirring occasionally, for 1 hour. Remove from heat and allow the soup to cool briefly.

2. Strain the soup, saving both broth and solids. Purée the vegetables in a food mill or processor until very smooth. Whisk this into the broth. Warm the soup, then taste and adjust the seasonings. Serve garnished with sliced celery and apple.

Variation

1. Do not purée the soup, but 15 minutes before serving, add the garnish and Leyden Dumplings (page 154). Then simmer until the dumplings are cooked, about 15 minutes.

Creamy Roasted Pepper Chili

Yield: 6 servings • Prep Time: 25 minutes • Cooking Time: 50 minutes

This creamy, Mexican-style chili is made from a variety of peppers. The flavor has a gentle, rich quality.

1. Preheat the broiler to high. Wash the peppers to remove all dust and dirt, then place them on a baking sheet about 4 inches from the broiler. Broil, turning 3 or 4 times, until they are charred and blistered on all sides. Do not overcook the peppers; the skin should be blackened, but the flesh should still be quite firm. Immediately remove the peppers from the oven, place them in a brown paper or plastic bag and fold the bag shut. When the peppers are cool enough to handle, remove them from the bag and, with a paring knife, peel them. Scrape out and discard the seeds. Place the poblanos in a blender or a food processor, fitted with the metal chopping blade. Purée until smooth. Slice the bell peppers into small dice and set them aside.

2. In a 3-quart saucepan, heat the butter until hot, but not smoking. Add the onion and sauté, stirring constantly, for 2 minutes. Reduce the heat to low and cook, stirring often, until very soft, about 15 minutes. Add the serrano pepper, garlic, potato, stock and milk. Stir in the puréed peppers, cumin, salt, cinnamon and pepper. Cover and simmer until the potato is tender, about 20 minutes. Mash the potatoes with the back of the spoon to give the soup body. Remove the soup from the heat. Stir in the diced bell peppers and cilantro. Garnish each soup bowl with a dollop of yogurt.

2 poblano peppers (page 172)
2 red bell peppers
1 yellow bell pepper
1 tablespoon butter
1 cup diced white onion
1 serrano pepper (page 173), seeded and diced
1 tablespoon minced garlic
1 russet potato, peeled and diced
4 cups light vegetable stock (page 38)
2 1/2 cups milk, light cream or 2 cups soy milk mixed with 1/4 cup dry soy milk powder
1 1/2 teaspoons ground cumin
1 teaspoon salt
1/4 teaspoon cinnamon
1/4 teaspoon black pepper
2 tablespoons minced cilantro or mint
3 tablespoons yogurt or sour cream

Variation

1. Stir 1/4 cup Cilantro Pesto (page 157) into the soup and serve the soup with Toasted Corn Tortillas (page 152).

Cucumber Tomato Soup

Yield: 6 servings • Prep Time: 20 minutes • Cooking Time: 2 minutes

2 tomatoes
1 medium red onion, quartered
2 cloves garlic, minced
1 small yellow bell pepper, diced
3 cucumbers, peeled, seeded
    and quartered
2 jalapeño peppers, seeded and
    minced
3 1/2 cups plain, nonfat yogurt
3 cups stock or carrot juice
1 large red potato, diced
    and steamed
2 teaspoons cumin powder
1/2 teaspoon salt
Pinch of cayenne pepper
1/3 cup minced mint leaves
    (or substitute cilantro)
1 tablespoon ghee (page 169)
    or peanut oil
1 teaspoon brown mustard seeds

An elegant and easy-to-prepare summertime soup that has the contrasting effect of cool, creamy yogurt and zing from jalapeños.

1. With the tip of a paring knife cut a cross just through the skin of each tomato on the blossom end. Also cut out a cone-shaped piece from the stem end of each. Bring 1 quart of water to a boil and plunge the tomatoes into the water. With a slotted spoon, roll them in the water so all surfaces are blanched. After about 45 seconds the skin at the cross cut should begin to loosen. As soon as this happens remove the tomatoes from the water and place them in a strainer in the sink. Immediately run cold water over them to stop the cooking. When the tomatoes are cool enough to handle, peel and cut them in half. Gently squeeze the seeds from inside each half, then place the tomatoes in a food processor or blender.

2. Add the onion, garlic, bell pepper, cucumber and jalapeño in the order listed, processing briefly after each addition. Mix in the yogurt and stock, then blend for 30 seconds. Transfer the soup to a mixing bowl and stir in the potatoes, cumin, salt, cayenne and mint. The soup may be prepared up to 2 days in advance to this point if refrigerated in an airtight container.

3. Just before serving, heat the ghee in a small skillet. When it is hot, but not smoking, add the mustard seeds and cook, stirring constantly, until the seeds pop, about 1 minute. Transfer immediately to a clean kitchen towel and pat dry. Add the seeds to the soup and serve immediately.

Egg Drop Soup

Yield: 6 servings • Prep Time: 25 minutes • Cooking Time: 50 minutes

1 piece burdock root (page 167)
1 tablespoon minced garlic
1 tablespoon minced ginger
1 carrot, sliced
1 stalk celery, sliced
1 onion, quartered
4 scallions, chopped
1 teaspoon salt
1/4 teaspoon white pepper
8 cups water
2 tablespoons soy sauce
2 tablespoons cornstarch
3 tablespoons cold water
3 eggs, beaten
1/3 cup minced cilantro

GARNISH:
3 tablespoons minced scallions
1 teaspoon toasted sesame oil

A gingery vegetable broth replaces chicken broth which is traditionally used as the base in this soup. Eggs are stirred in as a finishing touch for an interesting texture.

1. Combine the burdock, garlic, ginger, carrot, celery, onion, 4 scallions, salt, pepper and water in a 4-quart saucepan. Cover and bring to a boil. Reduce to a simmer and cook for 45 minutes. Remove from the heat and strain, reserving the liquid and discarding the soup solids. The soup may be prepared to this point up to 5 days in advance if refrigerated in an airtight container. It may be frozen for up to 6 months.

2. Return the soup to a clean saucepan and add the soy sauce. Taste and adjust the seasonings. Heat the soup to a simmer. Combine the cornstarch and water, then stir this into the soup. Allow the soup to boil just to thicken, then reduce to a simmer.

3. In a small bowl, beat the eggs until fluffy. Stir in the cilantro and beat again. Gradually pour the egg mixture into the center of the simmering soup in a very thin stream. As you pour, very gently stir the soup with a clockwise motion. The eggs should form thin strips as they cook. Do not beat or stir the soup too strongly because the eggs will become too finely shredded. Serve immediately topped with chopped scallions and a sprinkling of sesame oil.

Light Miso Soup

Yield: 6 servings • Prep Time: 10 minutes • Cooking Time: 25 minutes

Miso soup is consumed daily, often for breakfast, in traditional Japanese diets. This light and delicate version is virtually effortless to prepare.

1. In a 3-quart saucepan, combine the water, garlic, ginger root, scallions and daikon. Simmer, covered, for 20 minutes. Strain and return the broth to the saucepan. Discard the cooked vegetables.

2. Cut the tough stem from the softened wakame, then chop the leaf into 1/2-inch pieces. Whisk about 1/4 cup of the broth into the miso so that the mixture is very smooth, then set it aside. Add the sea vegetable and bamboo shoots to the saucepan of broth and simmer for just a minute. Stir in the miso and apple. Mix thoroughly and warm, but do not boil. Remove from the heat and divide evenly among 6 serving bowls. The soup should not be prepared ahead, nor should it be rewarmed.

8 cups water
2 cloves garlic, sliced
1 slice of ginger root about the size of a quarter, flattened
4 scallions, halved
1/4 cup daikon radish (page 168)
1 4-inch piece wakame (page 176), softened in warm water
3 tablespoons shredded bamboo shoots
1/2 cup mellow white miso (page 171)
1/4 cup shredded apple (optional)

Natto Miso Soup

Yield: 6 servings • Prep Time: 10 minutes • Cooking Time: 20 minutes

Natto Miso is made from barley and flavored with ginger. Its distinctive texture and aroma make it ideal for wintertime soups.

1. In a 4-quart saucepan, combine the water, garlic and carrot rounds. Simmer, covered, for 15 minutes or until carrots are just tender. Stir the water chestnuts, tofu and spinach into the broth and cook for 1 minute. Mix 1/4 cup of broth into the miso to form a paste, then stir the miso into the soup. Heat through, but do not boil.

2. Remove the soup from the heat and divide it evenly among 6 serving bowls. Sprinkle each bowl with minced scallions and a dash of sesame oil. Serve immediately.

8 cups water
2 cloves garlic, minced
3/4 cup carrot rounds (or decorative flowers, page 32)
1/4 cup water chestnut slices (fresh if available)
2 ounces soft tofu, cut in 1/2-inch cubes
1 cup chopped spinach leaves
2/3 cup natto miso (page 171)

GARNISH:
4 scallions, minced
1/2 teaspoon toasted sesame oil

Variation

1. Stir 1 cup cooked sweet rice into the soup just before serving.

Thick Miso Soup

Yield: 6 servings • Prep Time: 25 minutes • Cooking Time: 25 minutes

1 tablespoon peanut oil
1 cup sliced yellow onion
2 cloves garlic, minced
1 tablespoon minced ginger
1/4 cup sake
6 cups water
1/3 cup shredded burdock root
    (page 167)
1 cup shredded carrot
1 sweet potato, peeled and
    shredded
6 shiitake mushrooms (page 174),
    softened in warm water
1 cup broccoli flowerets
1/2 cup cubed jicama (page 170)
2 tablespoons rice syrup
    (page 172)
1 tablespoon kuzu (page 170)
2 tablespoons cold water
2 ounces soft tofu, cubed
1/4 cup dark miso (page 171)
1/3 cup light miso (page 171)

Sake and rice syrup add an unusual twist to this stew-like soup. The vegetables may be varied, but they should dominate so that the broth, thickened with kuzu, is only visible as a shimmering surface between bites.

1. Heat the peanut oil in a 4-quart saucepan and sauté the onion, garlic and ginger until the onion is translucent. Do not allow the garlic to brown. Add the sake and cook until the smell of alcohol evaporates. Add the water, burdock root, carrot, potato, mushrooms, broccoli, jicama and rice syrup. Simmer, covered, for about 8 minutes or until the vegetables are just tender.

2. Soften the kuzu in 2 tablespoons cold water and set aside. Combine the misos in a small bowl. Whisk about 1/4 cup of soup broth into the miso to form a smooth paste. Return this mixture to the soup. Stir in the kuzu, along with the tofu. Warm thoroughly until the soup is thickened, about 1 minute. Do not boil the soup. Serve immediately. The soup should not be prepared until just ready to serve, although the vegetables may be prepared and refrigerated well ahead.

South Indian Lentil Soup

Yield: 8 servings • Prep Time: 20 minutes • Cooking Time: 1 1/2 hours

1 1/2 cups yellow or brown
    lentils
8 cups water
1/2 teaspoon turmeric
2 cups diced tomatoes
1 cup diced carrot
1/2 cup diced celery
2/3 cup raw cashews
1 walnut-sized ball tamarind
    (page 175) (softened in 1 cup
    warm water or 2 tablespoons
    lemon juice)
1 tablespoon ground cumin
1 teaspoon coriander seeds
2 teaspoons fennel seeds
1 1/2 teaspoons salt
1/4 teaspoon hing (asafoetida)
    (page 170)
1/4 teaspoon black pepper
2 tablespoons ghee (page 169) or
    peanut oil
2 to 3 serrano peppers, seeded and
    diced
1 teaspoon brown mustard seeds

GARNISH:
Curried Chapati Strips (page 153)

This spicy lentil soup was inspired by the fine cooking of Nagarathna Rao in Mysore, South India.

1. Pick over the lentils to remove all rocks and debris. Rinse them well and place them in a bowl. Cover and set aside for 3 hours. Drain the lentils and place them in a 4-quart saucepan with 8 cups of water and the turmeric. Bring to a boil, stirring often. Reduce to a simmer, cover and cook, stirring often, for 1 hour.

2. Add the tomatoes, carrot, celery and cashews to the soup. Strain the tamarind through a tea strainer, pressing as much pulp through as possible. Discard the stringy pulp, and add the strained soaking liquid to the soup.

3. In a coffee grinder or mortar, grind the cumin, coriander seeds, fennel seeds, salt, hing, and black pepper until fine. Add this spice mix to the soup and cook for 30 minutes.

4. Meanwhile, heat the ghee in a small skillet until very hot, but not smoking. Add the serrano peppers and mustard seeds. Cook, stirring constantly, until the mustard seeds pop, about 1 minute. Stir this into the soup and simmer for 10 minutes. Serve immediately.

Gumbo Z'Herbes

Yield: 8 servings • Prep Time: 20 minutes • Cooking Time: 50 minutes

This soup is a zesty mixture of fresh garden greens, tomatoes and a pinch of Cajun-style spices. Whatever greens are on hand may be used, but I find the combination of watercress, kale and spinach particularly good.

1. In a 4-quart saucepan, heat the oil until hot, but not smoking. Add the onions and cook, stirring constantly, for 2 minutes. Reduce heat to low and cook, stirring often, until the onions have caramelized (they will be soft and brown), about 20 minutes. Raise heat slightly and add the flour. Cook, stirring constantly, until the flour turns light brown, about 10 minutes. Stir in the pepper, garlic, bay leaves, oregano, salt, cayenne and stock. Cover and bring to a simmer.

2. Meanwhile, steam the potato over rapidly boiling water until tender, about 10 minutes. Add the greens and continue to steam until tender, about 8 minutes. Transfer the greens and potato to a food processor and process until smooth. (Add up to 1 cup of soup broth to the processor if necessary to obtain a very smooth texture.) Stir the potato mixture into the soup and continue to simmer, stirring occasionally, for an hour. Stir in the parsley, taste and adjust the seasonings, then serve with steamed white or brown rice. The gumbo may be prepared up to 5 days in advance if refrigerated in an airtight container. It is best not frozen.

2 tablespoons olive oil
2 cups chopped onion
2 tablespoons flour
1 medium red pepper, seeded and
  chopped
2 tablespoons minced garlic
2 bay leaves
1 teaspoon dried oregano,
  crushed
1/2 teaspoon salt
1/4 teaspoon cayenne pepper
8 cups hearty vegetable stock
  (page 39)
1 large red skinned potato, diced
  (about 1 1/3 cups)
4 cups lightly packed watercress
  leaves
4 cups lightly packed kale leaves,
  chopped
4 cups lightly packed spinach
  leaves, chopped
1/2 cup minced parsley

Variation

1. Omit the potato and stir 1 1/2 cups soft bread crumbs into the soup with the greens. Serve Tabasco on the side.

Roasted Sweet Pepper Soup

Yield: 6 servings • Prep Time: 30 minutes • Cooking Time: 50 minutes

3 pounds red peppers
1 yellow bell pepper
2 medium red onions, diced
1 russet potato, cubed
2 cloves garlic sliced
6 cups light vegetable stock
  (page 38)
Salt to taste
1/2 teaspoon Five-Spice Powder
  (page 169)
1/4 cup minced scallions

Five-Spice Powder, a spice mix used in Chinese cooking, adds an anise undertone to this delicate soup.

1. Preheat the broiler to high. Rinse the peppers to remove all dirt, then place them on a baking sheet about 4 inches from the broiler. Cook, turning often until the surface of the peppers is charred and puffed, but not burned and flaked. Immediately transfer the peppers to a plastic bag to cool, then refrigerate for 2 hours or more before proceeding.

2. Peel the skin from the peppers, scraping any skin that sticks with a paring knife, if necessary. As the peppers are peeled, set them aside in a bowl to catch the juices. Split each pepper in half and remove seeds and ribs, but keep the juice. (Seeds and skin that slip into the juice may be strained out later.) Chop the red peppers into large pieces and place them in a 3-quart saucepan. Cut the yellow pepper into small dice and set aside.

3. Add the onion, potato, garlic and stock to the saucepan. Bring to a boil, stirring frequently. Reduce heat to a simmer and cook, covered, stirring occasionally, until the onion is tender, about 35 minutes.

4. Remove the soup from the heat and cool slightly. Strain and discard the vegetables, reserving the liquid. Purée the red pepper mixture through the fine blade of a food mill or in a food processor. Return the soup to the pan, whisk in the pepper purée, then season the soup to taste with salt and Five-Spice Powder. Warm, stir in the yellow peppers and top with minced scallions.

Variation

1. Cut 3 ounces of firm tofu into tiny dice. In a small bowl, combine 1 1/2 tablespoons soy sauce, 1/4 teaspoon Five-Spice Powder, and 2 tablespoons barley malt powder (page 167). Mix well. Add the tofu and marinate 2 hours. Just before serving the soup, quickly cook the tofu (in its marinade) in a small skillet over medium heat for about 5 minutes. Drain and stir the tofu into the soup.

Creamy Kale Soup with Parmesan Garlic Butter

Yield: 6 servings • Prep Time: 25 minutes • Cooking Time: 1 1/2 hours

Carrot stock serves as a base to sweeten the strong, meaty quality of kale. For a very successful dairy-free variation of this soup, you may substitute soy milk for the cream enrichment, 1/3 cup mellow white miso for the cheese, and 1 tablespoon soy margarine for the butter called for in the Parmesan butter.

4 leeks, cleaned and chopped
2 russet potatoes, peeled and cubed
6 cups chopped kale, stems removed
1 1/2 cups dry white wine
7 cups carrot vegetable stock or light vegetable stock (page 38)
4 whole cloves garlic, peeled
2 sprigs parsley
1 bay leaf
1 teaspoon salt
1/4 teaspoon white pepper
1/4 teaspoon nutmeg
2 teaspoons fennel seeds, toasted and ground (page 33)
1 cup, packed, parsley leaves
1/2 cup grated Parmesan
1 tablespoon butter
1/2 cup low-fat crème fraîche (page 34), cream or whole milk (optional)

1. Place the leeks in a 4-quart saucepan with the potatoes and 1 cup of kale. Add 1 cup of the wine and cook over high heat, stirring constantly, until the alcohol has evaporated, about 3 minutes. Add the stock, 2 garlic cloves, parsley sprigs, bay leaf, salt, pepper, nutmeg and 1/2 teaspoon ground fennel. Bring the soup to a boil, stirring often. Reduce the heat and simmer, covered, for 1 hour.

2. As the soup cooks, fit the processor bowl with the metal chopping blade. With the motor running, drop the remaining garlic into the bowl and process until minced, about 10 seconds. Add the parsley leaves to the bowl and, with a pulse action, process until finely minced, about 1 minute. Add the Parmesan, remaining fennel and butter, and process until smooth. This Parmesan butter may also be prepared by hand, using a garlic press for the garlic and mincing the parsley as finely as possible. The butter may be prepared ahead and refrigerated in an airtight container for 5 days, or frozen for 2 months.

3. Strain the soup into a large bowl. Remove the bay leaf and parsley from the cooked vegetables. Purée the vegetables in a food processor or blender until absolutely smooth and whisk this mixture into the reserved broth. This soup base may be prepared ahead and refrigerated in an airtight container for 3 days, or it may be frozen for 2 months.

4. Before serving, warm the soup base until piping hot. Remove it from the heat and whisk in the crème fraîche or other enrichment. Taste and adjust the seasonings. Keep the soup warm over low heat as you prepare the kale.

5. Place the remaining kale in a large strainer and rinse it well. Heat a 10-inch skillet over medium-high heat. Add as much of the kale as you can to the skillet and toss it gently, allowing the water that clings to the leaves to cook the kale. As the volume cooks down, add the remaining kale and toss until just wilted. Add 1/2 cup of wine and continue to cook until the kale is tender, but still a vibrant green, about 6 minutes. Stir 2 tablespoons of the Parmesan butter into the cooked kale and add the cooked greens to the soup. Pass the remaining butter so that guests may season their soup to taste.

Creamy Leek Soup with Cardamom

Yield: 6 servings • Prep Time: 25 minutes • Cooking Time: 1 1/4 hours

3 pounds leeks, cleaned and
    chopped
6 cloves garlic, sliced
2 tablespoons butter
1 tablespoon olive oil
3 tablespoons flour
5 cups hearty vegetable stock
    (page 39)
3 cups milk or soy milk
1 teaspoon ground cardamom
1/2 teaspoon salt
1/4 teaspoon black pepper
1/4 teaspoon ground nutmeg
Pinch of cayenne
4 sprigs fresh parsley
1 bay leaf
1 ounce dried porcini
    mushrooms (page 172),
    softened in warm water
1/2 pound button mushrooms,
    sliced
2 tablespoons lemon juice
1/4 cup minced parsley
1/2 cup milk, crème fraîche (page
    34) or soy milk

Few spices entice the senses more than freshly ground cardamom. When used with discretion, it produces a sublime undertone, whereas an excess has a bitter effect. The combination of leek and cardamom was a favorite of the fourth-century Emperor Heliogabalus.

1. In a 4-quart saucepan over medium heat, sauté the leeks and garlic in 1 tablespoon of butter and the olive oil, until they are very soft, about 20 minutes. Turn heat to high, sprinkle with the flour and cook, stirring constantly, for about 1 minute. Whisk in the stock, then add the milk, cardamom, salt, pepper, nutmeg, cayenne, sprigs of parsley and bay leaf. Cover and simmer, stirring occasionally, for 30 minutes.

2. Remove the soup from the heat and cool briefly. Strain the solids, saving the broth. Remove the parsley and bay leaf from the leeks, then transfer the leeks to a food processor or blender. Purée until very smooth, scraping the sides of the bowl down and adding liquid as necessary to obtain a very smooth consistency. Whisk the solids back into the soup broth.

3. Drain the porcini mushrooms, reserving their liquid, and chop them. Heat the remaining butter in a skillet over medium heat. Add both types of mushrooms and cook, stirring constantly, for about 1 minute. Squeeze the lemon juice over the mushrooms, reduce heat to medium, and continue to cook, stirring often, until the fresh mushrooms are very soft, about 7 minutes. Stir them into the soup and add the reserved porcini liquid. The soup may be prepared ahead up to 4 days in advance if refrigerated in an airtight container. Before serving, heat the soup to piping hot. Whisk in the minced parsley and the milk, then remove immediately from the heat. Taste and adjust the seasonings. Serve at once.

Cream of Sorrel Soup with Pear Butter

Yield: 6 servings • Prep Time: 25 minutes • Cooking Time: 50 minutes

4 leeks, cleaned and chopped
2 russet potatoes, peeled and
    cubed
1 cup dry white wine
7 cups hearty vegetable stock
    (page 39)
1 Anjou pear, peeled, halved
    lengthwise, and seeded
4 whole cloves garlic, peeled
2 sprigs parsley
1 teaspoon salt
1/4 teaspoon pepper
1/4 teaspoon nutmeg
4 cups sorrel, stems removed and
    chopped

Sorrel's lemony bite is softened by the sweet undertone of pear. This soup may also be prepared with a combination of sorrel and spinach if you prefer a less distinctive sorrel taste.

1. Place the leeks in a 4-quart saucepan with the potatoes. Add the wine and cook over high heat, stirring constantly, until the alcohol has evaporated, about 3 minutes. Add the stock, pear, garlic, parsley sprigs, salt, pepper and nutmeg. Bring to a boil, stirring often. Reduce heat and simmer, covered for 15 minutes, or until the pear is soft. (A very ripe pear will soften more quickly.) Remove the pear from the soup and set it aside. Continue simmering the soup for 30 minutes. Add 1 cup of sorrel to the soup, then cook it for another 10 minutes. Remove the soup from the heat and leave it uncovered to cool.

2. As the soup cooks, prepare the pear butter. Fit the processor bowl with the metal chopping blade. Add the parsley leaves to the bowl and, with a pulse action, process until finely minced, about 1 minute. Add the pear halves and process until smooth. Add the miso, bread crumbs and butter, then blend thoroughly. Transfer the mixture to a small bowl and refrigerate until ready to use. This butter may be prepared up to 3 days in advance if refrigerated in an airtight container.

3. Strain the cooked soup, reserving the liquid. Purée the strained vegetables in a food processor or blender, adding cooking liquid as necessary to obtain a very smooth texture. Whisk the purée into the reserved broth. This soup base may be prepared ahead and refrigerated in an airtight container for 5 days. It may be frozen for 2 months.

4. Shred the remaining sorrel and set it aside. Before serving, warm the soup base until piping hot. Stir in 2 tablespoons of the pear butter. Remove the soup from the heat and whisk in the crème fraîche. Stir in the shredded sorrel, then taste and adjust the seasonings.

1/2 cup, packed, parsley leaves
1/4 cup miso (page 171)
1/4 cup soft bread crumbs
1 tablespoon butter
1/2 cup low-fat crème fraîche (page 34) or soy cream (page 36)

Creamy Watercress Soup with Toasted Walnut Butter

Yield: 6 servings • Prep Time: 25 minutes • Cooking Time: 1 1/4 hours

Whole watercress leaves, stirred in just before serving, give this soup an unmistakably fresh character. It may be served as is or, for a more complex flavor, Toasted Walnut Butter can be whisked in as well.

1. Place the leeks in a 4-quart saucepan with the potatoes. Add the wine and cook over high heat, stirring constantly, until the alcohol has evaporated, about 3 minutes. Add the stock, garlic, parsley, bay leaf and salt, nutmeg and pepper. Bring to a boil, stirring often. Reduce heat and simmer, covered, for 45 minutes. Add 2 cups watercress and continue to cook until the watercress is very tender, about 10 minutes.

2. As the soup cooks prepare the walnut butter. Place the walnuts in the bowl of a food processor fitted with the metal chopping blade and process until smooth. (You may also use a blender.) Add the miso or Parmesan and mix well. The butter may be prepared ahead and refrigerated in an airtight container for up to a week.

3. Strain the cooked soup into a large bowl. Remove the bay leaf and parsley from the cooked vegetables, then purée the vegetables in a food processor or blender until absolutely smooth. Whisk the purée into the reserved broth. This soup base may be prepared ahead and refrigerated in an airtight container for 3 days or it may be frozen for 2 months.

4. Before serving, warm the soup base until piping hot. Remove from the heat and whisk in 1 1/2 tablespoons of walnut butter and cook to distribute. For a slightly richer tasting soup, stir in the milk, then taste and adjust the seasonings. Stir in the remaining watercress and cook for 1 minute. Serve immediately with additional walnut butter on the side.

4 leeks, cleaned and chopped
2 Idaho potatoes, cubed
1 1/2 cups dry white wine
7 cups light vegetable stock (page 38)
2 cloves garlic, peeled
2 sprigs parsley
1 bay leaf
1 teaspoon salt
1/4 teaspoon nutmeg
1/8 teaspoon freshly ground black pepper
6 cups watercress, stems removed
3/4 cup milk (optional)

TOASTED WALNUT BUTTER:
1/2 cup walnuts, toasted (page 33)
3 tablespoons mellow white miso (page 171) or 1/4 cup grated Parmesan

Jerusalem Artichoke Soup with Sweet Mochi Crusts

Yield: 6 servings • Prep Time: 25 minutes • Cooking Time: 1 hour

1/4 cup lemon juice
2 pounds Jerusalem artichokes
   (sun chokes)
3/4 pound new potatoes
2 tablespoons olive oil
1 1/2 cups sliced white onion
3/4 pound mushrooms, sliced
4 cloves garlic
8 cups light vegetable stock
   (page 38) or water
1 1/2-inch square piece of
   Parmesan crust, if available*
1/4 teaspoon white pepper
1 bay leaf
4 sprigs flat leaf parsley
1 cup milk or 2/3 cup crème
   fraîche (page 34)

TOPPING:
1/4 cup grated Parmesan
1/4 cup low-fat ricotta
2 tablespoons minced parsley
4 ounces fresh mochi (page 172)
6 sprigs parsley

*Note: The inedible crust, cut from the end of a piece of Parmesan cheese, is frequently used in traditional Italian soups to give depth and intensity of flavor. The crust is removed before the soup is served.

Jerusalem artichokes, also known as sun chokes, are not actually related to the globe artichoke at all. They are, instead, the eatable root of a sunflower which is native to North America. Nonetheless, when cooked their haunting aftertaste is highly reminiscent of their namesake. With that in mind, this recipe pairs their flavor with olive oil, mushrooms, lemon and Parmesan—ingredients frequently used to complement traditional artichoke dishes.

1. Fill a mixing bowl with water and stir in 2 tablespoons of lemon juice. Using a paring knife, peel the Jerusalem artichokes, working around as many of the bumps and crevices as possible, but also working quickly as the artichokes will turn grey rapidly once they are exposed to the air. Cut each root into rough cubes and immediately drop them into the acidulated water. Peel and cube the potatoes and drop them into the water too. This step will retard discoloring in both vegetables.

2. Heat the olive oil in a 4-quart saucepan over medium high heat until hot, but not smoking. Add the onions and toss for 1 minute. Reduce heat to low and cook, stirring often, until the onions are translucent, about 10 minutes. Do not allow the onions to brown. Turn heat to medium and add the mushrooms. Cook for about a minute, until the mushrooms just begin to soften. Add the reserved lemon juice and continue to cook, stirring constantly, until the mushrooms are softened completely, about 8 minutes.

3. Add the garlic, stock, cheese crust, pepper, bay leaf and sprigs of parsley. Drain the Jerusalem artichokes and potatoes, and add them to the saucepan. Bring the soup to a boil, stirring often. Reduce to a simmer and cook, stirring occasionally, until the artichokes and potatoes are very tender, about 40 minutes. Remove from the heat and cool briefly.

4. Strain the soup, reserving the broth. Remove the Parmesan crust and purée the rest of the soup solids in a processor or blender until very smooth. Whisk the purée into the reserved broth. Add the milk or cream and warm thoroughly. Taste and adjust the seasonings. The soup may be prepared up to 4 days in advance if refrigerated in an airtight container. It does not freeze well.

5. Just before serving, prepare the topping. Preheat the oven to 375°F. Combine the Parmesan, ricotta and minced parsley, then set aside. Cut the mochi into strips that are about 1/2 inch by 3 inches. Place them on a baking sheet and bake until puffed and hard on the outside, but still soft inside, about 8 minutes. Cut a slice in the side of each piece of mochi and fill with the Parmesan mixture. Divide the mochi among the soup bowls and pour soup over. Garnish each bowl with a sprig of parsley. Serve immediately.

Vichyssoise

Yield: 6 servings • Prep Time: 25 minutes • Cooking Time: 1 hour

Use only the white part of the leeks to obtain a beautiful, creamy white color. Save the leek tops to season a stock, or trim off tough ends and steam the greens to serve as a salad. Vichyssoise is traditionally served cold but makes an elegant hot first course as well. For a less elegant soup it may also be served hot and without being puréed.

1. Combine the leeks, potatoes, and wine in a 3-quart saucepan. Bring to a boil and cook, stirring constantly, until the alcohol smell has disappeared, about 3 minutes. Add the stock, salt, pepper, nutmeg, cayenne, parsley sprigs and bay leaf. Return to the boil. Reduce to a simmer, cover and cook, stirring occasionally, for about an hour. Remove from the heat and cool.

2. Strain the soup, reserving the liquid. Remove and discard the bay leaf from the soup solids, then purée them through the fine blade of a food mill or in a food processor until very smooth. Whisk the solids into the reserved soup broth. The soup may be prepared up to 4 days in advance if refrigerated in an airtight container. It may also be frozen for up to 2 months.

3. Before serving, whisk 1/3 cup of the crème fraîche into the chilled soup. Taste and adjust the seasonings. Serve in individual bowls, topped with a dollop of remaining cream and a sprinkling of parsley. To serve hot, warm the soup until piping hot. Remove it from the heat and whisk in 1/3 cup of the crème fraîche. Taste and adjust the seasonings.

6 cups sliced leeks, white part only
1 pound russet potatoes, peeled and cubed
1/2 cup dry white wine
8 cups hearty vegetable stock (page 39)
1 teaspoon salt
1/4 teaspoon white pepper
1/4 teaspoon nutmeg
Pinch of cayenne
3 parsley sprigs
1 bay leaf
1/2 cup crème fraîche (page 34) or milk
2 tablespoons minced parsley

Rose Petal Vichyssoise

Yield: 6 servings • Prep Time: 25 minutes • Cooking Time: 1 1/4 hours

Beets give this soup its subtle sweetness and rich, rose-colored appearance.

1. Combine the leeks, onion, beets, potatoes, and wine in a 3-quart saucepan. Bring to a boil and cook, stirring constantly, until the alcohol smell has disappeared, about 3 minutes. Add the stock, salt, pepper, cayenne, mint stems, and return to the boil. Reduce to a simmer, cover and cook, stirring occasionally, for about an hour. Remove from the heat and cool.

2. Strain the soup broth into a large bowl. Purée the soup solids in a food processor or blender until very smooth. Whisk the solids into the reserved soup broth. The soup may be prepared up to 4 days in advance if refrigerated in an airtight container.

3. Before serving, whisk 1/3 cup of the crème fraîche into the chilled soup. Taste and adjust the seasonings. Serve in individual bowls, topped with a dollop of remaining cream and a sprinkling of mint with a lemon wedge on the side. To serve hot, warm the soup until piping hot. Remove it from the heat and whisk in 1/3 cup of the crème fraîche. Taste and adjust the seasonings.

3 cups sliced leeks, white part only
3 cups sliced red onion
1 pound beet root, peeled and cubed
3/4 pound Idaho potatoes, peeled and cubed
1/4 cup dry white wine
10 cups hearty vegetable stock (page 39)
1 teaspoon salt
1/4 teaspoon pepper
Pinch of cayenne
3 sprigs mint
1/2 cup crème fraîche (page 34) or milk
2 tablespoons minced mint
6 lemon wedges

Sweet Potato Vichyssoise

Yield: 6 servings • Prep Time: 20 minutes • Cooking Time: 1 1/4 hours

6 cups sliced leeks, white part only (8 to 10 leeks)
1 pound garnet yams, peeled and cubed
1/4 pound russet potatoes, peeled and cubed
1/2 cup dry white wine
8 cups hearty vegetable stock (page 39)
2 tablespoons lemon juice
1 teaspoon salt
1/4 teaspoon pepper
Pinch of cayenne
3 sprigs mint
1/2 cup crème fraîche (page 34) or soy cream (page 36)
2 tablespoons minced mint
6 lemon wedges

Thick and slightly sweet with a gentle orange color, this soup is the perfect complement to a simple main course. Serve it hot or cold.

1. Combine the leeks, yams, potatoes, and wine in a 4-quart saucepan. Bring to a boil and cook, stirring constantly, until the alcohol smell has disappeared, about 3 minutes. Add the stock, lemon juice, salt, pepper, cayenne and mint stems. Return the soup to the boil. Reduce to a simmer, cover and cook, stirring occasionally, for about 1 hour. Remove the soup from the heat and cool.

2. Strain the soup, reserving the liquid. Purée the soup solids in a food mill or processor, adding cooking liquid as necessary to obtain a very smooth consistency. Whisk the solids into the reserved soup broth. The soup may be prepared to this point up to 4 days in advance if refrigerated in an airtight container.

3. Before serving, whisk 1/3 cup of the crème fraîche into the chilled soup. Taste and adjust the seasonings. Serve cold in individual bowls, topped with a dollop of cream and a sprinkling of mint with a lemon wedge on the side. To serve hot, warm the soup until piping hot. Remove it from the heat and whisk in 1/3 cup of the crème fraîche. Taste and adjust the seasonings.

4 • Soup Meals

French Onion Soup

Yield: 8 servings • Prep Time: 20 minutes • Cooking Time: 50 minutes

Onion soup, topped with a bubbly crust of cheese, is an earmark of French cooking and each chef has his own idea as to what the "perfect" version may be. Few are made, as this one is, with a vegetable stock, but this variation on a classic theme works exceedingly well. The croutons may be prepared several days in advance if stored in an airtight container. Select medium-sized onions that are firm throughout and have crisp, tight skins.

1. Cut each onion in half and peel them, leaving the root end intact. (This facilitates cutting without allowing the onions to fall apart.) Cut the yellow onions into rough dice that are about 1/2 inch in size and slice the red onions into 1/4-inch thick rounds. Discard root ends.

2. Heat the butter and oil in a 4-quart sauce pan over medium heat. When it is very hot, but not smoking, add the onions and cook, stirring constantly until they begin to wilt, about 5 minutes. Reduce heat to low and continue to cook, stirring occasionally, for about 30 minutes or until the onions have reduced to about 1/3 their original volume and are very lightly browned. Do not allow them to burn.

3. Turn heat to high and cook briskly for about 1 minute, stirring constantly, until the onions are sizzling hot. Sprinkle the flour over the onions and stir to distribute evenly.

4. Reduce heat to medium and continue to cook, stirring often until the flour has turned a nutty brown, 10 to 15 minutes. Again turn the heat to high and gradually add 3 cups of stock, whisking constantly to prevent lumps from forming in the broth. Add the brandy and cook for 1 minute, then reduce heat to low and add the remainder of the stock all at once. Stir in the bay leaf, parsley, salt and pepper. Half cover and cook, stirring occasionally, for about 20 minutes.

5. Taste and adjust the seasonings. Remember that the Gruyère and Parmesan will add more saltiness to the soup. Combine the Gruyère and bread crumbs. Preheat the broiler to high. Ladle the hot soup into eight ovenproof serving bowls. Place a crouton, Parmesan side down, in the center of each and cover the entire surface of the soup with the grated Gruyère mixture. Broil until the cheese crust is lightly browned and bubbly. Serve immediately.

6. To prepare the croutons, preheat the oven to 325°F. Place the bread on a baking sheet and brush both sides of each slice with melted butter. Bake until lightly browned, about 10 minutes. Sprinkle cheese on each slice of bread and return the baking sheet to the oven until the cheese has melted and the croutons are golden brown, about 7 minutes. Transfer to a cake rack to cool. The croutons may be prepared and stored in an airtight container several days in advance.

3 pounds yellow onions
1 pound red onions
2 tablespoons butter
1 tablespoon vegetable oil
3 tablespoons unbleached flour
8 cups hearty vegetable stock
  (page 39)
1/4 cup brandy or cognac
1 bay leaf
2 sprigs parsley
1/2 teaspoon salt
1/8 teaspoon pepper
1/4 cup grated Gruyère
1/4 cup dry bread crumbs

CROUTONS:
8 slices French bread
3 tablespoons butter, melted
6 tablespoons grated Parmesan
  cheese

Caramelized Onion Soup with Arame and Carrots

Yield: 8 servings • Prep Time: 15 minutes • Cooking Time: 40 minutes

Arame is one of the mildest types of sea vegetables. Here it is combined with the sweet taste of caramelized onions and carrots for a splendid effect.

1 1/2 cups arame (page 167)
1 tablespoon peanut oil
3 pounds onion, sliced very thin
2 tablespoons rice syrup
   (page 172)
1/2 teaspoon salt
1/4 teaspoon black pepper
7 cups kombu stock (page 40) or
   light vegetable stock (page 38)
1 tablespoon minced garlic
1 tablespoon minced ginger root
1/2 pound carrots, cut in julienne
   strips
3 tablespoons cornstarch
4 tablespoons cold water
1 scallion, shredded
1/4 cup shredded daikon
   (page 168)

GARNISH:
1 teaspoon toasted sesame oil
3 tablespoons sesame seeds

1. Rinse the arame in several changes of hot water. Set it aside in a small bowl, cover it with boiling water and prepare the soup.

2. Heat the peanut oil in a 2-quart saucepan over medium-high heat until hot, but not smoking. Add the onions and cook, stirring constantly, until they begin to soften, about 3 minutes. Reduce the heat to low and continue to cook, stirring frequently, until they are translucent and are beginning to brown, about 20 minutes. Add the rice syrup, salt and pepper, and continue to cook, stirring often, until the onions are evenly browned and have caramelized, about 15 minutes.

3. Add the stock, garlic and ginger. Turn the heat to high and bring the soup to a boil. Stir well, reduce to a simmer and cook for 5 minutes. Add the carrots and continue to cook until they are just tender, about 8 minutes. In a small bowl, combine the cornstarch with cold water and mix to a smooth paste, then stir it into the soup. Turn the heat to high and bring the soup to a boil, stirring constantly. Remove from the heat.

4. Drain the arame and stir it, the daikon and the scallions into the soup. Cover and set aside for one minute, to plump the vegetables. Transfer the soup to individual soup bowls or a large tureen. Sprinkle sesame oil and seeds over the soup and serve immediately.

Variation

1. Ladle soup into ovenproof serving bowls. Top with grated mochi and broil for 5 minutes. Alternatively, place baked strips of mochi in each bowl, top with soup, and serve.

Lentil Soup

Yield: 6 servings • Prep Time: 20 minutes • Cooking Time: 3 hours

This is a classic lentil soup with the addition of sun-dried tomatoes and spinach.

1 cup brown lentils
8 oil-soaked sun-dried tomatoes
   (page 174), drained and
   chopped
1 medium onion, diced
3 stalks celery, sliced
3 small carrots, diced
1 tablespoon olive oil
2 teaspoons garlic
9 cups light vegetable stock
   (page 38) or water

1. Rinse lentils well to remove all dirt and grit. If the sun-dried tomatoes you are using are not packed in oil, place them in a small bowl and cover with boiling water to soften for about 20 minutes then drain before using. Place the lentils in a 6-quart saucepan with the sun-dried tomatoes, onion, celery, carrots, olive oil, garlic and stock. Bring to a boil, then simmer for 5 minutes. Skim and discard foam that rises to the surface. Add the pepper, then reduce to a simmer. Cover half way and continue to simmer, stirring occasionally, for 2 1/2 hours.

2. When all of the lentils and the onion are very tender, mash about 1/4 of the lentils against the side of the pan with the back of a cooking spoon. Leave the rest intact. Stir in the salt, spinach and tomato paste. Cook until the spinach is tender, about 5 minutes, stirring constantly. Remove from the heat, taste and adjust the seasonings. The soup may be prepared up to 5 days in advance if refrigerated in an airtight container. It does not freeze well.

Freshly ground pepper
1 teaspoon salt
2 cups chopped spinach leaves
2 teaspoons tomato paste

Variations

1. Add 1 1/2 cups peeled, cubed winter squash (butternut, delicata, etc.) to the soup along with the carrots.

2. Just before serving, arrange thin slices of Raclette cheese or wedges of mild goat cheese on top of each bowl, then brown.

Lentil Gruyère Soup

Yield: 6 servings • Prep Time: 20 minutes • Cooking Time: 1 1/2 hours

While visiting Lyons in the south of France, I once had a salad of lentils with Gruyère, apples and garden fresh chard. The memorable combination serves as inspiration for this delightful soup.

1. Rinse lentils well to remove all dirt and grit. Place them in a 6-quart sauce-pan with the onion, olive oil, garlic, 1/2 cup of apple and the stock. Bring the soup to a boil, then simmer for 5 minutes as you skim and discard foam that rises to the surface. Add the pepper, bay leaf and thyme, then reduce to a simmer. Cover and continue to cook, stirring occasionally, until the lentils are very soft, about 2 hours.

2. Mash about 1/4 of the lentils against the side of the pan with the back of a cooking spoon. Leave the rest intact. Stir in the chard, salt, mustard and vinegar. Cook until the chard is tender, about 5 minutes, stirring constantly.

3. Remove the soup from the heat. Remove and discard the bay leaf then taste the soup and adjust the seasonings. Stir in the Gruyère cubes and diced apples. Serve at once.

1 cup brown lentils
1 medium onion, diced
1 tablespoon olive oil
2 teaspoons garlic
1/2 cup diced Granny Smith apple, cut in tiny dice
8 cups tomato vegetable stock (page 39) or 3 cups tomato juice and the rest water
Freshly ground black pepper
1 bay leaf
1/4 teaspoon dried thyme
3 cups chopped Swiss chard leaves, stems removed
1/2 teaspoon salt
1 1/2 teaspoons Dijon mustard
1 1/2 tablespoons balsamic vinegar

TOPPING:
4 ounces Gruyère cheese, cut into small dice
1 Granny Smith apple, peeled, cored and cut into small dice

Pot Au Feu

Yield: 6 servings • Prep Time: 30 minutes • Cooking Time: 3 1/2 hours • Resting Time: overnight

1/3 cup dried garbanzo beans, soaked overnight in cold water
6 ounces raw seitan (page 173)
2 carrots
2 whole cloves
1 yellow onion, peeled and halved
1 stalk celery, sliced
1 small turnip, quartered
1 parsnip, sliced
4 cloves garlic
1 bay leaf
4 sprigs fresh thyme or 1 teaspoon dried
4 sprigs fresh parsley
2 bay leaves
1 sprig fresh sage or 1/4 teaspoon dried
6 peppercorns
1 teaspoon salt
8 cups water
3 leeks, trimmed and cleaned
1 russet potato, diced
1 red onion, quartered
3/4 cup peas (fresh or frozen)

Had King Henry IV promised the people of France some seitan in every pot, rather than a chicken, the offer might not have gone down in history with such favor. Once you've tasted this extraordinary vegetarian version of the classic dish for which that offer was intended, you may wonder what twist history might have taken if wheat had been the focus of his offer. In this recipe any seasonal fresh vegetables may be steamed or grilled, then added to the soup in the final step of cooking.

1. Soak the garbanzo beans in cold water overnight. Quarter the seitan and shape each piece into a ball. The seitan may be prepared to this point up to 12 hours in advance.

2. Drain the garbanzos and place them in a 2-quart saucepan. Peel one of the carrots, cut it into 1-inch pieces and place them in the saucepan. Set the other carrot aside for a garnish. Stick the cloves into the yellow onion and add it along with the celery, turnip, parsnip, garlic and seasonings to the saucepan. Cover with 8 cups of water. Place over high heat and bring to a boil. Stir in the seitan balls, cover and reduce to a low simmer.

3. Simmer the pot au feu for 3 hours, stirring occasionally and checking to see that the water does not evaporate below the level of the vegetables. Strain the broth into a bowl. Pick the garbanzo beans and seitan out of the strainer and add them to the broth. Discard the cooked vegetables.

4. Refrigerate the broth, covered, overnight or for up to 3 days. Just before serving, steam the remaining carrot, leeks, potato and red onion. (Alternatively, the onion may be brushed with oil and grilled or broiled.) Add them, with the peas, to the broth to warm through. To serve, arrange beans and vegetables in each serving bowl. Slice the seitan and add it to the bowls. Taste the broth and adjust the seasonings. Pour this over the vegetables and top with a sprig of fresh parsley. Serve with Garlic Croutons (page 149) if desired.

Potato Soup with Sorrel and Mint

Yield: 6 servings • Prep Time: 15 minutes • Cooking Time: 1 1/4 hours

2 1/2 pounds russet potatoes, peeled and cubed
1 cup diced yellow onion
2 leeks, cleaned and diced
6 cups light vegetable stock (page 38)
1 tablespoon minced garlic
1/3 cup fresh mint leaves, chopped
1 1/2 teaspoons salt
1/4 teaspoon white pepper
1/4 teaspoon cayenne
2 cups sorrel leaves, stems removed

Potato softens the strong bite of sorrel while mint complements its lemony quality in this refreshing summer soup. Serve it hot or cold.

1. Combine the potatoes, onion, leeks, stock, garlic, 1 tablespoon mint, salt, pepper and cayenne in a 4-quart saucepan. Bring this to a boil, stirring often. Reduce to a simmer and cook, covered, until the onions are very tender, about 1 1/4 hours. Remove from the heat.

2. Strain the soup, saving the broth. Purée about 1/2 of the soup solids in a food processor or blender (or mash them by hand until fairly smooth). The soup may be prepared to this point up to 5 days in advance if refrigerated in an airtight container. Return all of the solids to the soup, transfer the soup to the cooking pot, and heat.

3. Stack the sorrel leaves and, with a sharp knife, shred them into 1/8-inch-wide strips. Remove the soup from the heat, stir in the sorrel, then the remaining mint. Taste and adjust the seasonings. The sorrel darkens and changes flavor as it sits, so the soup is best served immediately.

Winter Squash Stew

Yield: 6 servings • Prep Time: 25 minutes • Cooking Time: 3 1/2 hours

The base of this soup is a rich broth that matures and becomes sweet when refrigerated overnight. Tempeh, squash and leeks are bathed in a light coating of the soup, then each serving is garnished with pearl onions and peas.

1. Soak the cannellini beans in cold water overnight.

2. Drain the beans and place them with the carrot in a 3-quart saucepan. Stick the cloves into the yellow onion and add it along with the raisins, celery, turnip, parsnip, ginger, garlic, bay leaf, thyme, parsley, sage and peppercorns to the saucepan. Cover with 10 cups of water. Place over high heat and bring to a boil. Cover and reduce to a low simmer.

3. Simmer the soup for 2 1/2 hours, or until the beans are tender, stirring occasionally. Strain soup into a bowl. Pick the beans out of the strainer and discard the rest of the vegetables. Add the beans, salt and tempeh to the broth.

4. Refrigerate the broth, covered, overnight or for up to 3 days. Just before serving, add the leek, squash and onions to the broth. Cook them until just tender, about 20 minutes. Add the peas and cook another 5 minutes. To serve, arrange beans and vegetables in each serving bowl. Taste the broth and adjust the seasonings. Pour this over the vegetables and top with a sprig of fresh parsley.

Variation

1. Stir 2 tablespoons finely chopped pickled ginger and 2 tablespoons of rice syrup into the soup just before serving.

1/3 cup dried cannellini beans, soaked overnight in cold water
1 carrot
2 whole cloves
1 yellow onion, peeled and halved
1/2 cup raisins
1 stalk celery, sliced
1 small turnip, peeled and quartered
1 parsnip, peeled and sliced
2 teaspoons minced ginger
1 3-inch cinnamon stick
4 cloves garlic, sliced
1 bay leaf
4 sprigs fresh thyme or 1 teaspoon dried
4 sprigs fresh parsley
1 sprig fresh sage or 1/4 teaspoon dried
6 peppercorns
10 cups water
1 1/2 teaspoons salt
8 ounces tempeh, cubed (page 175)
4 leeks, trimmed and cleaned
3 cups winter squash cut in large dice (acorn, butternut, hubbard or a mixture of squash)
18 pearl onions, peeled
1 cup peas (fresh or frozen)

Slow Simmered Bean Pot

Yield: 6 servings • Prep Time: 35 minutes • Cooking Time: 3 1/2 hours

1/3 cup dried soy beans, soaked overnight in cold water
6 ounces raw seitan (page 173)
2 carrots
1 yellow onion, peeled and halved
1 3-inch piece daikon (page 168), cubed
1 stalk celery, sliced
1 small turnip, peeled and quartered
1 burdock root, scrubbed and sliced
4 cloves garlic
2 tablespoons minced ginger
1 star anise
6 peppercorns
2/3 cup soy sauce
1/2 cup dry sherry
3 tablespoons honey
7 cups water
2 red onions
6 whole, small leeks, trimmed and cleaned
1 1/2 cups small mushroom caps
1 small green or red pepper, seeded and cut into wedges
1 cup snow peas, strings removed
1/2 cup sliced water chestnuts
6 sprigs cilantro
2 tablespoons minced scallions

The classic Chinese method of red cooking in which foods are first cooked in oil then simmered in an aromatically seasoned broth was inspiration for the flavors in this recipe. The soup becomes rich and full after resting overnight; it is then simmered and spooned over an assortment of steamed vegetables for a beautiful presentation. Even though the recipe may seem rather drawn out, it is actually very simple to make once you begin, and the end result is exceptional. You may use other vegetables than those listed below, but keep in mind a balance of flavors, colors and textures.

1. Soak the soy beans in cold water overnight. Quarter the seitan and shape each quarter into a ball.

2. Drain the beans and place them in a 2-quart saucepan. Peel one of the carrots, cut it into 1-inch pieces and place them in the saucepan. Cut the other carrot into rounds or "roll cuts" (page 165), then set it aside in cold water for a garnish. Add the yellow onion, daikon, celery, turnip, burdock, garlic, ginger, star anise, peppercorns, soy sauce, sherry and honey to the saucepan. Cover with the soy sauce, sherry and water. Place over high heat and bring to a boil. Stir in the seitan balls, cover, and reduce to a low simmer.

3. Simmer the soup for 3 hours, stirring occasionally and checking to see that the liquid does not evaporate below the level of the vegetables. Strain the broth into a bowl. Pick the soy beans and seitan out of the strainer and add them to the broth. Discard the cooked vegetables which will have rendered their flavor to the broth. Refrigerate the broth, covered, overnight to allow flavors to mature. The broth may be prepared up to 3 days in advance.

4. Prepare each vegetable as garnish, keeping them separate so they may be arranged easily when serving the soup. Peel the onions, leaving root ends intact. Quarter them from top to root, then halve each quarter in the same direction. Be certain to leave the root end intact to hold the layers together. The onions may be brushed with oil and grilled or baked at 375°F. until browned (about 25 minutes) or they may be steamed until tender. Clean the leeks according to directions on page 170. Be careful to remove all tough tops and outer leaves. Set up a steaming rack in a saucepan and bring water beneath it to a boil. Add the carrots, cover and steam for 5 minutes. Add the leeks and mushrooms and cook for another 5 minutes. Add the peppers and continue to steam for 5 minutes. Add the snow peas and cook for 1 minute. (Keep water just below—not touching—the rack and always have the lid on except when adding the vegetables.) When the vegetables are cooked, transfer them immediately to a strainer and run cold water over them to stop their cooking. Dry the vegetables on a clean kitchen towel before serving. The vegetables may be prepared up to 24 hours before serving the soup.

5. To serve the soup, warm the broth with the beans and seitan. Arrange beans, vegetables and water chestnuts in each serving bowl. Slice the seitan and add it to the bowls. Taste the broth and adjust the seasonings. Pour this over the vegetables and top with a sprig of fresh cilantro.

Pepper Chili

Yield: 6 servings • Prep Time: 20 minutes • Cooking Time: 3 1/4 hours

A mixture of peppers, bulgar and sweet anasazi beans serves as the base of this spicy chili.

1. Pick over the beans to remove all stones and debris. Rinse in several changes of water, then soak in enough cold water to cover for 8 hours. Drain the beans and place them in a pressure cooker or saucepan with the 1 chopped onion, 1 green pepper, sliced garlic, 4 cups of water and 1 tablespoon oil. If pressure cooking, lock lid in place, bring to high steam and cook for 10 minutes. Place the cooker in the sink and run a strong current of cold water over it until the pressure drops completely. Unlock lid and check for doneness. If cooking in a standard saucepan, bring to a boil, reduce to a simmer, cover and cook, stirring from time to time, until the beans are tender, about 2 1/2 hours. Add more water if necessary to prevent burning. The beans may be cooked up to three days in advance and refrigerated in their cooking liquid before proceeding with the recipe.

2. Halve the ancho peppers, then pull off their stems, tear them in half and scrape out their seeds. Trim and discard any large ribs. Chop the anchos into 1-inch pieces. In a 4-quart saucepan, sauté the red onion in the remaining oil until soft, about 10 minutes. Add the beans, carrot, minced garlic, half of the red peppers, green pepper, ancho peppers, serranos, tomatoes, tomato paste, stock, salt, cumin, oregano, chili powder, and honey. Stir well. Simmer for 30 minutes then add the remaining red pepper and the bulgar. Continue to cook for 15 minutes. Stir in the mint and serve. The chili may be prepared up to 5 days in advance if refrigerated in an airtight container. It may be frozen for up to 3 months.

1 cup raw anasazi beans
1 yellow onion, chopped
1 small green pepper, seeded and chopped
4 cloves garlic, sliced
2 tablespoons vegetable oil
1 large red onion, chopped
1 large carrot, diced
6 cloves garlic, minced
2 large red peppers, seeded and chopped
1 green pepper, seeded and chopped
2 serrano peppers, seeded and minced
3 ancho peppers (page 167), softened in warm water
1 28-ounce can whole tomatoes
1 heaping tablespoon tomato paste
4 cups light vegetable stock (page 38)
1 1/2 teaspoons salt
3 teaspoons ground cumin
1 teaspoon oregano
3 tablespoons chili powder
1 tablespoon honey
3/4 cup bulgar, rinsed
1/3 cup minced mint or cilantro

Kidney Bean Chili

Yield: 6 servings • Prep Time: 20 minutes • Cooking Time: 2 1/2 hours

If you are looking for plain chili, this is it—no frills, simple to make and one that tastes like a "great bowl of chili." For a slightly more elaborate presentation, top each bowl with yogurt, sour cream or grated cheese.

2 cups raw kidney beans
2 yellow onions, chopped
4 cloves garlic, sliced
6 cups water
1 tablespoon vegetable oil
1 large red onion, chopped
1 stalk celery, diced
1 large carrot, diced
4 cloves garlic, minced
1 small green pepper, chopped
2 to 4 jalapeño peppers, seeded and minced
1 1-lb. can sliced tomatoes, drained
1 heaping tablespoon tomato paste
3 cups water or stock
1 1/4 teaspoons salt
2 1/2 teaspoons ground cumin
1 teaspoon oregano
2 tablespoons chili powder (or more to taste)
1 tablespoon honey

1. Pick over beans to remove all stones and debris. Rinse in several changes of water, then soak in enough cold water to cover for 8 hours. Drain beans and place them in a pressure cooker or saucepan with the 2 chopped onions, sliced garlic and 6 cups of water. With pressure cooking lock lid in place, bring to high steam and cook for 10 minutes. Place the cooker in the sink and run a strong current of cold water over it until the pressure drops completely. Unlock lid and check for doneness. If cooking in a standard saucepan, bring to a boil, reduce to a simmer, cover and cook, stirring from time to time, until the beans are tender, about 2 hours. The beans may be cooked up to 3 days in advance refrigerated in their cooking liquid before proceeding with the recipe.

2. In a 6-quart saucepan, sauté the red onion in the oil until soft, about 15 minutes. Add the beans and enough of their cooking liquid to equal 3 cups. (If there is not enough liquid, supplement it with stock or water.) Stir in the celery, carrot, garlic, peppers, tomatoes, tomato paste, stock, salt, cumin, oregano, chili powder and honey. Stir well, then simmer for 30 to 45 minutes, depending on how soft you wish the carrots to be. The chili may be prepared up to 5 days in advance if refrigerated in an airtight container. It may be frozen for up to 2 months.

Black Bean Chili with Corn

Yield: 6 servings • Prep Time: 25 minutes • Cooking Time: 3 hours

Fresh corn, red peppers and cilantro add a refreshing, light twist to this chili. It is mildly spicy as is, so serve a small bowl of "Hot Chili Paste" (page 157) alongside for guests to use with discretion.

2 cups raw black beans
2 yellow onions, chopped
4 cloves garlic, sliced
8 cups water
2 tablespoons vegetable oil
1 large red onion, chopped
1 large carrot, diced
4 cloves garlic, minced
2 large red peppers, seeded and chopped
2 to 4 jalapeño peppers, seeded and minced
1 28-ounce can whole tomatoes
1 heaping tablespoon tomato paste
3 cups water or stock
1 1/4 teaspoons salt
3 teaspoons ground cumin

1. Pick over beans to remove all stones and debris. Rinse in several changes of water, then soak in enough cold water to cover for 8 hours. Drain beans and place them in a pressure cooker or saucepan with the 2 chopped onions, sliced garlic, 6 cups of water and 1 tablespoon oil. With pressure cooking lock lid in place, bring to high steam and cook for 10 minutes. Place the cooker in the sink and run a strong current of cold water over it until the pressure drops completely. Unlock lid and check for doneness. If cooking in a standard saucepan, bring to a boil, reduce to a simmer, cover and cook, stirring from time to time, until the beans are tender, about 2 1/2 hours. They may be cooked up to 3 days in advance and refrigerated, with their cooking liquid, in an airtight container before proceeding with the recipe.

2. In a 4-quart saucepan, sauté the red onion in the remaining oil until soft, about 15 minutes. Add the beans, carrot, minced garlic, half of the red peppers, jalapeños, tomatoes, tomato paste, stock, salt, cumin, oregano, chili powder and honey. Stir well. Simmer for 30 minutes then add the remaining red pepper and the corn. Continue to cook for 10 minutes. Stir in the cilantro and serve.

1 teaspoon oregano
2 1/2 tablespoons chili powder
1 tablespoon honey
Kernels from 2 ears corn
  (or 1 1/2 cups frozen)
1/3 cup minced cilantro

Hot and Sour Soup

Yield: 8 servings • Prep Time: 25 minutes • Cooking Time: 25 minutes

The key to success in this soup is the variety of textures in combination with contrasting flavors. Chili paste with garlic, a prepared condiment available at Asian markets, adds the intense hot flavor. If you are cooking for non-adventurous diners, chili paste may be served separately and stirred in at the table.

1. Rinse the dried mushrooms and lily stems to remove all dirt. Place them in a large mixing bowl and cover with 3 cups boiling water. Place the arame in a small bowl and cover with boiling water. Set both bowls aside for at least 30 minutes to soften. Remove the mushrooms and lily stems from the water and squeeze them to remove excess water. Trim the tough stem ends from the mushrooms and shred them into matchstick-size pieces. If the ends of the lily stems are tough, cut them off, then shred the stems by pulling them apart lengthwise with your fingers. Drain the arame.

2. Place the mushrooms and lily stems in a 4-quart saucepan. Strain the soaking liquid into the saucepan through a tea strainer, then add the stock, ginger and garlic. Bring the soup to a boil, reduce to a simmer, cover and cook for 20 minutes. Add the arame, straw mushrooms, tofu, bamboo shoots, soy sauce, vinegar, white pepper and chili paste. Heat briefly. Taste and adjust the seasonings. Stir in the cornstarch mixture and bring to a boil, then remove from the heat and stir in the sprouts.

3. While the soup is still very hot, beat the eggs lightly with a fork. Hold a ladle with one hand and the bowl containing the eggs in the other. Stir the soup gently in a circular motion to create a quiet whirlpool effect. Pour the eggs in a thin stream into the soup to form threads of cooked egg in the soup. Do not stir the soup too vigorously at this point or the eggs will become too finely shredded. As soon as all of the egg is in, stop stirring. Transfer to serving bowls and garnish with a sprinkling of sesame oil and minced scallions.

6 dried shiitake mushrooms
  (page 174)
1 dried tree ear mushroom
  (page 168)
1/4 cup dried lily stems (page 171)
1/4 cup arame (page 167)
8 cups light vegetable stock
  (page 38)
1 tablespoon minced ginger root
1 tablespoon minced garlic
1/2 cup straw mushrooms
4 ounces firm style tofu,
  cut in small cubes
1/3 cup shredded bamboo shoots
3 to 4 tablespoons soy sauce
3 to 4 tablespoons red wine
  vinegar
1/4 teaspoon white pepper
1 teaspoon chili paste with garlic
  (or to taste)
3 tablespoons cornstarch
  dissolved in 5 tablespoons
  cold water
1/4 cup mung bean sprouts
2 eggs, beaten

GARNISH:
2 teaspoons toasted sesame oil
2 scallions, minced

Fancy Egg Drop Soup

Yield: 8 servings • Prep Time: 25 minutes • Cooking Time: 50 minutes

1 piece burdock root (page 167)
2 tablespoons minced garlic
1 tablespoon minced ginger
1 carrot, sliced
1 stalk celery, sliced
1 onion, quartered
4 scallions, chopped
1 teaspoon salt
1/4 teaspoon white pepper
8 cups water
2 tablespoons soy sauce
2 tablespoons cornstarch
3 tablespoons cold water
1/4 cup arame (page 167),
    softened in warm water
1 small cucumber, peeled, seeded
    and diced
3/4 cup straw mushrooms
    (page 174)
3 ounces firm tofu, cubed
10 snow peas, trimmed
3 eggs, beaten

GARNISH:
3 tablespoons minced scallions
1 teaspoon toasted sesame oil

This is an elaborate version of a simple egg drop soup. Served with steamed vegetables and tofu, this simple broth is transformed into a substantial meal.

1. Combine the burdock, 1 tablespoon garlic, ginger, carrot, celery, onion, 4 scallions, salt, pepper and water in a 4-quart saucepan. Cover and bring to a boil. Reduce to a simmer and cook for 45 minutes. Remove from the heat and strain, reserving the liquid and discarding the soup solids. The broth may be prepared up to 5 days in advance if refrigerated in an airtight container. It may be frozen for 3 months.

2. Return the soup to the clean saucepan and add the soy sauce. Taste and adjust the seasonings. Heat the soup to a simmer. Combine the cornstarch and cold water, then stir it into the soup. Allow the soup to boil, just to thicken, then reduce to a simmer. Stir in the arame, cucumber, mushrooms and tofu. Cook, stirring often, for 5 minutes. Add the snow peas to the soup, cover and set aside for 3 minutes.

3. In a small bowl, beat the eggs until fluffy. Pour them into the center of the simmering soup in a very thin stream. As you pour, very gently stir the soup in a clockwise motion. The eggs should form thin shreds as they cook. Do not beat or overstir the soup or the egg threads will become too fine. Serve immediately topped with chopped scallions and a sprinkling of sesame oil.

Three Bean Soup

Yield: 6 servings • Prep Time: 20 minutes • Cooking Time: 45 minutes

2 cups cooked kidney beans,
    drained
1 1/4 cups diced red onion
1 tablespoon minced garlic
1 teaspoon celery seeds
1/2 teaspoon salt
5 black peppercorns
7 cups hearty vegetable stock
    (page 39)
2 tablespoons honey
3 tablespoons balsamic vinegar
1 cup diced tomatoes
1/2 cup diced celery
1/2 cup diced green bell pepper
1/2 cup diced red bell pepper
1 cup green string beans,
    cut in 1-inch pieces (may use
    frozen)

The flavors and textures of an old-fashioned Three Bean Salad are echoed in this light-bodied soup. Serve it as is or over basmati rice as a substantial meal in itself.

1. In a 4-quart saucepan, combine the kidney beans, onion, garlic, celery seeds, salt, peppercorns and stock. Bring the soup to a boil, stirring often. Reduce to a simmer, cover and continue to cook, stirring occasionally, until the onions are tender, about 25 minutes.

2. Add the honey, vinegar, tomatoes, celery and peppers and continue to cook for 10 minutes. Stir in the green and wax beans and cook until they are just tender (about 15 minutes for fresh beans, 8 minutes for frozen).

3. Stir in the soy sauce, then taste and adjust the seasonings. The soup may be prepared to this point up to 3 days in advance if refrigerated in an airtight container. It does not freeze well. When ready to serve, combine the cornstarch with the water in a small bowl. Pour this mixture into the cooked soup and bring it to a boil, stirring constantly. Remove from the heat and serve immediately.

Variation

1. Add 2 ounces cooked seitan (page 173) to the soup with the kidney beans. Prepare the soup through Step 2. Strain the soup, reserving the solids. Reduce the broth to 4 cups. Chop the seitan, then combine all ingredients for the soup and warm. Serve topped with Sweet Onion Crisps (page 151).

Peanut Butter Soup

Yield: 6 servings • Prep Time: 15 minutes • Cooking Time: 50 minutes

Yes, peanut butter! Though it may be difficult to conceive of using it for anything more exotic than a sandwich, soup made from peanut butter is a common dish in many cuisines from West Africa and Indonesia to parts of the Caribbean. Even if you are unsure about the notion of peanut butter soup, give this soup a try.

1. Cube the tempeh and place it in a small mixing bowl with 2 tablespoons tamari, 1 tablespoon molasses and 1 teaspoon minced garlic. Set aside for 30 minutes.

2. Heat 1 1/2 tablespoons oil in a 4-quart saucepan until hot, but not smoking. Add the onion and cook, stirring constantly, for 2 minutes. Reduce the heat to medium, stir in the red and green peppers and continue to cook, stirring frequently, until the onion is very soft, about 10 minutes. Add the ginger root, remaining garlic and stock. Remove the ancho pepper from its soaking liquid. Tear off and discard the stem end. Slice the pepper open. Scrape out and discard the seeds and ribs. Chop the pepper and add it to the soup. Stir in the cumin, coriander, chili pepper flakes, turmeric, raisins and rice. Cover and bring the soup to a boil, then turn heat to low and cook, stirring occasionally, until the rice is tender, about 35 minutes.

3. Heat the remaining oil in a small skillet. Add the tempeh and cook, tossing frequently, until it is lightly browned. Pour the tempeh out onto a cutting board and chop it into small pieces, then stir it into the soup.

4. When the rice is tender, remove the soup from the heat. The soup may be prepared to this point up to 3 days in advance if refrigerated in an airtight container. In a small bowl, combine the remaining tamari and molasses with the peanut butter. Whisk in enough of the soup broth to make a smooth paste. Stir this back into the soup and warm briefly. Serve immediately, garnished with a sprinkling of scallions and cucumber.

1 cup yellow wax beans, cut in 1-inch pieces (may use frozen)
2 tablespoons soy sauce
2 tablespoons cornstarch
3 1/2 tablespoons water

4 ounces tempeh (page 175)
1/4 cup tamari (page 175)
2 tablespoons molasses
1 1/2 tablespoons minced garlic
3 tablespoons peanut oil
2 cups chopped onion
1 large red pepper, seeded and chopped
1 small green pepper, seeded and chopped
2 teaspoons minced ginger root
9 cups light vegetable stock (page 38)
1 ancho pepper (page 167), softened in hot water
1 1/2 teaspoons ground cumin
1/2 teaspoon ground coriander
1/4 teaspoon chili pepper flakes
1/8 teaspoon turmeric
3 tablespoons raisins
1/3 cup sweet rice
1/3 cup peanut butter

GARNISH:
1/4 cup minced scallions
1/4 cup chopped cucumber

Variation

1. Omit the rice and add 3 ounces cooked rice noodles or spaghetti to the soup just before serving.
2. Omit the peanut butter for an equally good—though extremely different—end result.

Lemon Tortilla Soup

Yield: 8 servings • Prep Time: 20 minutes • Cooking Time: 2 1/4 hours

A light, lemony broth is poured over baked corn tortilla strips just as the soup is served. For a more substantial soup, you may add 3 ounces of chopped tofu or tempeh to the broth as it cooks.

2 heads garlic
2 tablespoons olive oil
2 cups diced onion
3 russet potatoes, diced
2 cups diced carrot
1/2 cup diced celery
1 cup diced tomatoes
2 red bell peppers, seeded and chopped
3 jalapeño peppers, seeded and minced
2 tablespoons lemon juice
1 teaspoon oregano
1 1/2 teaspoons salt
1 scant teaspoon cumin seeds
1/4 teaspoon black pepper
10 cups water

TOPPING:
8 corn tortillas
1 1/2 cups grated Monterey Jack cheese (or use soy cheese)
1/4 cup minced cilantro
8 sprigs cilantro

1. Separate the garlic into cloves, but do not peel them. Discard the root ends of each head. In a 4-quart saucepan, heat the oil until hot, but not smoking. Add the onion and cook, stirring constantly, for 1 minute. Reduce the heat to medium and continue to cook, stirring often, until the onion is translucent, about 10 minutes. Add the garlic, potatoes, carrots, celery, tomatoes, red pepper, jalapeños, lemon juice, spices and water. Bring to a boil, stirring often, then reduce to a simmer and cook, covered, for 2 hours. Check the water level as the soup cooks. It should not boil down below the surface of the vegetables. Add more if necessary.

2. Strain the soup, saving the broth and discarding the vegetables. Taste and adjust the seasonings. The soup may be prepared up to 5 days in advance if refrigerated in an airtight container. It may also be frozen for up to 3 months.

3. Preheat the oven to 375°F. Have the soup warming. Place 4 of the tortillas on a clean work surface. Combine the grated cheese with the minced cilantro, then sprinkle this mixture evenly over the tortillas. Top each with a reserved tortilla, forming a "sandwich." Place them on a baking sheet, and slice the "sandwiches" into 1/2-inch-wide strips. Bake the tortillas until the cheese melts, about 8 minutes. Arrange the tortilla strips in 8 serving bowls, then top with soup and garnish with a sprig of cilantro.

Fava Bean and Noodle Soup

Yield: 4 servings • Prep Time: 25 minutes • Cooking Time: 45 minutes

The classic Italian Zuppa di Fagioli con la Pasta usually incorporates ham and/or salt pork as a key ingredient. For a vegetarian version, I've relied on the heavenly taste of fresh fava beans (cooked cannellini beans may also be used) accented by capers and a bountiful amount of basil. Freshly grated Parmesan may be passed at the table.

8 cups hearty vegetable stock (page 39)
2 cups shelled fresh fava beans (if unavailable, use cooked cannellini beans)
2 tablespoons olive oil
2 cups diced red onion
1/3 cup diced celery
1 cup diced carrot
3 tablespoons minced garlic
2 tablespoons barley malt powder (page 167) (or 1 tablespoon molasses)
1/2 teaspoon dried sage
1/2 teaspoon dried thyme
1/2 teaspoon dried oregano
1/4 teaspoon dried red pepper flakes

1. Bring the stock to a boil in a 4-quart saucepan. Add the fava beans and return to the boil. Reduce heat slightly and cook for 5 minutes. Drain the beans, reserving the broth. Slice the tough skin of each bean with the tip of a paring knife, then slip off and discard the skin. Set the beans aside. If using cannellini beans, omit this step.

2. Heat the oil in the saucepan until hot, but not smoking. Add the onions and celery, and cook, stirring constantly, for 1 minute. Reduce the heat to low and continue to cook, stirring often, until the onions are very soft, but not browned, about 15 minutes. Pour the reserved broth over the onions. Add the carrots, garlic, barley malt powder, sage, thyme, oregano and pepper flakes. Cover and

reduce to a simmer. Cook, stirring occasionally, until the vegetables are very tender, about 40 minutes.

3. Place about 1/3 of the beans in a food processor or blender. Purée, adding up to 1/4 cup of soup broth to obtain a smooth consistency. Transfer these and the whole beans to the soup. The soup may be prepared to this point up to 3 days in advance if refrigerated in an airtight container.

4. Bring the soup to a boil, then add the salt, pepper and spaghetti and cook until the pasta is al dente (about 1 minute for fresh noodles, 8 minutes for dried). Stir in the red pepper, peas, parsley, basil and capers. Taste and adjust the seasonings (remember that Parmesan added at the table will increase the saltiness). Transfer the soup to a large tureen or individual bowls and serve. Pass grated Parmesan for guests to use as desired.

1/2 teaspoon salt
1/4 teaspoon black pepper
1/2 cup spaghetti noodles, broken into 1-inch pieces
1 cup diced red bell pepper
1/2 cup peas (may use frozen)
1/4 cup minced Italian parsley
1/2 cup chopped basil leaves
3 tablespoons capers

Oriental Bean and Noodle

Yield: 8 servings • Prep Time: 25 minutes • Cooking Time: 1 hour

A flavorful broth packed with vegetables, noodles and beans, this simple soup is a meal in itself. A dish of cilantro "pesto" may be passed for those guests with an insatiable garlic tooth.

1. In a 4-quart saucepan, sauté the onions in the oil until translucent, about 10 minutes. Add the garlic and ginger and cook for another minute. Stir in the tomatoes, carrots, celery, yam, soy beans and stock. Add the dulse, cilantro sprigs and pepper. Bring the soup to a boil, stirring often. Reduce to a simmer, cover and cook, stirring occasionally, for about 25 minutes, or until the vegetables are just tender.

2. Raise heat to a low boil. Add the soy sauce and honey, then stir in the soba noodles and continue to cook, stirring often, for 5 minutes. Add the bok choy and allow the soup to cook until the noodles are al dente, about 5 more minutes. Stir in the snow peas. Remove the soup from the heat and mix in the chopped cilantro. Serve at once.

2 cups diced yellow onion
2 tablespoons peanut oil
2 tablespoons minced garlic
1 tablespoon minced ginger
3 cups diced tomatoes
1 cup sliced carrot
3/4 cup sliced celery
1 yam, peeled and diced
1 cup cooked soy beans (or garbanzos)
5 cups hearty vegetable stock (page 39)
1/4 cup (not packed) dulse (page 168)
4 sprigs cilantro
1/4 teaspoon white pepper
3 tablespoons soy sauce
2 teaspoons honey or sugar
4 cups chopped bok choy
1 cup snow peas
4 ounces soba noodles (page 174)
1/4 cup fresh cilantro, chopped

Minestrone

Yield: 6 servings • Prep Time: 20 minutes • Cooking Time: 35 minutes

Thick and robust, this soup is flavored with the scent of rosemary and topped with freshly grated Parmesan. It improves in flavor if prepared a day or so ahead, but if you plan to do so, add the noodles just before serving to keep them al dente.

2 cups sliced red onion
3 tablespoons olive oil
2 cloves garlic
3 cups diced tomatoes
1 cup sliced carrot
3/4 cup sliced celery
1 cup cooked cannellini beans
    (or Great Northern)
1 cup diced red potato
5 cups hearty vegetable stock
    (page 39)
1/4 cup (not packed) dulse
    (page 168)
4 sprigs parsley
2 teaspoons rosemary
1 teaspoon dried marjoram
1 teaspoon oregano
1/4 teaspoon black pepper
2 cups shredded cabbage
3/4 cup string beans
1/4 cup ziti noodles

GARNISH:
Freshly grated Parmesan
1/3 cup pesto (page 157)

1. In a 4-quart saucepan, sauté the onion in the olive oil until translucent, about 10 minutes. Add the garlic and cook for another minute. Stir in the tomatoes, carrots, celery, cannellini beans, potato and stock. Add the dulse, parsley, rosemary, marjoram, oregano and pepper. Bring the soup to a boil, stirring often. Reduce to a simmer, cover and cook, stirring occasionally, for about 25 minutes, or until the vegetables are just tender. The soup may be prepared to this point up to 5 days in advance if refrigerated in an airtight container.

2. Raise heat so the soup is at a low boil, then stir in the cabbage and string beans. Cook for 10 minutes. Add the noodles and continue to cook until it is just al dente. Remove from the heat and serve at once sprinkled with freshly grated Parmesan. A dish of pesto may be passed for those guests with an insatiable garlic tooth.

Cauliflower and Garbanzo Bean Soup

Yield: 8 servings • Prep Time: 20 minutes • Cooking Time: 30 minutes

This is a warming winter soup with traditional tastes of India.

2 tablespoons lemon juice
1 large head cauliflower
1 1/2 tablespoons peanut oil
1 1/2 cups diced sweet onion
    (Vidalia, if possible)
2/3 cup diced celery
2/3 cup diced carrot
2 tablespoons curry powder
1 cup chopped tomatoes
1 cup cooked garbanzo beans
1 tablespoon minced garlic
8 cups hearty vegetable stock or
    carrot stock (page 39)
1 teaspoon salt
1 bay leaf
1 teaspoon garam masala
    (page 169)
1/2 cup shelled peas
    (may use frozen)
1/4 cup minced mint

1. Fill a medium-sized mixing bowl with water and add the lemon juice. Trim and discard the leaves and tough stems from the cauliflower. Cut the rest into small flowerets, trimming any tough skin from the stems of the flowerets. As you cut up the cauliflower, drop it immediately into the bowl of water and set aside for 30 minutes. This helps to retain the white color of the cauliflower.

2. Heat the peanut oil in a 4-quart saucepan over high heat until hot, but not smoking. Add the onion and reduce the heat to medium. Cook, stirring constantly until the sizzling sound of cooking subsides, about 2 minutes. Continue to cook, stirring often, until the onions are translucent, about 10 minutes. Add the celery, carrot and curry powder and cook, stirring often, for 5 minutes. Add the tomato, garbanzos, garlic, stock, salt, bay leaf and garam masala. Drain the cauliflower and stir it into the soup. Reduce the heat to a simmer, then cover and cook until the cauliflower is just tender, about 15 minutes.

3. Stir the peas into the soup and cook for 3 to 4 minutes, until crisp. If you are using frozen peas, simply stir them into the soup, remove it from the heat and allow it to stand for a minute. Just before serving add the mint. Serve hot or at room temperature.

Variation

1. Chop 3 ounces simmered seitan (page 173). Add it to the soup instead of the garbanzos.

Black Bean Soup

Yield: 6 servings • Prep Time: 20 minutes • Cooking Time: 3 1/2 hours

The addition of lime adds a wonderfully light and harmonious touch to this version of the Cuban classic. Traditionally, the soup is served with a garnish of chopped onion, hard boiled egg or tomato. For variation, try Cumin Scented Croutons (page 150) and a squeeze of lime.

1 1/2 cups dried black beans
6 cups water
4 cups diced yellow onion
3 cloves garlic, peeled and left
    whole
9 peppercorns
2 bay leaves
2 teaspoons cumin seeds
1/2 teaspoon dried epazote
    (page 168) (optional)
2 cups chopped tomatoes
3 tablespoons minced garlic
1 jalapeño pepper, seeded and
    minced
1 lime, sliced
3 teaspoons ground cumin
1 1/2 teaspoons dried oregano
1 teaspoon salt
1/4 cup minced fresh parsley
1/4 cup minced fresh mint

GARNISH:
Cumin Scented Croutons
    (page 150)
Lime triangles

1. Pick over the beans and discard all rocks and debris. Rinse the beans well in several changes of cold water, then place them in a large bowl and cover with cold water. Set aside to soak for 12 hours.

2. Drain the beans. Discard the soaking liquid, rinse and drain again. Place the beans in a 6-quart soup pot or pressure cooker, and add the 6 cups of water. Cover and place over high heat, stirring frequently to prevent beans from sticking to the bottom of the pan. As the beans come to a boil foam will begin to rise to the surface. Reduce to a simmer, then skim and discard the foam until no more appears. Add 1 1/2 cups diced onion, 3 whole cloves garlic, the peppercorns, bay leaves, cumin seeds and epazote. Cover and return to a boil over high heat, then reduce to a simmer and cook, stirring occasionally, until the beans are tender, about 2 hours. As the beans cook, add water as necessary so that they remain covered with liquid. If you are using a pressure cooker, remove the pan from the heat before adding the onion and other seasoning ingredients. Lock the lid in place, then place the cooker over high heat. When high steam is reached, cook for 10 minutes exactly. Immediately remove the cooker from the heat and place it in the sink under cold running water to quickly release the pressure. Alternatively, you may use 6 cups of canned beans.

3. Once the beans are cooked, drain them, saving their liquid, and place them in a 3-quart pot. Measure their cooking liquid and add enough stock or water to equal 6 cups. (If you are using canned beans, drain and rinse, then add 6 cups of stock.) Stir the tomato into the pot, add the remaining onion, minced garlic, jalapeño, lime, cumin, oregano and salt. Cover and simmer, stirring occasionally, for 1 hour. Stir in the parsley and mint. Continue to cook for 10 minutes. Taste and adjust the seasonings. Remove the lime slices and epazote before serving. The soup may be prepared up to 5 days in advance if refrigerated in an airtight container. It may be frozen for 2 months. To serve, top each bowl with cumin croutons and serve lime wedges on the side.

Gingery Azuki Bean Soup

Yield: 8 servings • Prep Time: 20 minutes • Cooking Time: 3 hours

2 cups dried azuki beans
1 teaspoon Szechwan pepper-
    corns (page 174), wrapped in
    cheesecloth
2 dried red chili peppers
8 cups cold water
1 1/2 cups chopped yellow onion
3 cloves garlic, peeled and left
    whole
2 1/4-inch slices ginger, smashed
    with the side of a knife
2 cups chopped tomatoes
    (may use canned)
1/2 cup Shaoxing (rice wine) or
    dry sherry
8 dried shiitake mushrooms
    (page 174), softened in hot
    water and quartered
1/4 cup fermented black beans
    (page 168), crushed
1 cup diced yellow onion
1 cup minced scallion
3 tablespoons minced ginger
3 tablespoons minced garlic
1 green bell pepper, seeds and
    white membrane removed,
    diced
1 red bell pepper, seeds and
    white membrane removed,
    diced
1/4 cup tamari (page 175)
3 tablespoons maple syrup

GARNISH:
5 teaspoons toasted sesame oil
1/3 cup minced cilantro leaves
3 tablespoons minced pickled
    ginger (or to taste)
1/4 cup minced scallion

Delicate and sweet azuki beans are paired with ginger and fermented black beans in this filling soup. If you use canned beans, add the Szechwan peppercorns to the soup as it cooks and additional pickled ginger before serving.

1. Pick over the beans and discard all rocks and debris. Rinse the beans well in several changes of cold water, then place them in a large bowl and cover with cold water. Set aside to soak for 12 hours.

2. Heat a small heavy skillet until very hot. Add the Szechwan peppercorns and toss until they release their aroma and begin to darken. Pour them immediately into a mortar or electric spice grinder and grind finely. (If you do not have either a mortar and pestle or electric grinder, wrap the peppercorns in cheesecloth before adding them to the soup. This way you will be able to remove them before serving the soup.) Heat the pan again and quickly brown the chili peppers. Set them aside.

3. Drain the beans. Discard the soaking liquid, rinse and drain the beans again. Place them in a 6-quart soup pot or pressure cooker, and add the 8 cups of water. Cover and place over high heat, stirring frequently to prevent beans from sticking to the bottom of the pan. As the beans come to a boil foam will begin to rise to the surface. Reduce to a simmer, then skim and discard the foam until no more appears. Add the onions, garlic, ginger, and peppers. Cover and return to a boil over high heat, then reduce to a simmer and cook, stirring occasionally, until the beans are tender, for about 2 hours. If you are using a pressure cooker, remove the pan from the heat after adding the onion and other seasoning ingredients. Lock the lid in place, then place the cooker over high heat. When high steam is reached, cook for 9 minutes exactly. Immediately remove the cooker from the heat and place it in the sink under cold running water to quickly release the pressure. The cooked beans may be refrigerated in an airtight container for up to 3 days before continuing with the recipe.

4. Place cooked beans and 6 cups of cooking liquid in a 4-quart soup pot or Dutch oven. Add water to the cooking liquid if necessary to equal 6 cups. Remove and discard the pieces of cooked ginger. Add the tomatoes, Shaoxing, mushrooms, black beans, onions, scallions, ginger, garlic, peppers, tamari and maple syrup. Simmer, covered, for 1 1/2 hours, stirring often. Just before serving, stir the sesame oil and cilantro into the soup. Taste and adjust the seasonings. Serve in individual bowls sprinkled with minced scallions and pickled ginger.

Creole Pecan Chowder

Yield: 6 servings • Prep Time: 25 minutes • Cooking Time: 1 hour

This chowder has a unique blend of flavors and textures. The broth's heat is tamed by the addition of crisped vegetable dumplings and pecan topping. Although the ingredients list and directions are long, the recipe is actually quite simple to make. Each component may be prepared in advance, then assembled just before serving.

1. In a 4-quart saucepan, heat 2 tablespoons butter over medium high heat until the bubbles begin to subside, but the butter has not browned. Add the onions and sauté, stirring constantly, for about a minute, then reduce the heat to low and continue to cook, stirring often, until the onions are translucent, about 8 minutes. Add the celery, bell pepper and garlic. Continue to cook, stirring often until the vegetables are all soft, about 25 minutes.

2. Turn the heat to medium and sprinkle with flour. Cook, stirring constantly, until the flour turns a nutty brown, about 8 minutes. Add the tomatoes. Stir and scrape the bottom of the pan to incorporate all bits of flour. Cook for about 3 minutes, stirring constantly, then add the stock, paprika, oregano, thyme, sage, salt and cayenne. Cover and simmer, stirring occasionally until the onions are very soft, about 25 minutes. Remove the broth from the heat. It may be prepared up to 5 days in advance if refrigerated in an airtight container.

3. Remove the soup from the heat and allow it to cool briefly. Strain the soup solids from the broth, saving the liquid. In a food processor or blender, purée the soup very finely. Stir this back into the broth and return the soup to the saucepan.

4. Grate the tofu and combine it in a small mixing bowl with the zucchini, carrot and lemon juice. Season to taste with salt, pepper and cayenne. Stir in the egg and flour, then mix to blend thoroughly. The batter will be sticky so dust your hands with flour to facilitate shaping the dumplings. Form the zucchini mixture into 2-inch oval "patties." Dust the dumplings with flour and set them aside on a lightly floured plate. Melt the butter over medium-high heat in a 10-inch skillet. Sauté the dumplings, loosening them from the pan and flipping with a pancake turner once or twice, until they are lightly browned, about 8 minutes. Transfer them to a paper towel as you finish the soup. The dumplings may be prepared to this point up to 24 hours in advance if stored in one layer in an airtight container in the refrigerator.

5. In a blender or food processor, combine the ingredients for the Pecan Crumble. Purée until evenly ground. Set the crumble aside. It may be prepared up to 5 days in advance if refrigerated in an airtight container.

6. To serve the soup, place dumplings in each bowl, ladle the soup over and sprinkle with Pecan Crumble. Serve immediately.

3 tablespoons butter
1 1/2 cups diced onion
3/4 cup diced celery
1/3 cup diced green bell pepper
4 cloves garlic, minced
3 tablespoons flour
1 cup diced tomato
6 cups kombu stock (page 40)
   or light vegetable stock
   (page 38)
1 teaspoon paprika
1 teaspoon oregano
1/2 teaspoon thyme
1/2 teaspoon sage
1/2 teaspoon salt
1/4 teaspoon cayenne

DUMPLINGS:
3 ounces frozen tofu, thawed and
   pressed (page 175)
2/3 cup grated zucchini
1/2 cup grated carrot
1 tablespoon lemon juice
Salt, pepper and cayenne to taste
1 egg, beaten
2 1/2 tablespoons flour
2 tablespoons butter

PECAN CRUMBLE:
1/3 cup minced parsley
1 cup toasted pecans (page 33)
1/4 cup scallion tops
1/4 teaspoon salt

Variation

1. Whisk 1 cup buttermilk, yogurt or cream into the broth. Omit the dumplings and serve with Corn Bread (page 148).

Chili Rojo Gumbo

Yield: 6 servings • Prep Time: 20 minutes • Cooking Time: 2 hours

Traditional tastes of the Southwest are added to a typical Cajun Gumbo resulting in this fiery full-meal soup.

1/2 pound okra
2 ancho peppers
2 teaspoons olive oil
1 1/2 cups chopped yellow onion
1 tablespoon flour
2 stalks celery, sliced
1 small green pepper, seeded and chopped
1 medium red pepper, seeded and chopped
2 serrano peppers, seeded and minced
1 tablespoon minced garlic
1 cup chopped tomatoes
2 bay leaves
1/2 teaspoon salt
1/4 teaspoon cayenne pepper
3 cups tomato stock (page 38) or water
5 ounces tempeh, chopped (page 175)
1 to 2 tablespoons red wine vinegar (to taste)
1/2 cup minced cilantro

1. Trim stem ends from okra, then slice each piece into 1-inch pieces. Cover a baking sheet with a clean kitchen towel. Place okra on the towel and sprinkle with salt and pepper. Allow it to rest at room temperature for 30 minutes. Holding the ancho peppers under cold tap water, pull off their stems, tear them in half and scrape out their seeds. Trim and discard any large ribs. Chop the chilies into 1-inch pieces and place them in a small bowl. Cover with hot water and set aside to soften for 30 minutes.

2. In a 4-quart saucepan, heat the oil until hot, but not smoking. Add the onions and cook, stirring constantly, for 2 minutes. Reduce heat to low and cook, stirring often, until onions have caramelized (they will be soft and brown), about 20 minutes.

3. Raise heat slightly and add the flour. Cook, stirring constantly, until the flour turns light brown. Add the okra and cook for 5 minutes. Stir in the celery, peppers, garlic, tomatoes, bay leaves, salt, cayenne, and stock. Drain the ancho chilies, saving 1/2 cup of their soaking liquid, then add the chilies and reserved liquid to the gumbo. Cover and simmer, stirring often, for 1 1/2 hours. Add water as the gumbo cooks if the liquid evaporates below the top surface of the okra.

4. Stir in tempeh, vinegar and cilantro. Continue to cook for 10 minutes. Serve hot. The gumbo may be prepared up to 3 days in advance if refrigerated in an airtight container. It may be frozen for 1 month.

Thai Mushroom and Coconut Soup with Lemon Grass

Yield: 8 servings • Prep Time: 15 minutes • Cooking Time: 25 minutes

Galangal, lime leaves and lemon grass may be found in most Asian markets. Dried lemon grass may be substituted for the fresh, if necessary. Ginger root may also replace the galanga, and a squeeze of fresh lime juice gives a hint of the correct flavor if the leaves are unavailable.

3 cups mushroom stock (or mushroom soaking liquid and light vegetable stock to equal 3 cups)
5 cups coconut milk (page 37)
1 1-inch piece kombu (page 170)
4 dried shiitake mushrooms (page 174), softened in 2 cups warm water
4 stalks lemon grass (page 171) (or 4 tablespoons dried)

1. Combine the stock and coconut milk in a 2-quart saucepan. Wipe the kombu off with a damp cloth and add it to the broth. Remove the shiitake mushrooms from the soaking liquid. Trim and discard tough stems, then slice the mushrooms into 1/4-inch strips. Add them to the soup.

2. Trim top stems and tough outer leaves from each piece of lemon grass, leaving stalks 5 to 6 inches long. To prepare, place a stalk on the counter and lay the flat side of a cleaver or large knife over the end of the lemon grass. Slap the

cleaver with the heel of your hand to smash and flatten the stalk. Roll the stalk over, move the cleaver up the stalk and slap it again. The lemon grass must be flattened open to contribute maximum flavor. Slice the stalk into 3-inch pieces. Repeat with the remaining lemon grass and add them all to the soup.

3. Rinse the galangal, then slice it into very thin rounds. Using the broad side of the cleaver, flatten each piece by slapping it, then scrape it against the cutting board with the dull edge of the knife. Add the galangal, garlic, 3 lime leaves, salt, soy sauce, honey and peppercorns to the soup. Cover and bring to a boil, then reduce the heat and simmer gently for 20 minutes. Remove and discard the piece of kombu.

4. Stir the straw mushrooms, tofu and bok choy leaves into the soup and cook for 5 minutes. Stir in the remaining lime leaves or lime juice and cilantro. Serve immediately with scallions sprinkled on top.

1 2 1/2-inch piece galangal (page 169) or ginger
3 cloves garlic, sliced thin
6 lime leaves (page 171) or 1 tablespoon lime juice
1/4 teaspoon salt
2 to 3 tablespoons soy sauce
2 teaspoons honey or sugar
4 peppercorns, finely crushed
1 16-ounce can whole straw mushrooms (page 174), drained and rinsed
4 ounces tofu
1 1/2 cups chopped bok choy leaves
3 tablespoons cilantro leaves
4 scallions, minced

Variations

1. Sauté 3 to 4 dried red chili peppers in 2 teaspoons of peanut oil until they turn black, about 1 minute. Add them to the soup with the shiitake mushrooms.
2. Stir 1/4 cup rinsed wakame into the soup with the straw mushrooms.

Old-Fashioned Split Pea

Yield: 6 servings • Prep Time: 15 minutes • Cooking Time: 2 hours

This is a thick and wholesome soup in which carrot and parsnip enhance split peas' natural sweetness.

1. Rinse split peas well to remove all dirt and grit then cover with cold water and soak for 8 hours. Drain the peas and place them in a 4-quart saucepan with the onion, carrot, parsnip, celery, garlic and 8 cups of water. Bring the soup to a boil, then simmer for 5 minutes as you skim and discard foam that rises to the surface. Add the pepper, nutmeg and cayenne, then reduce to a simmer. Cover and continue to cook, stirring occasionally, for 2 hours or until the peas are very soft. As the soup cooks, add more water if necessary to prevent the peas from sticking to the pan and burning.

2. Mash about 1/4 of the cooked peas against the side of the pan with the back of a cooking spoon. Stir in the salt and parsley, then taste and adjust the seasonings. The soup may be prepared up to 4 days in advance if refrigerated in an airtight container. It may be frozen up to 1 month.

1 cup green split peas
2 cups diced onion
1 1/2 cups carrots, cut in small dice
1 small parsnip, cut in small dice
1 stalk celery, cut in small dice
1 tablespoon minced garlic
8 cups water
1/2 teaspoon freshly ground black pepper
1/4 teaspoon nutmeg
Pinch of cayenne
1 1/2 teaspoons salt
1/4 cup minced parsley

Spicy Split Pea

Yield: 6 servings • Prep Time: 15 minutes • Cooking Time: 1 1/2 hours

1 cup green split peas
1 1/2 cups diced sweet onion
  (Vidalia, if available)
1 cup chopped tomatoes
  (or 1 16-ounce can, drained)
1 cup carrots in small dice
1 tablespoon minced garlic
1 teaspoon ginger
8 cups water
2 dried red chili peppers
1 4-inch cinnamon stick
2 teaspoons ground cumin
1/4 teaspoon ground coriander
Pinch of nutmeg
Freshly ground black pepper
1 1/4 teaspoons salt
1 red pepper, seeded and cut in
  small dice
1/4 cup minced basil

This spicy variation of a classic split pea soup has become a family favorite. Depending on your taste and the rest of the meal, you may serve it as is, a rather thick soup, or add additional water for a lighter broth. If you make it thinner, you may wish to increase the salt slightly to compensate.

1. Rinse the split peas well to remove all dirt and grit, then cover with cold water and soak for 8 hours. Drain the peas and place them in a 4-quart saucepan with the onion, tomatoes, carrots, garlic, ginger and water. Bring to a boil, then simmer for 5 minutes as you skim and discard foam that rises to the surface. Add the chili peppers, cinnamon, cumin, coriander, nutmeg and pepper. Reduce to a simmer, then cover and continue to cook, stirring occasionally, for 2 hours or until the peas are very soft.

2. Mash about 1/4 of the peas against the side of the pan with the back of a cooking spoon and leave the rest intact. Stir in the salt and diced red pepper. Continue to cook for 10 minutes. Remove from the heat, add the basil, then taste and adjust the seasonings.

Variation

1. Stir 1 1/2 cups chopped fresh spinach leaves into the soup just before serving. Serve with Cinnamon Croutons (page 150).

Spicy Baked Cauliflower Soup

Yield: 6 servings • Prep Time: 15 minutes • Cooking Time: 1 3/4 hours

1 medium-sized head cauliflower
1 cup nonfat yogurt
1/2 cup minced onion
1 1/2 tablespoons minced ginger
1 tablespoon minced garlic
1 teaspoon ground cinnamon
2 teaspoons garam masala
  (page 169)
1/2 teaspoon turmeric
1/8 teaspoon ground cardamom
1 teaspoon salt
1 tablespoon honey
4 cups hearty vegetable stock
  (page 39)
2 tablespoons peanut oil
1/3 cup diced red bell pepper
2 tablespoons minced mint or
  cilantro

This is one of the simplest recipes imaginable. A whole head of cauliflower is bathed in a spicy yogurt mixture, then baked and puréed. The result is a rich, sweet and spicy-tasting cauliflower soup.

1. Rinse the cauliflower and trim off all leaves and tough outer stems. In a 9-inch square baking dish, combine the yogurt, onion, ginger, garlic, cinnamon, garam masala, turmeric, cardamom, salt and honey. Blend well. Place the raw cauliflower in the bowl and turn it to coat evenly with the yogurt marinade. Cover and refrigerate for at least 30 minutes or up to 24 hours.

2. Preheat the oven to 400°F. Pour 1/2 cup of stock and the oil over the cauliflower. Cover the baking dish with a lid that does not touch the cauliflower. (If you do not have a lid that fits, poke 4 toothpicks into the cauliflower and lay a foil tent over it so that the pan is sealed, but the cauliflower has air circulating around it.) Place the pan in the preheated oven. After 15 minutes, reduce the heat to 300°F. Continue to bake the cauliflower until very tender, about 1 1/2

hours more. Cut the cooked cauliflower into pieces and place them in a food processor or blender. Scrape all of the cooked marinade into the processor as well and purée until the cauliflower is a finely ground, even texture.

3. Transfer the purée to a 3-quart saucepan and whisk in the remaining stock. Warm briefly, then taste and adjust the seasonings. Serve topped with diced red pepper and minced mint.

South Indian Gumbo

Yield: 6 servings • Prep Time: 25 minutes • Cooking Time: 2 hours

Okra, known as "Ladies' Fingers" in India, is common in many curries. Its thickening quality, which manifests with long cooking, gives this gumbo an appealing sheen.

1/2 pound okra
4 teaspoons peanut oil
2 to 4 dried red chili peppers
1 1/2 cups chopped onion
1 cup sliced celery
1 cup diced carrot
2 teaspoons minced ginger root
1 tablespoon minced garlic
1 small green pepper, seeded and chopped
1 medium red pepper, seeded and chopped
1 cup chopped tomatoes
1 3-inch stick cinnamon
2 teaspoons ground cumin
1 1/2 teaspoons garam masala (page 169)
1/2 teaspoon crushed fennel seeds
1/2 teaspoon salt
1/4 teaspoon turmeric
3 cups water or light vegetable stock (page 38)
1/4 cup split green mung beans
1/3 cup minced cilantro

GARNISH:
1 to 2 serrano peppers (page 173), seeded and minced
1 teaspoon brown mustard seeds

1. Trim stem ends from okra, then slice each piece into 1-inch pieces. Cover a baking sheet with a clean kitchen towel. Place the okra on the towel and sprinkle with salt and pepper. Allow it to rest at room temperature for 30 minutes.

2. In a 4-quart saucepan, heat 2 teaspoons of oil until hot, but not smoking. Add the chili peppers and cook quickly, tossing constantly, until they turn black, about 1 minute. Remove the peppers from the pan and set them aside. Return the pan to the heat and add the onions. Cook, stirring constantly, for 2 minutes. Reduce heat to low and cook, stirring often, until onions have caramelized, about 20 minutes.

3. Stir the okra into the onions and cook for 5 minutes. Stir in the celery, carrot, ginger, garlic, peppers and tomatoes. Add the reserved chili peppers, cinnamon, cumin, garam masala, fennel seeds, salt, turmeric and water. Rinse the beans and stir them into the soup. Cover and simmer, stirring often until the beans are tender, about 1 1/2 hours. Add additional water as the gumbo cooks, if the liquid evaporates below the top surface of the okra.

4. Stir in the beans and cilantro and continue to cook for 10 minutes. The soup may be prepared to this point up to 3 days in advance if refrigerated in an airtight container. It may be frozen for up to 1 month.

5. Just before serving, heat the remaining oil in a small skillet until it is hot, but not smoking. Add the peppers and toss for 30 seconds. Stir in the mustard seeds and continue to cook, stirring constantly, until they pop, about 1 minute. Transfer the mixture to the soup and serve.

Variation

1. Replace the mung beans with cooked kidney beans. Add the beans after the soup and seasonings have cooked for 30 minutes.

Creole Gumbo

Yield: 6 servings • Prep Time: 15 minutes • Cooking Time: 2 hours

1/2 pound okra
2 teaspoons olive oil
1 large onion, chopped
1 tablespoon flour
2 stalks celery, sliced
1 small green pepper, seeded and chopped
1 medium red pepper, seeded and chopped
2 cloves garlic, minced
1 cup chopped tomatoes
2 bay leaves
1/2 teaspoon salt
1/4 teaspoon cayenne pepper
3 cups water or light vegetable stock (page 38)
1/4 teaspoon file powder
5 ounces cubed firm tofu
1/2 cup minced parsley

Filé powder (ground sassafras root) is sometimes considered an essential part of any gumbo. Though many gumbos are made without it, I include it here for its subtle taste and thickening quality.

1. Trim stem ends from okra, then slice each piece into 1-inch pieces. Cover a baking sheet with a clean kitchen towel. Place okra on the towel and sprinkle with salt and pepper. Allow it to rest at room temperature for 30 minutes.

2. In a 4-quart saucepan, heat the oil until hot, but not smoking. Add the onions and cook, stirring constantly, for 2 minutes. Reduce heat to low and cook, stirring often, until onions have caramelized (they will be soft and brown), about 20 minutes.

3. Raise heat slightly and add the flour. Cook, stirring constantly, until the flour turns light brown. Add the okra and cook for 5 minutes. Stir in the celery, peppers, garlic, tomatoes, bay leaves, salt, cayenne and stock. Cover and simmer, stirring often, for 1 1/2 hours. Add water as the gumbo cooks if the liquid evaporates below the top surface of the okra.

4. Sprinkle the file into the gumbo and stir in tofu and parsley. Continue to cook for 10 minutes. The gumbo may be prepared up to 3 days in advance if refrigerated in an airtight container.

Red Lentil Dal

Yield: 4-6 servings • Prep Time: 20 minutes • Cooking Time: 1 hour

1 cup red lentils
1 small butternut (or other winter squash)
2 cups diced onion
1 1/2 tablespoons ghee (page 169) or peanut oil
1 tablespoon minced ginger
8 whole cardamom pods, smashed
2 1/2 teaspoons crushed fennel seeds
1/4 teaspoon ground cloves
1/4 teaspoon ground coriander
8 cups water
1/8 teaspoon hing (asafoetida) (page 170)
1/4 teaspoon turmeric
1 3-inch cinnamon stick
1/4 cup raisins
1 teaspoon salt
1/4 teaspoon black pepper
1 cup chopped spinach (or other green)

Dal is a term used in India to categorize beans. Many soup-type dishes are made from them. Although they vary to extremes in terms of consistency and spiciness, these dishes are also referred to as dal.

1. Pick over the lentils to remove all dirt and debris, then place them in a strainer. Do not rinse them until just before you add them to the soup or they will clump together; set them aside. Halve the squash, then peel it and scrape out and discard the seeds. Cut the meat into 3/4-inch cubes and set them aside.

2. In a 4-quart saucepan, sauté onions in 1 1/2 tablespoons of ghee over medium heat until they are very soft, about 20 minutes. Stir in the ginger, cardamom, fennel seeds, cloves and coriander. Raise heat slightly and cook for about a minute, stirring constantly.

3. Rinse the lentils, rubbing them to remove all dust and dirt. Add them to the soup, then stir in 8 cups of water, the hing, turmeric and cinnamon stick. Bring the soup to a simmer, then cook, stirring occasionally, for 15 minutes. Add the squash, raisins, salt and pepper. Continue to cook, stirring occasionally, for 15 minutes or until the squash is tender. Stir in the spinach, cover, remove from the heat and set aside for 5 minutes.

4. Heat the remaining ghee in a small skillet. When it is hot, but not smoking, add the peppers and mustard seeds. Cook, stirring constantly, until the seeds pop, about 1 minute. Transfer immediately to a paper towel and blot to remove excess oil. Add the pepper mixture to the soup, then stir in the mint. Taste and adjust the seasonings. The soup may be prepared up to 4 days in advance if refrigerated in an airtight container. It does not freeze well.

GARNISH:
2 teaspoons ghee (page 169) or peanut oil
2 fresh serrano peppers, chopped (page 173)
1/2 teaspoon brown mustard seeds
2 tablespoons minced mint

Split Green Gram Soup with Millet

Yield: 6 servings • Prep Time: 25 minutes • Cooking Time: 1 1/2 hours

Split green gram (split green mung beans) may be found in good Asian markets. It is a very delicate bean, with a unique light texture and taste. If it is not available, red or brown lentils or split peas may be substituted.

1 1/2 cups split green gram
3 cups diced onion
1/2 teaspoon turmeric
10 cups water or vegetable stock
1/2 cup millet
2/3 cup minced mint
1 teaspoon anise seed, crushed
5 black peppercorns
10 fenugreek seeds
1/2 teaspoon cumin seeds
1/2 teaspoon coriander seeds
Pinch of hing (asafoetida) (page 170)
1 1/2 teaspoons salt
2 teaspoons minced garlic
1 teaspoon minced ginger
3 tablespoons ghee (page 169) or butter
2 cups diced tomatoes
A 1-inch ball tamarind (page 175), softened in warm water
1 tablespoon molasses (optional)
1/2 teaspoon brown mustard seeds
2 to 3 dried red chili peppers or fresh serrano peppers
Mint sprigs

1. Pick over the beans to remove all dirt and debris. Rinse well, then soak in cold water for 2 hours. Drain the beans and place them in a 4-quart saucepan with 6 cups of water, 1 cup onion and the turmeric. Place over high heat and bring to a boil. Reduce to a simmer, skim and discard foam that rises to the surface. Cover and cook, stirring occasionally, until the beans are very tender, about 1 hour. If using a pressure cooker, after the foam is removed, lock the top in place, bring to high steam and cook for 5 minutes. Immediately release the pressure under cold running water. Set the beans aside.

2. Heat a small skillet over high heat. Add the millet and stir until lightly toasted, about 1 1/2 minutes. (It will darken slightly, but should not burn.) Remove from the heat immediately. In a separate 2-quart saucepan, combine the millet with 3 cups water, 1 cup onion and 1/2 teaspoon salt. Cover and bring to a boil. Reduce to a simmer and cook, stirring occasionally, until the millet is tender, about 25 minutes. Toss in 1/4 cup of minced mint, then fluff the millet, cover it and set aside.

3. Place the anise seed, peppercorns, fenugreek, cumin seeds, coriander seeds, asafoetida and 1 teaspoon of salt in a blender. Grind until fine. Add the remaining onion, garlic and ginger. Continue to purée until smooth.

4. Heat 2 tablespoons ghee in a skillet. Add the onion purée and cook, stirring often, for 15 minutes. Add this mixture to the cooked beans, then stir in the tomatoes. Strain the tamarind through a tea strainer, discarding the seeds and stringy pulp. Add the strained pulp and soaking water along with the molasses to the soup. Cook, stirring often, for 30 minutes.

5. Heat the remaining 1 tablespoon of ghee in a small skillet over high heat. Add the mustard seeds and chili peppers. Cook, stirring constantly, until the seeds pop, about 1 minute. Transfer immediately to the soup, then stir in the remaining mint. Taste and adjust the seasonings. To serve, arrange a ring of millet in each flat serving bowl and ladle soup into the center. Garnish each bowl with a sprig of mint.

Black Bean Soup with Posole

Yield: 6 servings • Prep Time: 25 minutes • Cooking Time: 3 1/2 hours

2 cups dried black beans
  (or 4 cups cooked beans)
3 tablespoons olive oil
3 cups diced onion
8 cloves garlic, sliced
1 cup frozen posole
12 cups water or vegetable stock
1 1/2 teaspoons salt
1 cup diced fresh tomatoes
8 sun-dried tomatoes (page 174),
  softened in hot water
2 to 5 chipolte peppers (page
  168), softened in hot water
1 teaspoon dried thyme
1 teaspoon dried oregano
1 1/2 teaspoons ground cumin
1 teaspoon anise seed, crushed
4 tablespoons butter or
  margarine (optional)
1/2 cup minced cilantro
6 cilantro sprigs

Posole, or hominy, has a potent aroma, yet its surprisingly mild flavor blends with and complements the flavors in this spicy soup. You may use either frozen or canned posole. Canned posole takes far less time to cook, but the texture of frozen posole is superior.

1. Pick over the beans to remove all dirt and debris. Rinse well, then soak in cold water for 8 hours. Drain the beans and place them in a 6-quart saucepan with 6 cups of water, 1 tablespoon olive oil, 1 cup onion and half the garlic. Place over high heat and bring to a boil. Reduce to a simmer, skim and discard foam that rises to the surface. Cover and cook, stirring occasionally, until the beans are very tender, about 2 hours. If using a pressure cooker, after the foam is removed, lock the top in place, bring to high steam and cook for 10 minutes. Immediately release the pressure under cold running water. The beans may be prepared up to 3 days ahead to this point if refrigerated; keep them in their cooking liquid in an airtight container.

2. In a separate 2-quart saucepan, combine the posole with 5 cups water and bring to a boil. Cook, stirring occasionally, until the corn pops open, about 1 1/2 hours. Add 1 cup onion, 3 cloves garlic, 1 teaspoon salt and continue to cook until fully tender, about 1 hour. Add water as the posole cooks to prevent it from sticking and burning. (If using canned posole, drain and rinse it well, then skip the preliminary cooking and allow only 25 minutes for the second stage of cooking.) When it is fully cooked the posole should have absorbed all of its cooking water. The posole may be partially cooked up to 24 hours in advance. It must be removed from the heat after adding the onions and cooking for 30 minutes. Before serving the soup, simmer the partially cooked posole gently for 30 minutes, stirring often and checking to be certain it has enough water so that it does not stick and burn.

3. When the beans are cooked, drain them and measure their cooking liquid. Adjust it by adding more water, so that you have 5 cups of liquid. Place the beans in a 6-quart saucepan. Mash about 1/3 of them with the back of a fork, and leave the rest whole. Add the cooking liquid and fresh tomatoes, then set aside.

4. Purée the remaining onions in a blender. Add up to 1/4 cup of the bean cooking liquid, if necessary, to obtain a smooth consistency. Drain the sun-dried tomatoes, saving their liquid. Purée the tomatoes in a blender, adding up to 1/4 cup of their soaking liquid, if necessary, to get a smooth consistency. Drain the chipoltes, remove their stems and seeds, then add them to the tomato purée with the garlic, thyme, oregano, cumin, anise seed and salt. Purée until smooth.

5. Heat the remaining oil in a skillet. Add the onion purée and cook, stirring often, for 15 minutes. Stir in the tomato purée and cook another 5 minutes. Add this to the beans and cook, stirring often, for 45 minutes. Taste and adjust the seasonings.

6. To serve, finish cooking the posole just as you want to serve the soup. When the posole has absorbed all of the liquid, stir in the butter (optional) and cilantro. Arrange a ring of posole in each flat serving bowl and ladle soup into the center. Garnish each bowl with a sprig of cilantro.

Pot Au Feu
Seasonal vegetables and seitan are simmered in
a sophisticated broth in this memorable soup.
(page 70)

Italian Garden Soup
*Shavings of fontina cheese serve as a delicate
garnish in this refreshing soup. (page 95)*

Roasted Eggplant Soup
*Broiled tomato slices top this delicately
flavored soup. (page 115)*

Cranberry Apple Gazpacho
The bite of cranberries is mellowed by the addition of apple juice in this festive holiday soup. (page 46)

Black Bean Posole Soup
A hearty soup accented by the smokey undertone of chipotle peppers. (page 90)

**Beet and Fennel Consommé
with Gorgonzola Won Tons**
*The crystal clear broth of this elegant soup has a
divine balance of tastes. (page 42)*

Lotus Petal Soup
A light and flavorful carrot-ginger broth.
(page 44)

Artichoke Soup with Orange and Saffron
The haunting aroma of saffron makes this soup
irresistible. (page 100)

Garlic Scented Spinach Soup with Feta
A full-bodied spinach soup enriched with feta
and topped with filo. (page 113)

Udon Noodle Soup
*The traditional flavors of mirin and tamari serve
as the base for the broth in this satisfying soup.*
(page 109)

Tree Oyster Bisque
A rich, lowfat bisque, gently flavored with cayenne and cognac. (page 51)

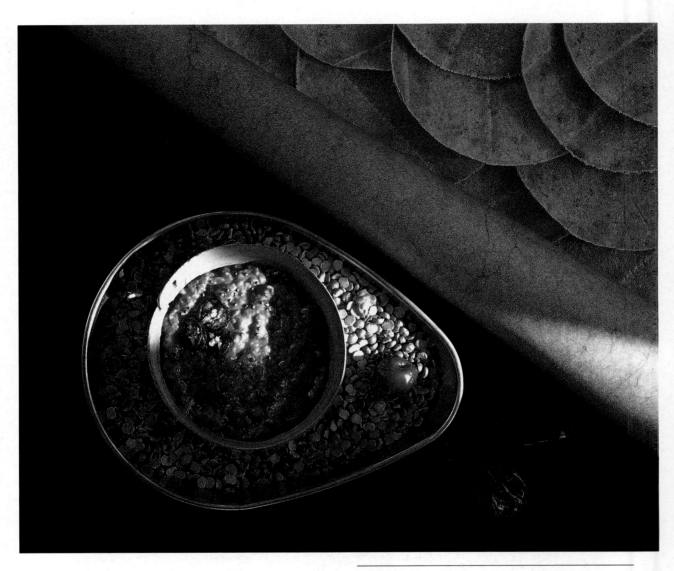

Spicy Split Pea Soup
A simple, spicy variation on an all-time favorite.
(page 86)

Grand Marnier Surprise
*Succulent poached dried figs served in a creamy
millet soup make a sublime dessert. (page 136)*

Caramelized Pear Soup
A creamy dessert soup accented with a swirl of chocolate. (page 128)

Midnight Sun
Star anise accents the rich taste of blueberries in this dessert soup. (page 139)

Mixed Fruit Soup
A refreshing assortment of fruit bathed in a delicate fruit broth. (page 130)

Red Bean Soup with Basmati Rice

Yield: 6 servings • Prep Time: 25 minutes • Cooking Time: 2 1/2 hours

Inspired by red beans and rice, this soup was made famous in New Orleans. The alluring aroma of basmati rice is an ideal match for this delicately spiced version of the original dish.

1. Pick over the beans to remove all dirt and debris. Rinse well, then soak in cold water for 8 hours. Drain the beans and place them in a 4-quart saucepan with 6 cups of water, 1 tablespoon olive oil, 1 cup onion and half the garlic. Place over high heat and bring to a boil. Reduce to a simmer, skim and discard foam that rises to the surface. Cover and cook, stirring occasionally, until the beans are very tender, about 2 hours. If using a pressure cooker, after the foam is removed, lock the top in place, bring to high steam and cook for 9 minutes. Immediately release the pressure under cold running water.

2. In a separate 2-quart saucepan, combine the rice with 2 1/4 cups water, 1 cup onion and 3 cloves garlic. Cover and bring to a boil. Reduce to a simmer and cook until all water is absorbed and the rice is tender, about 25 minutes. Stir the butter (optional) and 1/4 cup of the parsley into the rice. Keep the rice warm in a low oven until the soup has finished cooking.

3. When the beans are cooked, drain them and measure their cooking liquid. Adjust it by adding more water, so that you have 5 cups of liquid. Place the beans in a 4-quart saucepan. Mash about 1/3 of them with the back of a fork, and leave the rest whole. Add the cooking liquid, fresh tomatoes and celery, then set aside.

4. Place the remaining onion and garlic in a blender and purée until smooth. Add the black pepper, celery seeds, thyme, marjoram, anise seed and salt. Purée to blend smooth.

5. Heat the remaining oil in a skillet. Add the onion purée and cook, stirring often, for 15 minutes. Add this to the beans and cook, stirring often, for 45 minutes. Stir in the remaining parsley, then taste and adjust the seasonings.

6. To serve, arrange a ring of rice in each flat serving bowl and ladle soup into the center. Garnish each bowl with a sprig of parsley and pass the Tabasco.

2 cups raw red beans
  (or 4 cups cooked beans)
12 cups water or vegetable stock
  (3 quarts)
3 tablespoons olive oil
3 cups diced onion
8 cloves garlic, sliced
1 1/2 cups basmati rice
4 tablespoons butter (optional)
1/2 cup minced parsley
2 cups diced tomatoes
1 cup diced celery
8 black peppercorns
1 teaspoon celery seeds
1 teaspoon dried thyme
1 teaspoon dried marjoram
1 teaspoon anise seed, crushed
1/2 teaspoon salt
Tabasco Sauce

Anasazi Bean Soup with Rum

Yield: 6 servings • Prep Time: 15 minutes • Cooking Time: 3 hours

1 cup dried anasazi beans
1 cup diced onion
1 1/2 tablespoons minced garlic
1/2 cup diced parsnip
6 cups water
2 chipolte peppers (page 168),
    softened in hot water
2 ancho peppers (page 167),
    softened in hot water
2 cups coconut milk (page 37)
2 to 4 tablespoons Jamaican
    dark rum
4 sprigs parsley
1 bay leaf
1/2 teaspoon dried oregano
Freshly ground black pepper
1/2 teaspoon salt
3/4 cup chopped bell pepper
    (mixed colors if desired)
2 cups chopped tomatoes
1/2 cup chopped cilantro

The sweet taste and delicate, non-mealy texture of anasazi beans become richer and even more flavorful when cooked with coconut milk and rum. Chipolte peppers add their unique hot and smoky character.

1. Pick over the beans to remove all stones and debris. Rinse the beans well, then cover them with cold water and allow them to soak for at least 8 hours. Drain the beans and place them in a 3-quart saucepan with the onion, garlic, parsnip, and water. Bring to a boil, stirring occasionally. Reduce to a simmer and cook for 5 minutes, skimming and discarding any foam that rises to the surface.

2. Drain the dried peppers and pull each apart. Remove the stems and scrape out all seeds. Chop them finely, then stir them into the soup. Add the coconut milk, 2 tablespoons rum, the parsley, bay leaf, oregano and pepper. Cover and simmer, stirring occasionally, until the beans are tender, about 3 hours. As the soup cooks, check the water level to be certain that it does not evaporate below the surface of the beans. The soup may be prepared to this point up to 4 days in advance if refrigerated in an airtight container. It may also be frozen for up to 3 months.

3. Just before serving, heat the soup to a boil. Add the salt, chopped peppers and tomatoes. Cook, stirring often, until the peppers are soft, about 15 minutes. Remove from the heat. Stir in the cilantro, then taste and adjust the seasonings. Ladle the soup into 1 large or several small serving bowls. Arrange cornmeal biscuits on top. Drizzle the remaining rum over the soup and arrange biscuits on top. Alternatively, omit this final addition of rum and simply serve with cornbread (page 148) alongside.

Lone Star Bourbon Soup

Yield: 6 servings • Prep Time: 25 minutes • Cooking Time: 2 hours

1 cup dried black-eyed peas
1 cup diced onion
1 1/2 tablespoons minced garlic
1/2 cup diced celery
1/2 cup diced parsnip
2/3 cup minced pitted prunes
8 cups water
6 tablespoons bourbon
1 small sprig fresh thyme
    or 1/2 teaspoon dried
4 sprigs parsley
1 bay leaf
1/4 teaspoon ground nutmeg

The humble black-eyed pea is often ignored except on New Year's Day when Hoppin' John is served. But it is a versatile bean with well-balanced taste and texture. In addition, it cooks quickly—no soaking required. In this soup the beans are combined with bourbon and prunes, then greens are stirred in as a finishing touch. For a playful (and exceedingly tasty) presentation, diamond-shaped Cornmeal Biscuits are placed in the center of each bowl of soup to form a star.

1. Pick over the beans to remove all stones and debris. Rinse the beans well and place them in a 4-quart saucepan with the onion, garlic, celery, parsnip, prunes and water. Bring to a boil, stirring occasionally. Reduce to a simmer and cook for 5 minutes, skimming and discarding any foam that rises to the surface.

2. Add 1/4 cup bourbon, the thyme, parsley, bay leaf, nutmeg, pepper and cayenne. Cover and simmer, stirring occasionally, until the beans are tender, about 1 1/2 to 2 hours. The soup may be prepared to this point up to 4 days in advance if refrigerated in an airtight container. It may also be frozen for up to 3 months.

3. Just before serving, heat the soup to a boil. Add the salt, remaining bourbon and chopped greens. Cook, stirring often, until the greens are a vibrant color and are tender, about 5 minutes. Remove from the heat. Place about 2 tablespoons of cheese in each serving bowl and ladle soup over. In the center of each bowl, arrange Cornmeal Biscuits (page 148) in a star pattern and serve at once.

Freshly ground black pepper
Pinch of cayenne
1/2 teaspoon salt
4 cups chopped greens
  (collard, mustard, kale or a
  mixture)
1/2 cup grated Gruyère (or other
  Swiss cheese)

Great Tongues of Fire!

Yield: 8 servings • Prep Time: 20 minutes • Cooking Time: 3 1/4 hours

Tongues of fire beans are beautiful, large and flat, with wine-colored flame shapes lapping each bean. They are sweet and slightly mealy. The flaming finish to this soup is a play on the name of the bean itself.

1. Pick over the beans to remove all stones and debris. Rinse the beans well, then cover them with cold water and allow them to soak for at least 8 hours. Drain the beans and place them in a 6-quart saucepan with the onion, garlic, parsnip and stock. Bring to a boil, stirring occasionally. Reduce to a simmer and cook for 5 minutes, skimming and discarding any foam that rises to the surface.

2. Add the celery, raisins, carrot, cinnamon stick, parsley, bay leaf, oregano and pepper. Cover and simmer, stirring occasionally, until the beans are tender, about 3 hours. As the soup cooks, check the water level to be certain that it does not evaporate below the surface of the beans. The soup may be prepared to this point up to 4 days in advance if refrigerated in an airtight container. It may also be frozen for up to 3 months.

3. Just before serving, heat the soup to a boil. Add the salt, escarole and Parmesan. Cook, stirring often, until the escarole is soft, about 8 minutes. Remove from the heat, stir, then taste and adjust the seasonings. Ladle the soup into one large, or several small serving bowls. Arrange Parmesan cups on top. When at the table, drizzle the cognac over the soup, between the crusts and immediately ignite the cognac. Serve at once.

1 cup dried tongues of fire beans
  (substitute scarlet runners or
  limas)
1 1/2 cups diced onion
8 cloves garlic, sliced
1/2 cup diced parsnip
8 cups light vegetable stock
  (page 38)
1 cup diced celery
1/2 cup raisins
1 cup diced carrot
1 3-inch cinnamon stick
4 sprigs parsley
1 bay leaf
1/2 teaspoon dried oregano
Freshly ground black pepper
1/2 teaspoon salt
2 cups escarole leaves, chopped
1/4 cup Parmesan cheese
  (optional)
8 Parmesan Cups (page 150)
1/4 cup cognac

5 • Variations & Themes

Italian Garden Soup

Yield: 6 servings • Prep Time: 30 minutes • Cooking Time: 35 minutes

This refreshing soup is almost like a salad—an assortment of fresh vegetables, lightly basted by a small amount of flavorful broth. Serve it topped with grated Parmesan cheese if desired.

1. Preheat the broiler to high. Wash the peppers to remove all dust and dirt, then place them on a baking sheet about 4 inches from the broiler. Broil, turning 3 or 4 times, until they are charred and blistered on all sides. Do not overcook the peppers. The skin should be blackened, but the flesh should still be quite firm. Immediately remove the peppers from the oven, place them in a brown paper bag and fold the bag shut. This will allow steam to separate the skin from the meat. When the peppers are cool enough to handle, remove them from the bag and, with a paring knife, peel them. Scrape out and discard the seeds, then slice the peppers into thin strips. Set aside.

2. In a 2-quart saucepan, bring 1 quart of water to a boil. At the stem end of each tomato, cut out a cone-shaped piece of core that is about 1 inch deep. With the tip of a paring knife, cut a cross in the blossom end of each tomato, just through the skin. Drop the tomatoes into the boiling water and cook, turning once or twice, until the skin at the blossom end just begins to peel back, about 30 seconds. Drain the tomatoes immediately and run cold water over them to stop their cooking. Peel the tomatoes and cut them in half, then squeeze the seeds and juice from each half. Chop the peeled and seeded tomatoes. Set them aside.

3. In a 2-quart saucepan, heat the oil until hot, but not smoking. Add the onions, reduce heat to medium and cook, stirring often, until wilted, about 10 minutes. Add the garlic, salt, pepper, parsley, oregano, pepper flakes and stock. Bring to a fast simmer, cover, and cook for 5 minutes. Add the zucchini and yellow squash, then continue to cook until they are just tender, about 8 minutes. Stir in the chard and fennel, and cook until the chard is a bright green color and just tender, about 5 minutes.

4. Remove the soup from the heat and stir in the peeled peppers and basil. Taste and adjust the seasonings. Place arugula in each bowl and ladle the soup over the leaves. Sprinkle with the chopped tomatoes, Parmesan or Fontina cheese and olives (if desired), then serve immediately. The soup is best prepared and eaten immediately.

1 red bell pepper
1 yellow bell pepper
2 large ripe tomatoes
2 tablespoons olive oil
1 1/2 cup sliced red onions
1 tablespoon minced garlic
1 teaspoon salt
1/4 teaspoon white pepper
4 sprigs parsley
1 sprig oregano or
   1 teaspoon dried
Pinch of red pepper flakes
3 cups hearty vegetable stock
   (page 39)
1 zucchini, sliced
1 yellow crookneck squash,
   sliced
2 cups green chard leaves,
   torn into pieces
1 small fennel root, tops
   removed and bulb sliced thin
1/2 cup basil leaves, shredded
3/4 cup arugula leaves
2 ounces Parmesan cheese, grated

OPTIONAL GARNISH:
2 tablespoons sliced black olives
Shavings of Fontina cheese

English Garden Soup

Yield: 6 servings • Prep Time: 25 minutes • Cooking Time: 1 hour

1 cup pearl onions
3 tablespoons olive oil
2 teaspoons rice syrup (page 172)
    or sugar
1/2 teaspoon salt
1/4 teaspoon black pepper
1 1/2 cups small Brussels sprouts
2 leeks, cut in julienne strips
5 cups hearty vegetable stock
    (page 39)
1 cup cubed red-skinned
    potatoes (skin on)
1 sprig fresh thyme
    (1 teaspoon dried)
3 sprigs parsley
2 carrots, sliced
1 cup chopped savoy cabbage
1 cup English peas
    (may use frozen, thawed)
Pinch of nutmeg
1 head Boston lettuce

TOPPING:
6 ounces mild goat cheese, sliced
1/4 cup toasted walnuts

This soup has a natural, stylized look. Whole pearl onions, Brussels sprouts and green peas are cupped in soft, green lettuce leaves. Leeks and carrots are then arranged alongside. For a tasty and elegant finish, each serving is topped with sliced goat cheese and walnuts.

1. To prepare the onions, carefully peel them, leaving the root ends intact. With the tip of a paring knife make a cross mark that is about 1/8 inch deep, in the root end of each onion. In a small skillet, heat 1 tablespoon oil until hot, but not smoking. Add the onions and cook, tossing often, until they just begin to brown, about 5 minutes. Reduce heat to low, cover the skillet and continue to cook the onions, tossing frequently, until they are soft throughout, about 25 minutes. Raise the heat slightly, add the rice syrup, sprinkle with salt and pepper and cook until browned, about 5 minutes. Set aside.

2. Trim tough outer leaves from the Brussels sprouts and cut the stem end flush with the bottom of each. As with the onions, make a cross mark in the stem end. Steam them over rapidly boiling water until just tender, about 10 minutes. Transfer to a strainer and run cold water over them to stop their cooking and retain their color. When completely cold, turn the Brussels sprouts out onto a clean kitchen towel to dry while preparing the rest of the soup.

3. In a 2-quart saucepan, heat the remaining oil until hot, but not smoking. Add the leeks, reduce heat to medium and cook, stirring often, until wilted, about 10 minutes. Add the stock, potatoes, thyme and parsley. Bring to a fast simmer, cover, and cook for 5 minutes. Add the carrots and Brussels sprouts. Continue to cook until the Brussels sprouts and potatoes are just tender, about 20 minutes. Stir in the cabbage and fresh peas (if using frozen, do not add them now, but just before serving the soup). Cook until the cabbage turns a bright green color and is just tender, about 4 minutes.

4. Remove the soup from the heat. Discard the thyme branch and parsley and stir in the onions. Taste and adjust the seasonings. Place a lettuce leaf in each serving bowl. Ladle soup broth over the lettuce. With a slotted spoon, transfer Brussels sprouts and peas to the lettuce "boats." Arrange leeks and carrots beside the leaves and add additional broth if necessary. Float a piece of cheese in the center of each bowl. Sprinkle walnuts over top and serve. The soup is best prepared just before eating, though the Brussels sprouts and onions may be cooked well ahead and all other preparation may be completed a day in advance.

Mushroom Patch Soup

Yield: 6 servings • Prep Time: 20 minutes • Cooking Time: 1 hour

A variety of mushrooms contribute contrasting colors and textures to this light, lemon-flavored soup. Roasted red pepper and green peas add a balance of color and taste. If fresh shiitakes are available, they are preferable.

1. Preheat the broiler to high. Wash the pepper to remove all dust and dirt, then place it on a small baking sheet about 4 inches from the broiler. Broil, turning 3 or 4 times, until it is charred and blistered on all sides. Do not overcook the pepper; the skin should be blackened, but the flesh should still be quite firm. Immediately remove the pepper from the oven, place it in a brown paper bag and fold the bag shut. This will allow steam to separate the skin from the meat. When the pepper is cool enough to handle, remove it from the bag and, with a paring knife, peel it. Scrape out and discard the seeds, then slice the pepper into thin strips. Set it aside.

2. In a 3-quart saucepan heat the oil and butter until hot but not smoking. Add the onions and sauté, stirring constantly, for 2 minutes. If using dried shiitake, add them, then reduce heat to low and continue to cook, stirring frequently, until the onions are lightly browned, about 25 minutes.

3. When the onions have caramelized in this way, raise the heat to medium and add all of the remaining mushrooms. Toss them for about 2 minutes, until the button mushrooms have just begun to soften. Add the lemon juice and cook, stirring constantly for another 2 minutes. Add the garlic, rice syrup, salt, nutmeg, pepper, red pepper flakes, parsley and stock. Reduce to a simmer and cook for 15 minutes, then add the tarragon and peas.

4. Remove the soup from the heat and stir in the pepper strips. Taste and adjust the seasonings. Place a lettuce leaf in each bowl. Pour the soup over the lettuce, sprinkle Gruyère and almonds over each bowl and serve. The soup is best prepared and eaten immediately.

1 red bell pepper
1 tablespoon olive oil
1 tablespoon butter
1 1/2 cup sliced white onions
6 sliced shiitake mushrooms
 (softened in warm water if
 dried)
1 1/2 pounds button mushrooms,
 sliced
8 morel mushrooms, quartered
 lengthwise
2 cloud ear mushrooms, shredded
 (softened in warm water if
 dried)
1/2 pound tree oyster mushrooms,
 diced
1 package enoki mushrooms,
 root ends trimmed
3 tablespoons lemon juice
1 tablespoon minced garlic
1 1/2 tablespoons rice syrup (page
 172) or 1/2 tablespoon honey
1 teaspoon salt
1/2 teaspoon nutmeg
1/4 teaspoon pepper
1/8 teaspoon crushed red pepper
 flakes
4 sprigs parsley
4 cups mushroom stock (page 38)
1 cup English peas
 (may use frozen, thawed)
3 tablespoons chopped fresh
 tarragon
1 head Boston lettuce

GARNISH:
2 ounces Gruyère cheese, grated
1/4 cup sliced almonds, toasted

Simple Vegetable Soup

Yield: 8 servings • Prep Time: 20 minutes • Cooking Time: 45 minutes

When you first think of making a vegetarian soup, this may well be what you have in mind— seasonal vegetables cooked in a complementary broth and seasoned with fresh herbs. Below you will find suggestions for each season. The preparation is the same for each, so I simply list different ingredients to suit the time of year.

FALL VEGETABLES
2 cups diced yellow onion
4 leeks, cleaned and diced
3 cloves garlic, minced
2 tablespoons olive oil
3/4 cup dry white wine
10 cups hearty vegetable broth
1 1/2 cups red potatoes, cubed
2 cups carrot rounds
1/2 cup diced parsnip
1 cup diced kohlrabi
2 sprigs lovage (if available)
4 sprigs parsley
3/4 teaspoon dried thyme
   (or 1 1/2 teaspoons fresh)
1 bay leaf
1 teaspoon salt
1/4 teaspoon black pepper
1 cup shredded cabbage
1 cup chopped kale

SPRING VEGETABLES
1 cup diced white onion
8 scallions, minced
2 tablespoons olive oil
3/4 cup dry white wine
10 cups light vegetable broth
   (made with 4 rhubarb stems)
1 pound new red potatoes,
   scrubbed
1 cup sliced carrot
1/2 cup diced celery
6 sprigs parsley
1/4 teaspoon dried thyme
   (or 1/2 teaspoon fresh)
1 bay leaf
1 teaspoon salt
1/2 pound asparagus, cut in
   2-inch pieces
1/2 cup diced jicama (page 170)
3 tablespoons snipped chives

Fall Variation

1. In a 6-quart saucepan, sauté the onion, leeks and garlic in the olive oil over medium heat, stirring often, until the onion is soft, about 10 minutes. Add the wine and cook until the alcohol has evaporated, about 2 minutes. Stir in the remaining ingredients except the cabbage and kale. Simmer partially covered for 45 minutes, or until the vegetables are just tender. Stir in the greens and continue to cook until they are tender, but still a vibrant color, about 8 minutes. Taste and adjust the seasonings. Serve as is or with Garlic Croutons (page 149).

Spring Variation

1. Cook as in the original recipe, leaving the asparagus, jicama and chives out until the last 8 minutes of cooking.

Summer Variation

1. Proceed as with the original recipe, waiting to add the zucchini, yellow squash, peas, cucumber and spinach and chervil until the last 8 minutes of cooking.

Winter Variation

1. Proceed with the recipe as above, adding all of the ingredients after the onions are cooked. Simmer for 1 1/2 hours.

SUMMER VEGETABLES

1 1/2 cups diced onion
1 cup diced leeks
2 tablespoons olive oil
6 cloves garlic
1 carrot, sliced
1 stalk celery, diced
10 cups light vegetable or
   mushroom stock (page 38)
4 sprigs parsley
1 bay leaf
1/4 teaspoon dried thyme or
. 1/2 teaspoon fresh

1 teaspoon salt
1/4 teaspoon black pepper
2 cups chopped fresh tomatoes
1 cup sliced zucchini
1 cup sliced yellow crookneck squash
1/2 cup English peas
1 small cucumber, peeled, seeded
   and diced
2 cups chopped spinach leaves
3 tablespoons minced chervil

WINTER VEGETABLES

2 cups diced yellow onion
4 leeks, sliced
4 cloves garlic
3 tablespoons olive oil
2 cups cubed winter squash
1 carrot, sliced
1 turnip, peeled and diced
1 stalk celery, sliced
10 cups hearty vegetable stock
   (page 39)
6 sprigs parsley

2 bay leaves
1/2 teaspoon dried thyme,
   or 1 teaspoon fresh
1/4 teaspoon dried oregano
1 teaspoon salt
1/4 teaspoon black pepper
1/4 teaspoon ground
   nutmeg

Winter Vegetable Stew

Yield: 8 servings • Prep Time: 20 minutes • Cooking Time: 1 1/4 hours

1. In a 6-quart saucepan, sauté the onion and leeks in the olive oil over medium heat until the onion is translucent, about 8 minutes. Add the wine and cook until the alcohol has evaporated, about 1 minute. Stir in the remaining ingredients, except the cabbage and macaroni. Simmer partially covered for 45 minutes, or until the vegetables are just tender.

2. Add the cabbage and macaroni to the soup and cook for an additional 8-10 minutes or until the macaroni is just barely done. Taste and adjust the seasonings. Serve as is or with Crusty Garlic Croutons (page 149).

1 pound yellow onion, diced
4 leeks, cleaned and diced
2 tablespoons olive oil
3/4 cup dry white wine
10 cup hearty vegetable stock
   (page 39)
1 pound red potatoes, cubed
3 cups cubed acorn or butternut
   squash (or a combination)
2 cups carrot rounds
1 cup celery slices
1 cup diced turnip
4 sprigs parsley
1/4 teaspoon dried thyme
   (or 1/2 teaspoon fresh)
1 bay leaf
1 teaspoon salt
2 cups chopped cabbage
1/4 cup elbow macaroni

Summer Squash Bake

Yield: 6 servings • Prep Time: 15 minutes • Cooking Time: 1 1/4 hours

Summer squash and tomatoes have such high water content that when baked they virtually transform spontaneously into soup. Their flavors merge gracefully with the aroma of basil in this exceedingly simple recipe.

1. Preheat the oven to 350ºF. Layer the vegetables, butter, rice, spices and stock, in the order listed, into a 4-quart baking dish (or Dutch oven). Cover with a piece of wax paper or baking parchment, and then place a tight-fitting lid on top. Bake in the center of the oven for 1 hour. Remove from the oven, then stir in the basil and continue to cook until the rice is tender, about 5 minutes.

2. Stir the olives into the soup, then taste and adjust the seasonings. Line serving bowls with lettuce leaves and ladle the soup into the bowls. Serve immediately with freshly grated Parmesan alongside. This soup is best made and eaten immediately.

2 cups sliced onion
4 cloves garlic, sliced
2 small zucchini, sliced
   (about 3 cups)
2 small yellow crookneck squash,
   sliced (about 3 cups)
1 small fennel root, sliced thin
   (about 1 1/2 cups) or use 1 cup
   sliced celery
1 cup diced bell pepper (red,
   green, yellow or a mixture)
2 pounds tomatoes, cored and
   chopped (about 3 cups)
2 tablespoons melted butter
1/2 cup long grain brown rice
1 teaspoon salt
1/4 teaspoon black pepper
Leaves from 1 sprig fresh thyme
   or 1 teaspoon dried
6 cups hearty vegetable stock
   (page 39)
3/4 cup fresh basil leaves

TO SERVE:
1/4 cup sliced black olives
1 small head lettuce (Boston or
   bibb)
Grated Parmesan (optional)

Artichoke Soup with Orange and Saffron

Yield: 4 servings • Prep Time: 20 minutes • Cooking Time: 1 hour

6 large globe artichokes or
    1 1-pound can artichoke
    bottoms packed in water
1 lemon
3 tablespoons olive oil
1 1/2 cups sliced leeks,
    white part only
1 cup diced onion
2 tablespoons toasted garbanzo
    flour (or wheat flour)
6 cups hearty vegetable stock
    (page 39)
1/2 teaspoon salt
1/4 teaspoon white pepper
1/2 teaspoon ground saffron or
    chopped saffron threads
2 unpeeled Vanencia oranges,
    sliced 1/2 inch thick and
    seeds removed
4 sprigs parsley

GARNISH:
2 tablespoons minced parsley
Saffron threads (optional)

The unusual use of saffron and orange in combination with artichoke is inspired by classic Mediterranean flavors. The result is a soup with an extremely beautiful light orange hue and a mouth-watering taste.

1. To prepare the fresh artichokes, fill a large mixing bowl with water. Squeeze the lemon juice into the water and drop in the lemon halves. Using a wavy-edged knife, saw the leaves off one artichoke, about 1 1/2 inches from the stem end. Then, using a paring knife, cut off all remaining leaves where they attach to the bottom of the artichoke, so that the bottom is neatly trimmed. With a spoon, scrape the choke from the center of the artichoke, then cut the bottom into quarters and place it in the acidulated water. Repeat this with the remaining artichokes. This will retard discoloration. If you are using canned artichokes, simply drain, rinse and quarter them.

2. In a 3-quart saucepan, heat the oil until hot but not smoking. Add the leeks and onion. Sauté, stirring constantly, for 2 minutes. Reduce the heat to low and cook, stirring often, until the leeks are wilted, about 10 minutes. Raise heat to medium and sprinkle with flour. Cook for 1 minute, stirring constantly. Whisk in the stock. Add the salt, pepper, saffron, orange slices and sprigs of parsley. Drain the artichokes and stir them into the soup. Cover and simmer until the oranges are very tender, about 45 minutes.

3. Remove the soup from the heat and cool briefly. Spoon the orange slices from the soup and set them aside. Pour the soup through a strainer, reserving the broth. Purée the soup solids in a food processor or blender until smooth. Return the purée to the broth. Taste and adjust the seasonings. The soup may be prepared up to 5 days in advance if refrigerated in an airtight container. It may be frozen for 1 month.

4. Trim and save the rind from 2 of the oranges; discard the rest. Cut the rind into small dice and use as a garnish sprinkled on top of the soup, along with a sprinkling of minced parsley. Alternatively, you may sprinkle a few saffron threads over each serving. Their color will bleed nicely into the surface of the soup as the bowl rests at the table.

Curried Zucchini Soup

Yield: 8 servings • Prep Time: 15 minutes • Cooking Time: 30 minutes

The marriage of zucchini with the delicate flavors of this curry blend is very successful. Garbanzo flour adds a subtle, wholesome undertone that harmonizes the curry.

1. Heat the ghee over medium heat in a 3-quart saucepan until hot but not smoking. Add the onion and sauté for 2 minutes. Reduce the heat to medium and continue to cook, stirring often, until translucent, about 10 minutes. Add the ginger and garlic, reduce heat to low, and continue to cook for 2 minutes, stirring constantly so that the garlic does not burn.

2. Turn the heat to high. Sprinkle the flour over the onions and cook, stirring constantly, until the flour begins to brown, about 2 minutes. Stir in the tomatoes and mix well. Add the stock, zucchini, cumin, salt, coriander seeds, cinnamon, turmeric, cloves and mace. Bring the soup to a boil, then reduce to a simmer and cook, covered and stirring frequently, for 25 minutes, or until the vegetables are tender.

3. Remove the cinnamon and strain the vegetables, saving the broth. Purée the vegetables using the fine blade of a food mill or a food processor. Whisk the puréed vegetables into the broth. The soup may be prepared ahead to this point and stored in an airtight container in the refrigerator for up to 4 days. It may be frozen for 2 months.

4. Before serving, warm the soup until piping hot. Whisk about 1/4 cup of soup into the tahini, then stir this back into the soup. Keep it warm, but do not allow it to boil. Taste and adjust the seasonings.

5. Heat two teaspoons of ghee in a small pan over medium heat. Add the mustard seeds and cook, stirring constantly, until the seeds begin to pop and have blackened slightly, about 1 minute. Pour the seeds into the soup. Ladle the soup into individual serving bowls and sprinkle red pepper over each bowl as a garnish.

1 1/2 tablespoons ghee (page 169) or vegetable oil
2 cups diced white onion
2 teaspoons minced ginger root
2 teaspoons minced garlic
3 tablespoons toasted garbanzo flour (may use wheat flour)
1 pound chopped ripe tomatoes
6 cups light vegetable stock (page 38)
3 pounds small zucchini, sliced
1 teaspoon ground cumin
1/2 teaspoon salt
1/2 teaspoon coriander seeds
1 4-inch stick cinnamon
1/4 teaspoon turmeric
1/8 teaspoon ground cloves
1/8 teaspoon mace
3 tablespoons tahini (page 175) (optional)

GARNISH:
2 teaspoons brown mustard seeds
2 teaspoons ghee (page 169) or vegetable oil
1 small red bell pepper, diced

Variations

1. Stir 1/4 cup rinsed basmati rice into the soup with the stock. Increase the salt to 1 teaspoon and add 2 cinnamon sticks.

2. Stir 3/4 cup buttermilk into the finished soup.

Artichoke Soup with Mushrooms and Capers

Yield: 4 servings • Prep Time: 25 minutes • Cooking Time: 50 minutes

This soup has a delicate but rich-tasting broth filled with whole pieces of artichoke and mushroom. Each mouthful begins with the seductive aroma of porcini mushrooms, is followed by capers' salty undertone, and ends with the lingering taste of artichoke.

6 large globe artichokes
  or 1 1-pound can artichoke
  bottoms packed in water
1 lemon (if fresh artichokes are
  used)
3 tablespoons olive oil
1 cup sliced shallots (8 to 10
  shallots)
3/4 cup diced red onion
2 tablespoons flour
1/2 cup dry white wine
6 cups hearty vegetable stock
  (page 39)
1 tablespoon minced garlic
1/2 teaspoon salt
1/4 teaspoon black pepper
Pinch of nutmeg
Pinch of cayenne
1 sprig fresh thyme or
  1 teaspoon dried
4 sprigs Italian parsley
1 ounce dried porcini
  mushrooms (page 172),
  softened in 1 cup warm
  water
1/2 pound button mushrooms,
  quartered
1 1/2 cups sliced carrots
2 tablespoons capers
2 tablespoons minced Italian
  parsley

1. To prepare the fresh artichokes, fill a large mixing bowl with water. Squeeze the lemon juice into the water and drop in the lemon halves. Using a wavy-edged knife, saw the leaves off one artichoke about 1 1/2 inches from the stem end. Then, using a paring knife, cut off all remaining leaves where they attach to the bottom of the artichoke, so that the bottom is neatly trimmed. With a spoon, scrape the choke from the center of the artichoke, then cut the bottom into quarters and place it in the acidulated water. Repeat this with the remaining artichokes. This will retard discoloration. If you are using canned artichokes, simply drain, rinse and quarter them.

2. In a 3-quart saucepan heat the oil until hot but not smoking. Add the shallots and onions, then sauté, stirring constantly, for 2 minutes. Reduce the heat to low and cook, stirring often, until the onions are very soft, about 15 minutes. Raise the heat to medium and sprinkle the flour over the onions. Cook for 1 minute, stirring constantly. Whisk in the wine and allow it to cook until the smell of alcohol evaporates, about 3 minutes. Stir in the stock, garlic, salt, pepper, nutmeg, cayenne, thyme and parsley sprigs. Drain the artichokes and stir them into the soup. Cover and simmer for 25 minutes.

3. Add the mushrooms (including the liquid from the porcini) and sliced the carrots. Continue to cook until the carrots are tender, about 15 minutes. Stir in the capers and parsley then taste and adjust the seasonings. The soup may be prepared up to 5 days in advance if refrigerated in an airtight container.

Tarragon Scented Asparagus Soup

Yield: 6 servings • Prep Time: 20 minutes • Cooking Time: 25 minutes

The sweet aroma of tarragon is an exceptionally good complement to the taste of asparagus. This soup is light and fresh-tasting, and it is simple to prepare.

1 1/2 pounds asparagus
1 1/2 tablespoons butter
2 teaspoons olive oil
1 large leek, chopped
2 cloves garlic, minced
1/2 pound red potatoes, diced
6 cups light vegetable stock
  (page 38)
3 sprigs fresh tarragon or
  3 teaspoons dried
1/2 teaspoon salt
1/4 teaspoon pepper
Pinch of nutmeg

1. Rinse the asparagus. Break off each spear just above the woody bottom section and discard the tough bottom piece of stem. Peel the asparagus. To do this, lay each spear on the work surface. Place the blade of a swivel-edged peeler about an inch from the tip, and peel the skin off to the bottom of the spear. Turn the asparagus to peel all sides and repeat with the remaining spears. Chop the asparagus into 1-inch pieces. Set aside 12 tips to use as a garnish.

2. In a 2-quart saucepan heat the butter and oil until hot but not smoking. Add the leek and garlic and sauté, stirring often, until the leeks are soft, about 10 minutes. Add the diced potatoes and continue to cook until the potatoes are

beginning to soften, about 10 minutes. Stir in the asparagus and stock. Bring the soup to a boil, reduce the heat to low, and season with 1 sprig of tarragon, the salt, pepper and nutmeg.

3. Cover and simmer the soup until the asparagus is tender, but still green, about 10 minutes. Remove the soup from the heat immediately and strain the vegetables, reserving the liquid. (If the asparagus is left in the pan and in contact with the warm soup liquid the entire soup will take on an army green hue.)

4. Purée the vegetables, using the fine disk of a food mill or a processor, adding liquid to obtain a smooth consistency. Return the broth to the saucepan and bring to a boil. Cook until it is reduced to about 4 1/2 cups. Stir the liquid into the vegetables. The soup may be prepared to this point 3 days in advance if refrigerated in an airtight container.

5. To prepare the garnish, steam the reserved asparagus tips until bright green and just tender, about 5 minutes. Remove them from the heat and transfer them to a strainer, then immediately run cold water over them to stop their cooking. Allow them to drain thoroughly. Remove the leaves from the remaining tarragon stems and mince the leaves finely. Just before serving, heat the soup briefly. Stir in the minced tarragon, taste and adjust the seasonings. Garnish each bowl with asparagus tips.

Cucumber Yogurt Soup

Yield: 6 servings • Prep Time: 20 minutes

The look of this soup is as enticing as its taste. It has dramatic contrast in color: pale green soup, garnished with dark purple dulse and streaks of balsamic vinegar. The look is balanced by the flavor: cool cucumbers and yogurt spiked with garlic.

4 large cucumbers, peeled, seeded and cubed
3 scallions, minced
2 teaspoons minced garlic
1 teaspoon salt
1/2 teaspoon white pepper
3 tablespoons chopped fresh dill or chives
2 1/4 cups yogurt
2/3 cup light vegetable stock (page 38), chilled

GARNISH:
2 tablespoons balsamic vinegar
Chopped dulse (page 168)

1. In a large mixing bowl, combine the cucumber, scallions, garlic, salt, pepper and dill. Refrigerate for 2 hours. Place the cucumber mixture in a food processor or blender and purée, scraping the bowl as necessary until the mixture is evenly ground. Transfer the soup to a large bowl.

2. Whisk the yogurt and chilled stock into the soup. Serve immediately or refrigerate, covered, for up to a day. Ladle into soup bowls. Place about a teaspoon of vinegar in the center of each bowl and gently swirl it into the soup. Sprinkle each bowl with dulse and serve immediately.

Variations

1. Substitute basil for the dill.

2. Substitute fresh carrot juice for the stock and stir 1/4 cup minced red bell peppers into the soup just before serving.

Spicy Cucumber Soup with Mint

Yield: 6 servings • Prep Time: 15 minutes

The cooling taste of cucumber, mirrored by mint, is contrasted in this soup with hot spices typical of India.

4 large cucumbers, peeled,
   seeded and cubed
   (about 4 cups)
1/4 cup minced red onion
1 teaspoon minced garlic
1 teaspoon minced ginger root
1 serrano pepper, seeded and
   minced
1 teaspoon ground cumin
1/8 teaspoon ground cinnamon
Pinch of ground coriander
Pinch of cayenne
2 tablespoons rice syrup
   (page 172)
1 1/2 teaspoons salt
1/2 teaspoon white pepper
3 tablespoons chopped fresh
   mint
3 1/2 cups buttermilk
2 tablespoons kuzu (page 170)
3 tablespoons cold water
2/3 cup light vegetable stock
   (page 38)

GARNISH:
2 teaspoons vegetable oil
2 tablespoons brown mustard
   seeds

1. In a large mixing bowl, combine the cucumber, onion, garlic, ginger, serrano pepper, cumin, cinnamon, coriander, cayenne, rice syrup, salt, pepper and mint. Refrigerate at least 30 minutes. Place the vegetables in a food processor or blender and purée until very smooth. Transfer the soup to a large bowl.

2. Whisk the buttermilk into the soup. Crush the kuzu and dissolve it in cold water. Stir this into the vegetable stock and scald. Pour the kuzu mixture into the soup. Taste and adjust the seasonings. The soup may be prepared to this point up to 2 days in advance if refrigerated in an airtight container. It does not freeze well. Just before serving, ladle into soup bowls. Heat the vegetable oil in a small skillet until hot but not smoking. Add the mustard seeds and cook, stirring constantly, until the seeds pop, about 1 minute. Transfer immediately to a paper towel and pat excess oil from the seeds. Sprinkle the seeds over each bowl and serve immediately.

Plantain Bisque

Yield: 6 servings • Prep Time: 20 minutes • Cooking Time: 50 minutes

The sweet flavor of baked plantains is highlighted by a combination of lime and roasted garlic in this unusual soup.

2 ripe (black) plantains
6 whole (unpeeled) cloves
   garlic
3 tablespoons lime juice
1 tablespoon butter
1 cup diced yellow onion
1/2 cup minced carrot
1 stalk celery, minced
2 teaspoons ground cumin
1/8 teaspoon ground mace
6 cups light vegetable stock
   (page 38)
1 1/2 teaspoons salt
1/2 teaspoon saffron threads
1/4 teaspoon black pepper
1 tablespoon kuzu (page 170),
   crushed
2 tablespoons cold water
1/4 cup minced cilantro

1. Preheat the oven to 350°F. Rinse the plantains and pierce each several times through the skin, with the tine of a fork. Place the plantains on a baking sheet. Wrap the garlic in foil and put it on the sheet as well. Bake both for 50 minutes to 1 hour, turning once as they cook, until both are soft when squeezed. Remove the baking sheet from the oven. When the plantains are cool enough to handle, peel them and cut them into pieces then put them in a food processor or blender. Squeeze each clove of garlic into the processor or blender bowl, then add 2 tablespoons of lime juice. Purée the mixture, scraping the bowl as necessary and adding up to 1/2 cup of water to obtain a smooth texture.

2. As the plantains bake, heat the butter in a 2-quart saucepan over medium heat until hot but not smoking. Add the onions and sauté for about a minute. Reduce the heat to low, add the carrot, celery, cumin, and mace and continue to cook, stirring frequently, for about 15 minutes or until the onions are soft.

3. Turn the heat to high and add the stock. Cover and bring to a boil. Reduce the heat to low, stir in the salt, saffron, and pepper and simmer, covered, until all vegetables are soft, about 30 minutes.

4. Whisk the plantain purée into the soup. Combine the kuzu with cold water and stir the thickener into the soup. Bring to a boil and whisk to blend. Taste and adjust the seasonings. Remove from the heat, stir in the cilantro and serve immediately, piping hot.

Succotash Chowder

Yield: 8 servings • Prep Time: 25 minutes • Cooking Time: 45 minutes

Flavors of the South and North unite in this light chowder. Serve as is or topped with Pepper Crackers (page 152).

2 yellow onions, diced
1 stalk celery, sliced
2 tablespoons butter
1 cup fresh lima beans
   (may use frozen)
1 cup diced red potato
5 1/2 cups milk or soy milk
2 1/2 cups light vegetable stock
   (page 38)
2 ears sweet corn
   (or 1 1/2 cups frozen)
1 cup green beans, cut in
   2-inch pieces
1 carrot, minced
1 small red pepper, minced
1 teaspoon salt
1/4 teaspoon black pepper
1/2 teaspoon paprika
Pinch of cayenne
1 1/2 tablespoons arrowroot
2 1/2 tablespoons cold water
1/4 cup minced chervil or
   parsley

1. Sauté the onion and celery in the butter over medium heat, stirring frequently, until it has softened and is beginning to brown, about 15 minutes. Do not allow the onion to burn. Add the lima beans, potato, milk and stock and bring to a boil. Reduce to a simmer and cook, stirring often, for 5 minutes.

2. As the soup cooks, prepare the corn. Shuck each ear, break in half and remove the kernels from the cobs by standing each ear on the cutting surface, broken side down, and shaving off the kernels from the tip of the corn, down.

3. Add the corn, green beans, carrot and red pepper to the soup and cook briefly. Stir in the salt, pepper, paprika and cayenne. Cover halfway and simmer until the beans are tender, but still a vibrant color, about 15 minutes.

4. In a small bowl combine the arrowroot and water. Mix until smooth, then stir this into the soup. Bring the soup to a boil. Stir in the chervil and ladle into serving bowls.

Variation

1. Add 2 cups diced tomato to the soup along with the carrot. Whisk 1/4 cup of soup broth into 1 tablespoon of tomato paste, then stir this in with the arrowroot. Replace the chervil with shredded basil.

New England Style Chowder

Yield: 4 servings • Prep Time: 25 minutes • Cooking Time: 25 minutes

1 pound firm tofu
1/4 cup sweet rice vinegar
1 tablespoon sugar or
   2 tablespoons rice syrup
   (page 172)
1 cup diced white onion
3 tablespoons butter
2 tablespoons flour
3 cups kombu stock (page 40)
2 cups diced red potatoes
3 cups milk or soy milk
1 teaspoon salt
1/4 teaspoon black pepper
1/8 teaspoon ground nutmeg
1/2 cup ricotta cream or tofu
   cream (page 35)
3 tablespoons minced parsley

The debate is endless as to which is better, Manhattan or New England Clam Chowder. Without clams you might say it's a moot point, but I beg to differ. Here is a New England-style version with "mock" clams that rivals even the best bowl of chowder Gloucester has to offer. The tofu must be frozen then marinated, so you must begin this recipe at least a day ahead.

1. Drain the tofu and slice it into 1-inch pieces. Wrap each piece in plastic wrap and freeze until solid. Thaw the tofu then place it on a cutting board. Put a second board on top and weight this down to extract as much water as possible. Leave it for 30 minutes to an hour at room temperature.

2. Combine the vinegar and sugar in a mixing bowl. Grate the pressed tofu with the largest holed grating your grater has (not the slicing surface), and add it to the vinegar. Set aside for 30 minutes.

3. In a 2-quart saucepan, sauté the onions in the butter until translucent, about 10 minutes. Sprinkle the flour over and cook, stirring constantly, for 3 minutes. Stir in the stock very slowly to avoid lumping. Drain the tofu and add it to the soup with the potatoes, milk, salt, pepper and nutmeg. Cover and simmer until the potatoes are tender, about 20 minutes.

4. Place a spoonful of ricotta cream in the bottom of each bowl and ladle the soup over. Sprinkle with parsley and serve with oyster crackers.

Ginger Broccoli Soup with Cashews

Yield: 6 servings • Prep Time: 25 minutes • Cooking Time: 45 minutes

1 1/2 cups diced carrot
1/2 cup diced onion
1/4 cup diced scallions
2 tablespoons minced ginger
1 1/2 tablespoons minced garlic
1/4 cup raw cashews
10 cups hearty vegetable stock
   (page 39)
1/2 teaspoon salt
1/4 teaspoon pepper
Pinch of cayenne
1 bunch broccoli
2 tablespoons soy sauce
1 tablespoon rice syrup (page 172)
2 tablespoons cornstarch
   dissolved in 3 tablespoons
   water

GARNISH:
3 tablespoons cashew halves,
   toasted (page 33)

The classic combination of broccoli and cashews is accented here with an undertone of ginger in this simple purée.

1. Combine the carrot, onion, scallions, ginger, garlic, cashews and stock in a 4-quart saucepan. Cover and bring to a boil. Stir in the salt, pepper and cayenne, then reduce the heat and simmer the soup until the vegetables are tender, about 30 minutes.

2. Cut the stem from the broccoli and trim the tough outer layer from the stems. Cut them into 1/2-inch pieces. Trim and discard the tough outer layer from broccoli flower stems, then cut the flowers into 1-inch pieces. You should have about 9 cups of broccoli. Add the broccoli to the soup, and continue to cook until the broccoli is tender, but still very green, about 12 minutes. Remove immediately from the heat and strain the soup into a large mixing bowl. This will insure that the broccoli remains a vibrant green color.

3. When the vegetables have cooled, purée them finely in a food processor or blender. Stir them back into the broth and return to a clean saucepan. Stir in the soy sauce and rice syrup. Combine the cornstarch and water and add this mixture to the soup. Warm the soup just to the boil so that it thickens. Serve immediately garnished with toasted cashews. The soup may be prepared up to 5 days in advance if refrigerated in an airtight container. It does not freeze well.

Cinnamon Chili

Yield: 6 servings • Prep Time: 25 minutes • Cooking Time: 45 minutes

A generous amount of tempeh serves as the initial focus of this soup and makes this chili a substantial meal in itself. The flavor is complex but light; balsamic vinegar lends a rich, full flavor while the scent of cinnamon lingers on the palate. Use a mixed grain tempeh for optimal variety in taste and texture. For a less spicy chili, omit the pasilla chilies.

12 ounces tempeh (page 175)
3 cups diced tomatoes
1/2 cup diced celery
4 cups hearty vegetable stock (page 39)
1 3-inch piece stick cinnamon
1/2 teaspoon salt
2 tablespoons balsamic vinegar
2 to 3 ancho peppers (page 167), softened in warm water
2 pasilla peppers (page 172), softened in warm water (optional)
1 1/4 cups chopped white onion
6 cloves garlic, peeled
1 teaspoon dried thyme
1 teaspoon dried marjoram
1 teaspoon cumin seeds
1/4 teaspoon ground cloves
6 black peppercorns
1/4 cup minced cilantro

1. Cut the tempeh into small dice, then place them in a 3-quart saucepan with the tomatoes, celery, stock, cinnamon and salt. Cook, stirring occasionally for 20 minutes. Remove from the heat and stir in the vinegar. Set aside.

2. Meanwhile, drain the peppers, saving their soaking liquid. Remove and discard the stems from the peppers, then cut them open and scrape out and discard the ribs and seeds. Cut the peppers into pieces, place them in a blender with 1/4 cup of the soaking liquid. Purée until very smooth, then transfer them to a small skillet.

3. Place the onion and garlic in the blender and purée with the thyme, marjoram, cumin seeds, cloves and peppercorns until finely ground. Add this mixture to the peppers and cook, stirring often, for 15 minutes. As the paste cooks, add more pepper soaking liquid as necessary, to prevent burning. Stir this paste into the cooked soup and simmer for 5 minutes. The soup may be prepared ahead to this point if refrigerated in an airtight container.

4. Before serving, stir in the cilantro. Taste and adjust the seasonings, adding more salt, vinegar or cinnamon as desired.

Tomato and Fennel Soup with Arborio Rice

Yield: 6 servings • Prep Time: 20 minutes • Cooking Time: 45 minutes

Classic tastes of Italy form the base of this soothing soup.

2 tablespoons fennel seeds, crushed
8 cups light vegetable stock (page 38)
1 1/2 pounds fennel bulb, sliced
1 pound white onions, sliced
3 cloves garlic, sliced
1 teaspoon dried oregano
1/4 teaspoon salt
1/4 teaspoon freshly ground black pepper
1 bay leaf
1/4 cup arborio rice
3 pounds tomatoes, cored and chopped
4 ounces Parmesan cheese, with crust
1 tablespoon tomato paste
1/4 cup minced Italian parsley

1. Place the fennel seeds in a tea ball or place them in the center of a small square of cheesecloth and tie it into a small sachet. In a 4-quart saucepan, combine the stock, fennel seeds, half of the fennel bulb, the onion and garlic. Bring the soup to a boil. Stir in the oregano, salt, pepper and bay leaf, then cover, reduce to a simmer and cook for 20 minutes.

2. Add the rice and tomatoes. Cut the crust from the cheese, set the cheese aside and add the crust to the soup. Stir in the tomato paste. Cook, stirring occasionally, for 30 minutes or until the rice is tender. Remove from the heat. The soup may be prepared ahead to this point and refrigerated in an airtight container for up to 4 days.

3. Remove the cheese crust and fennel seeds from the soup. Grate the Parmesan and stir it into the soup with the minced parsley. Taste and adjust the seasonings. Serve immediately.

Mysore Style Rasam

Yield: 8 servings • Prep Time: 20 minutes • Cooking Time: 2 1/4 hours

2/3 cup black-eyed peas
1/3 cup moong dal (skinned, split mung beans)
1 tablespoon peanut oil
1/4 teaspoon turmeric
1/4 teaspoon fenugreek
8 cups water
1 teaspoon-sized ball tamarind (page 175), soaked in 1/4 cup warm water or 1 tablespoon lemon juice
2 1/2 teaspoons anise seed
2 teaspoons ground cumin
2 teaspoons garam masala (page 169)
1/2 teaspoon ground coriander
1/4 teaspoon hing (asafoetida) (page 170)
1 1/2 cups chopped tomatoes
1 cup diced carrot
2/3 cup diced celery
1 cup small cauliflower flowerets
1 1/4 teaspoons salt
1/3 cup minced cilantro

GARNISH:
2 tablespoons peanut oil
2 to 4 serrano peppers
2 teaspoons brown mustard seeds

While living in Mysore, South India, I became particularly fond of rasam, a spicy tomato- and lentil-based broth that is served at many traditional meals. Every cook has their own version of the classic dish, some preparing a very thin broth and others making one that is thick and full of vegetables. Most cooks use a combination of beans and their own home-made rasam powder (combination of spices). This is a Westernized version of the classic.

1. Pick over the black-eyed peas and moong dal to remove all rocks and debris. Rinse them well and place them in a 4-quart saucepan with the water. Add the peanut oil, turmeric and fenugreek and bring to a boil, stirring often. Cover and reduce to a simmer, then cook, stirring occasionally, until the peas are very tender, about 1 1/2 hours.

2. Squeeze the tamarind pulp to release as much of it as possible, then press it through a tea strainer into the soaking liquid. Discard the remaining pulp and add the liquid to the soup. Stir in the remaining ingredients except the cilantro and garnish. Cover and simmer, stirring often, until the vegetables are very soft, about 45 minutes. As the soup cooks, add more water if necessary to keep the water level above all other ingredients.

3. Remove the soup from the heat and cool for 10 minutes. The soup may be prepared up to 5 days in advance to this point, if refrigerated in an airtight container. Just before serving, have the soup warm and stir in the cilantro. Taste and adjust the seasonings. In a small skillet heat the peanut oil until hot but not smoking. Add the minced serranos and mustard seeds. Cook, stirring constantly, until the seeds pop, about 1 minute. Transfer this immediately to a paper towel to drain the oil, then stir it into the soup. Serve with Lace Spice Crisps (page 159).

Soba Noodle Soup with Daikon

Yield: 6 servings • Prep time: 20 minutes • Cooking Time: 15 minutes

1/4 cup soy sauce
1 tablespoon mirin (page 171)
1 tablespoon sugar or honey
2 teaspoons minced garlic
1 teaspoon minced ginger
1 carrot, cut in julienne strips
4 ounces soba noodles (page 174)
4 cups kombu stock (page 40)
1 cup spinach leaves, chopped

GARNISH:
1/3 cup grated daikon (page 168)
1 sheet nori, torn into shreds (page 172)
3 scallions, minced

A very simple, cold soup topped with the delicate bite of grated daikon.

1. In a small saucepan, combine the soy sauce and mirin and place over high heat. When it boils and a white foam forms, add the sugar and cook for 30 seconds. Remove from the heat, transfer to a glass bowl and cover with a damp kitchen towel. Leave at room temperature for at least 2 hours, or preferably a couple of days.

2. Bring 2 quarts of water to a boil in a 3-quart saucepan. Add the garlic and ginger, then stir in the carrot and noodles. Cook, stirring occasionally until the noodles are al dente, about 8 minutes. Drain the noodles and place them in a large serving bowl.

3. Add the stock and spinach to the noodles, then toss with the soy sauce mixture. Cover and refrigerate immediately. The soup may be prepared up to a day in advance to this point. Place servings of cold soup into shallow bowls and garnish with a grated daikon, nori and scallions. Serve immediately.

Udon Noodle Soup with Vegetables

Yield: 6 servings • Prep time: 25 minutes • Cooking Time: 15 minutes

Use any assortment of vegetables you have on hand, but be certain to include a variety of tastes, textures and colors.

1/3 cup soy sauce
4 teaspoons mirin (page 171)
4 teaspoons sugar or honey
6 cups kombu (page 40)
  or light vegetable stock
  (page 38)
1 tablespoon minced garlic
2 teaspoons minced ginger
1 carrot, cut in julienne strips
4 ounces udon noodles (page 176)
3 cups chopped bok choy leaves
1 cup straw mushrooms
  (page 174)
1/4 cup sliced water chestnuts
1 small red pepper, peeled and
  diced
18 snow peas, strings removed
1/2 lime (optional)
4 scallions, minced

1. In a small saucepan, combine the soy sauce and mirin, then place over high heat. When it boils, add the sugar and cook for 30 seconds. Remove from the heat, transfer to a glass bowl and cover with a damp kitchen towel. Leave at room temperature for at least 2 hours, or preferably a couple of days.

2. In a 3-quart saucepan, combine the stock, garlic and ginger. Bring this to a boil, then add the carrots and noodles. Cook, stirring often, for 5 minutes. Add the bok choy and mushrooms. Continue to cook until the noodles are al dente.

3. Remove the soup from the heat and stir in the soy sauce mixture, water chestnuts, red pepper and snow peas. Cover and set aside for 1 minute. Squeeze in the lime juice (optional), then ladle the soup into individual serving bowls and garnish with a sprinkling of scallions. Serve immediately. The soup is best prepared and eaten immediately.

Variation

1. Substitute soba noodles for the udon.

Thai Peanut Soup

Yield: 6 servings • Prep Time: 15 minutes • Cooking Time: 50 minutes

This is a sublime, delicate soup with a hint of lemon and peanuts. It makes a fine start to a meal, or may be served as a light main course.

12 scallions, shredded
10 cloves garlic, sliced
4 lime leaves (optional)
3 dried red chilie peppers
2 teaspoons molasses
1 teaspoon salt
8 cups water
4 stalks lemon grass (page 171)
1 2-inch piece galangal (page 169)
  or ginger
3 ounces rice stick noodles
  (page 172)
3 tablespoons + 1 teaspoon
  smooth peanut butter
1 cup bean sprouts
3/4 cup straw mushrooms
  (page 174)
3 tablespoons soy sauce
2 tablespoons lime juice

TOPPING:
2 tablespoons chopped roasted
  peanuts
3 scallions, minced
Sprigs of fresh cilantro

1. In a 4-quart saucepan, combine the scallions, garlic, lime leaves, chilies, molasses, salt and water. Trim top stems and tough outer leaves from each piece of lemon grass, leaving stalks 5 to 6 inches long. Place a stalk on the counter and lay the flat side of a cleaver or large knife over the end of the lemon grass. Slap the cleaver with the heel of your hand to flatten the stalk, then roll the stalk over, move the cleaver up the stalk and slap it again. (The stalks must be crushed open to release their flavor.) Slice the stalk into 2-inch pieces. Repeat with the remaining lemon grass and add it all to the soup. Rinse the galangal, then slice it into 1/4-inch thick rounds. Again using the side of the cleaver, flatten each piece and add it to the soup.

2. Bring the soup to a boil, then cover, reduce to a simmer and cook for 45 minutes. The soup may be prepared up to 3 days ahead to this point, if refrigerated in an airtight container. When ready to serve, strain the broth and bring it to a boil. Stir in the noodles and cook, stirring often, for 3 minutes. Meanwhile, ladle a small amount of the broth into the peanut butter, then stir this back into the soup. Add the bean sprouts, mushrooms, soy sauce and lime juice. Immediately remove the soup from the heat, cover and set aside for 5 minutes. Taste and adjust the seasonings. Serve garnished with a sprinkling of nuts, scallions and a sprig of cilantro.

Hazelnut Scented Squash Soup

Yield: 6 servings • Prep Time: 15 minutes • Cooking Time: 1 1/2 hours

3 pounds butternut squash
1 head garlic
1 large yellow onion
1 pound garnet yams
1 teaspoon olive oil
3/4 cup hazelnuts
3 to 4 cups light vegetable stock
   (page 38) or water
1 teaspoon salt
1/4 teaspoon black pepper

GARNISH:
1/4 cup plain nonfat yogurt
   (optional)
3 tablespoons minced parsley

The sweet taste of winter squash blends with onion, garlic and toasted hazelnuts to produce an intoxicating aroma and taste in this warming winter soup.

1. Preheat the oven to 400°F. Wash the squash, garlic, onion and yams under cold water, scrubbing well to remove all dirt. Place the unpeeled vegetables 1 inch apart on a large baking sheet. Drizzle olive oil over the garlic. Put the sheet in the oven on the middle rack, and reduce the heat to 375°F. Bake until the vegetables are very soft when squeezed, turning them several times and checking for doneness as they cook. The onion and garlic will be ready after about 50 minutes; the squash and yams will require about 1 1/2 hours. Remove each vegetable to a wire rack and cool after it is cooked. The vegetables may be baked and refrigerated, loosely covered, up to 4 days before proceeding with the recipe.

2. As the vegetables cook, place the nuts on a separate baking sheet in the oven and toast them, stirring several times, for about 12 minutes or until they are lightly browned to the core. Turn the nuts out onto a clean kitchen towel and rub them to remove the skins. If the skins do not come off easily, transfer the nuts to a wire mesh strainer and rub them to remove as much skin as possible. The fresher the nut, the easier the skin will be to remove when toasted.

3. Chop 6 to 8 nuts and set them aside for a garnish. Place the rest of the nuts in a food processor fitted with the chopping blade. Grind them, scraping the sides of the bowl several times, until they are very smooth and creamy. Transfer this hazelnut "butter" to a small bowl and set it aside. The nuts may be toasted, chopped and ground into butter several days in advance. Store at room temperature in an airtight container.

4. Remove the skin from the onion and chop it roughly. Place it in the processor and squeeze each clove of garlic from the skin into the chopping bowl. Purée the onion and garlic for about a minute, or until they are smooth. Cut the squash open lengthwise. Scrape out and discard the seeds. Remove the meat from the skin and add it to the processor. Halve the yams and scrape them from their skins into the bowl as well. Purée the soup mixture until very smooth. You may need to work in two batches, depending on the size of your processor.

5. Scrape the puréed vegetables into a large soup pot. Whisk in the stock. Place the soup over medium heat and warm thoroughly. Mix a small amount of the soup into the hazelnut butter then whisk the nut mixture into the soup. Taste and adjust the seasonings. Garnish each serving with a dollop of yogurt, minced parsley and chopped hazelnuts. The soup may be prepared up to 5 days in advance if refrigerated in an airtight container. It may be frozen for 2 months.

Pecan Scented Pumpkin Soup

Yield: 6 servings • Prep Time: 15 minutes • Cooking Time: 1 1/2 hours

For a festive look, serve this soup in miniature pumpkins. To do so, slice off the top of each and scrape out all seeds and strings. Steam the pumpkins for about 8 minutes, just long enough to seal their color but not so that they become overly soft and lose their shape.

1 3-pound pie pumpkin
1 head garlic
1 large yellow onion
1 large russet potato
1 teaspoon olive oil
3/4 cup pecan halves
4 cups light vegetable stock
   (page 38)
1/2 teaspoon salt
1/4 teaspoon black pepper

GARNISH:
1/4 cup plain nonfat yogurt
3 tablespoons minced parsley

1. Preheat the oven to 400°F. Wash the pumpkin, garlic, onion and potato under cold water, scrubbing well to remove all dirt. Place the vegetables 1 inch apart, on a large baking sheet. Drizzle olive oil over the garlic. Put the sheet in the oven on the middle rack, and reduce the heat to 375°F. Bake until the vegetables are very soft when squeezed, turning them several times and checking for doneness as they cook. The onion and garlic will be ready after about 50 minutes; the pumpkin will require about 1 1/4 hours. Remove each vegetable to a wire rack and cool after it is cooked. The vegetables may be baked and refrigerated, loosely covered, up to 4 days before proceeding with the recipe.

2. As the vegetables cook, place the pecans on a separate baking sheet in the oven and toast them, stirring several times, for about 10 minutes or until they are lightly browned to the core. Turn the nuts out onto a counter to cool.

3. Chop 6 to 8 pecans and set them aside for a garnish. Place the rest of the nuts in a food processor fitted with the chopping blade. Grind them, scraping the sides of the bowl several times, until they are very smooth and creamy. Transfer this pecan "butter" to a small bowl and set aside. The nuts may be toasted, chopped and ground into butter several days in advance. Store at room temperature in an airtight container.

4. Remove the skin from the onion and chop it roughly. Place it in the processor and squeeze each clove of garlic from the skin into the processor bowl. Purée the onion and garlic for about a minute, or until they are smooth. Cut the pumpkin open lengthwise. Scrape out and discard the seeds. Remove the meat from the skin and add it to the processor. Halve the potatoes and scrape them from their skins into the bowl as well. Purée the soup mixture until very smooth. You may need to work in two batches, depending on the size of your processor.

5. Scrape the puréed vegetables into a large soup pot. Whisk in the stock, place over medium heat and warm thoroughly. Mix a small amount of the soup into the pecan butter then whisk the nut mixture into the soup. Season the soup to taste with salt and pepper. Garnish each serving with a dollop of yogurt and a light sprinkling of parsley and chopped pecans. The soup may be prepared up to 3 days in advance if refrigerated in an airtight container. It may be frozen for 2 months.

Curried Pumpkin Soup

Yield: 8 servings • Prep Time: 25 minutes • Cooking Time: 3 hours

1 3-pound pumpkin
  (or other winter squash)
7 cups hearty vegetable stock
  (page 39)
1 tablespoon minced ginger
2 teaspoons minced garlic
2 tablespoons curry powder
  (or to taste)
2 teaspoons ground cumin
1/3 cup natto miso (page 171)
1 cup plain nonfat yogurt
1/3 cup minced cilantro

GARNISH:
1/4 cup minced scallions

Prepared curry powders vary in hotness, so adjust the amount used according to your personal preference and the intensity of the powder.

1. Preheat the oven to 400°F. Wash the pumpkin and place it on a baking sheet in the middle of the oven. Reduce the heat to 375°F and cook until the pumpkin is soft when squeezed, about 1 1/4 hours. Remove the pumpkin to a cake rack. When it is cool enough to handle, cut it in half, scrape out and discard the seeds, then place the meat in a food processor fitted with the grinding blade. Purée the pumpkin, scraping down the sides of the bowl often, until it is as smooth as possible. Set the purée aside.

2. In a 2-quart saucepan, combine the stock, ginger and garlic. Simmer, covered, for 25 minutes. Whisk 1 cup of the broth into the pumpkin purée, then return this to the soup. Add the curry and cumin, then place the soup over medium heat. Cook, covered and whisking often, until it is steaming hot throughout.

3. In a small bowl, combine the miso, 3/4 cup of the yogurt and the cilantro. Whisk until smooth, then stir this into the soup and warm again thoroughly. Do not boil the soup or the digestive enzyme in the miso will be killed and the yogurt may separate.

4. Transfer the soup into 1 large or several small serving bowls and sprinkle with minced scallions. Swirl the remaining yogurt into the center. Serve piping hot. The soup may be prepared up to 3 days in advance if stored in an airtight container. It may be frozen for up to 3 months.

Variation

1. Stir 1/3 cup Apple Chutney (page 156) into the finished soup and top with Garlic Croutons (page 149).

Garlic Scented Spinach Soup with Feta

Yield: 8 servings • Prep Time: 25 minutes • Cooking Time: 30 minutes

Spanokopita serves as the inspiration for this unusual soup. Delicate filo dough lids top each serving and chunks of softened feta are nestled throughout the thick soup.

1. Heat the olive oil in a 3-quart saucepan over high heat until hot but not smoking. Add the onion, reduce heat to medium, and cook, stirring frequently, for about 8 minutes, until the onion is wilted. Reduce heat to low and continue cooking for about 15 minutes, stirring often, until the onions are soft and translucent. Return heat to high. Sprinkle the flour over the onions and cook for 1 minute, stirring constantly. Whisk in the wine and cook until the smell of alcohol has evaporated, about 30 seconds. Add the stock and garlic, then cover and bring to a boil.

2. Place the thawed spinach on a clean kitchen towel. Draw the corners of the towel together and hold it over the sink. Twist the towel to squeeze the spinach into a ball and drain as much liquid as possible. Add the spinach to the soup. Stir in the orange zest, oregano, salt, pepper, nutmeg, and cayenne. Reduce to a simmer and cook, stirring occasionally, for 15 minutes. Stir in the parsley and scallions. Taste and adjust the seasonings. (Remember that the feta will add more salt.) The soup may be prepared up to 3 days in advance if refrigerated in an airtight container. It may be frozen for 2 months.

3. Prepare filo lids for individual serving bowls. Lay the filo sheets in a stack on a dry work surface. Turn 1 serving bowl upside down and place it on the dough to use as a guide. With the tip of a paring knife, cut the dough into rounds that are the size of the top of the bowl. Cover the dough with a lightly dampened towel to prevent the dough from drying out as you prepare the lids.

4. Preheat the oven to 400°F. Carefully separate 8 rounds of dough from the stack and place them on a baking sheet. Brush each round with melted ghee and cover with a second piece of filo. Brush again with ghee. Repeat this step until each round is 6 layers thick. (If the dough is old or has dried out, the sheets may not separate easily or they may crack. Use the best, non-cracked pieces of dough for the top layers.) Brush the top of each lid with ghee. The pastry may be prepared ahead, covered and refrigerated for a day, or frozen for up to a week before continuing with the recipe.

5. Bake the dough in the top of the preheated oven until slightly puffed and golden, about 20 minutes. Remove from the oven and transfer to a wire rack. The tops may be prepared several hours in advance and stored at room temperature if it is not a humid day. If the weather does not cooperate, they may be shaped and refrigerated ahead, but leave the baking until the soup is warming or they will lose their crispness.

6. To serve the soup, drain the feta and crumble it into 1/2-inch pieces. Divide the cheese evenly among 8 serving bowls. Heat the soup thoroughly and ladle it over the feta. Top each bowl with a filo lid and serve immediately.

1/2 tablespoon olive oil
2 cups chopped white onion
3 tablespoons flour
1/2 cup dry white wine
8 cups light vegetable stock
 (page 38)
8 cloves garlic, minced
2 10-ounce packages frozen
 chopped spinach, thawed
2 teaspoons grated orange zest
2 teaspoons dried oregano
1 1/2 teaspoons salt
1/4 teaspoon black pepper
1/4 teaspoon ground nutmeg
1/8 teaspoon cayenne pepper
1/2 cup minced parsley
1 1/2 cups minced scallions
6 ounces feta cheese

FILO LIDS:
1/2 pound filo dough, thawed
1/3 cup melted butter or ghee
 (page 169)

Sorrel Soup with Polenta Crusts

Yield: 8 servings • Prep Time: 40 minutes • Cooking Time: 30 minutes

1/2 tablespoon olive oil
1 cup chopped white onion
5 tablespoons flour
8 cups light vegetable stock
  (page 38)
8 cloves garlic, minced
1 10-ounce package frozen
  spinach, thawed
1/2 cup sun-dried tomatoes
  (page 174), softened in hot
  water
1 1/2 teaspoons salt
1/4 teaspoon black pepper
1/4 teaspoon ground nutmeg
1/8 teaspoon cayenne pepper
1/2 cup grated Parmesan
4 cups sorrel leaves, chopped
1/4 cup minced mint

POLENTA:
1 1/2 cups water
1/4 teaspoon salt
2 teaspoons minced garlic
1/2 cup polenta
1/4 teaspoon nutmeg
2 tablespoons butter (optional)

The lemony taste of sorrel in combination with mint has an exceedingly refreshing effect. Prepare the polenta crusts ahead, then warm in a hot oven just before serving.

1. Heat the olive oil in a 3-quart saucepan over high heat until hot but not smoking. Add the onion, reduce heat to medium, and cook, stirring frequently, for about 10 minutes, until the onion is wilted. Reduce heat to low and continue to cook, stirring often, until the onions are soft and translucent, about 10 minutes. Return the heat to high. Sprinkle the flour over the onions and cook for one minute, stirring constantly. Whisk in the stock and garlic. Cover and bring to a boil.

2. Place the thawed spinach on a clean kitchen towel. Draw the corners of the towel together, hold it over the sink, and squeeze the spinach into a ball, twisting the towel to drain as much liquid as possible. Add the spinach to the soup. Drain the sun-dried tomatoes and chop them thoroughly. Add them to the soup with the salt, pepper, nutmeg, and cayenne. Reduce to a simmer and cook, stirring occasionally, for 15 minutes. The soup may be prepared to this point up to 3 days in advance if refrigerated in an airtight container. Add the mint, Parmesan and sorrel and stir. Remove from the heat, cover and set aside for exactly 3 minutes. Taste and adjust the seasonings.

3. The polenta crusts may be prepared, except for the final baking, up to 3 days in advance. They should be refrigerated, tightly covered, until needed. In a medium saucepan, bring 1 1/2 cups of water to a boil. Add the salt and garlic, then stir the polenta into the water in a thin stream. Return to a boil, stirring constantly. Reduce heat to low and continue to cook, stirring constantly until the polenta is smooth and no longer grainy, about 25 minutes. Stir in the nutmeg and 1 tablespoon butter. Stir vigorously to blend. Pour the polenta into a 9-inch square baking dish and cool with a damp kitchen towel touching its surface. When cool, remove the towel and wrap the pan in a plastic bag. Refrigerate until ready to crisp.

4. Preheat the oven to 400°F. Melt the remaining butter. Brush the surface of the polenta with butter, then cut the polenta into attractive shapes. Place the polenta on a baking sheet and bake until crisped around the edges and lightly browned. To serve the soup, ladle hot soup into each serving bowl. Top each bowl with a polenta crust and serve immediately.

Roasted Eggplant Soup

Yield: 6 servings • Prep Time: 25 minutes • Cooking Time: 1 1/4 hours

Broiled Parmesan-topped tomatoes float on top of each bowl of soup for an irresistible final touch.

1. Preheat the oven to 375°F. Rinse the eggplants. With the tip of a paring knife, make a 1/4-inch-deep slashes over the entire surface of the eggplants. Place a slice of garlic on the side of the blade of the knife. Then put the tip of the knife into a slash and, using your thumb, slip the garlic into the slash. Remove the blade from the slash and repeat the process, until all of the garlic has been inserted.

2. Place the eggplants and onion on a baking sheet and cook them until tender, about 50 minutes (the onion will be soft when squeezed). The eggplant will take about 1 1/4 hours (it will have sunk down, but should not be shriveled). Remove each from the oven as it is cooked.

3. Meanwhile, cut rounds, about the diameter of the tomatoes, from the slices of bread. Place them on a separate baking sheet. Bake in the oven until golden brown, about 15 minutes. Cool on a cake rack.

4. Peel the skin from the onion and eggplants. Cut the onion into quarters then cube it. Scrape most of the seeds from the eggplant meat, then place it with the onion in a food processor or blender. Add the lemon juice. Purée the mixture until smooth, then transfer the purée to a 2-quart saucepan. Add the stock, salt, pepper, nutmeg and tomato paste. Warm thoroughly.

5. Place the tahini in a small bowl. Whisk in about 1/4 cup of the soup, stirring until the mixture is smooth. Stir this back into the soup and add the minced garlic. Warm briefly, then remove from the heat and stir in the basil. Taste and adjust the seasonings. The soup may be prepared up to 4 days in advance if refrigerated in an airtight container. Reheat before continuing with the recipe.

6. Preheat the broiler to high. Divide the hot soup among ovenproof soup bowls. Place 3 slices bread topped with a slice of tomato on each portion of soup, then sprinkle with Parmesan. Place the soup bowls on a baking sheet so that the surface of the tomatoes is about 3 inches from the heat. Broil quickly until the cheese is lightly browned. Remove from the oven and sprinkle with additional basil if desired. Serve immediately.

2 medium eggplants (about 2 pounds)
5 cloves garlic, sliced thin
1 large yellow onion
12 slices bread (whole wheat or sourdough), toasted
1 tablespoon lemon juice
6 cups hearty vegetable stock (page 39)
1 teaspoon salt
1/4 teaspoon pepper
1/4 teaspoon nutmeg
1 tablespoon tomato paste
1 1/2 tablespoons tahini (page 175)
1 clove garlic, minced
1/4 cup sliced basil

GARNISH:
4 tomatoes, sliced
1/4 cup grated Parmesan

Tomato Soup with Beets and Mint

Yield: 8 servings • Prep Time: 25 minutes • Cooking Time: 45 minutes

4 small beets, peeled and sliced
8 cups light vegetable stock
 (page 38)
1 3-inch cinnamon stick
2 tablespoons olive oil
1 1/4 pound white onions, sliced
6 cloves garlic, sliced
3 tablespoons flour
2 1/2 pounds tomatoes, cored
 and chopped
1/2 teaspoon salt
1/4 teaspoon freshly ground
 black pepper
1 bay leaf
4 sprigs fresh mint
1/3 cup minced fresh mint

When cooking tomato soup in India where tomatoes were plentiful but somewhat insipid in color, I added beets and the problem was remedied. Here, with high quality beets and tomatoes, the flavor combination is as rich as the color. Serve this soup hot or cold, topped with a Minted Yogurt Cheese (page 155).

1. In a 4-quart saucepan, combine the beets, stock and cinnamon. Bring to a boil, then cover, reduce to a simmer and cook for 30 minutes, or until the beets are tender. Strain the beets from the stock, saving both, but discarding the cinnamon.

2. Heat the oil in a 4-quart saucepan until hot but not smoking. Add the onions and cook, stirring constantly, for 2 minutes. Reduce the heat and add the garlic. Continue to cook, stirring often, until the onions are very soft and just beginning to brown, about 20 minutes.

3. Raise heat to high and sprinkle the flour over the onions. Stir to distribute it evenly. Cook, stirring constantly until the flour just begins to brown, about 3 minutes. Add about 1/3 of the chopped tomatoes, scraping the pan to loosen all of the flour from the bottom. Add the remaining tomatoes, stock, beets, salt, pepper, bay leaf and sprigs of mint. Bring to a boil, then cover and reduce to a simmer. Cook, stirring occasionally, for 20 minutes or until the beets are very tender.

4. Remove the soup from the heat and when it is cool enough to handle, purée it through the finest blade of a food mill (or purée it in a food processor and then press it through a fine mesh strainer). Stir in the fresh mint. The soup may be served hot or cold, topped with a drop of Minted Yogurt Cheese (page 155).

Mushroom Barley Soup

Yield: 6 servings • Prep Time: 20 minutes • Cooking Time: 1 hour

1/2 cup pearl barley
1 teaspoon salt
8 cups hearty vegetable stock
 (page 39)
2 tablespoons butter or
 vegetable oil
1 1/2 cups diced red onion
2 pounds mushrooms, sliced
2 tablespoons minced garlic
1 cup diced carrot
1 sweet potato, peeled and diced
1/4 teaspoon black pepper
2 tablespoons minced parsley
Pinch of cayenne
1/2 cup chopped basil

The classic combination of mushrooms and barley is augmented by the refreshing addition of basil.

1. Combine the barley, salt and half of the stock in a 3-quart saucepan and bring to a boil. Reduce to a simmer, cover and cook, stirring occasionally, until the barley is tender, about 25 minutes.

2. Meanwhile, heat the butter in a large skillet until hot but not smoking. Add the onions, stir and reduce heat to medium. Cook for about 5 minutes, then add the mushrooms and garlic. Continue to cook, stirring frequently, until the mushrooms are tender, about 10 minutes.

3. Add the mushroom mixture to the cooked barley. Stir in the remaining stock, carrot, potato, pepper, parsley and cayenne. Simmer gently, stirring occasionally, until the potato is tender, about 20 minutes. Stir in the basil, taste and adjust the seasonings. Serve immediately. The soup may be prepared up to 5 days in advance if refrigerated in an airtight container. It may also be frozen for up to 2 months.

Variation

1. Add 1/3 cup chopped sun-dried tomatoes (softened in hot water, then drained if dried) to the soup with the potatoes. To serve, ladle the soup into ovenproof bowls and top each bowl with 3 tablespoons grated Gruyère cheese. Broil until lightly browned.

2. Serve either version of the soup topped with a combination of 1 cup grated mochi mixed with 1 tablespoon olive oil, 1 tablespoon tahini and 1 teaspoon salt.

Barley Soup with Greens

Yield: 6 servings • Prep Time: 25 minutes • Cooking Time: 1 hour

Kale, spinach, sun-dried tomatoes and barley create an interesting interplay of textures and tastes in this satisfying soup.

1/2 cup pearl barley
3/4 teaspoon salt
8 cups hearty vegetable stock (page 39)
2 tablespoons butter
1 cup diced red onion
1/2 pound mushrooms, chopped
2 tablespoons minced garlic
1 parsnip, cut in small dice
1/8 teaspoon freshly ground black pepper
Pinch of cayenne
1/4 cup minced parsley
1/2 to 2/3 cup sun-dried tomatoes (page 174) (softened in warm water if not packed in oil)
2 cups kale leaves, chopped
3 cups chard or spinach leaves, chopped
3 tablespoons chopped black olives

1. Combine the barley, salt and half of the stock in a 3-quart saucepan. Bring to a boil, then reduce to a simmer. Cover and cook, stirring occasionally, until the barley is tender, about 25 minutes.

2. Meanwhile, heat the butter in a large skillet until hot but not smoking. Add the onions, stir and reduce heat to medium. Cook for about 5 minutes, then add the mushrooms and 1 tablespoon garlic. Continue to cook, stirring frequently, until the mushrooms are tender, about 10 minutes. Add this to the cooked barley. Stir in the remaining stock, parsnip, pepper, cayenne and parsley. Simmer gently, stirring occasionally, for 20 minutes. The soup may be prepared ahead to this point and refrigerated in an airtight container for up to 5 days. Rewarm before continuing with the recipe.

3. Drain and chop the sun-dried tomatoes, then set them aside. Heat the soup to a boil and stir in the tomatoes and kale. Cook, stirring often until the kale is tender, but still a vibrant color, about 5 minutes. Add the spinach and black olives, then continue to cook, stirring often until tender, about 2 minutes. Taste and adjust the seasonings. Serve immediately.

Variation

1. Top each serving of soup with 2 tablespoons crumbled feta cheese just before serving.

Asian Style Barley Soup

Yield: 6 servings • Prep Time: 20 minutes • Cooking Time: 1 1/4 hours

1/2 cup pearl barley
9 cups hearty vegetable stock
1/4 teaspoon salt
2 ounces burdock root (page 167), scrubbed and cut into 1/4-inch pieces
4 stalks lemon grass (page 171)
1 tablespoon peanut oil
2 cups diced yellow onion
3/4 pound button mushrooms, chopped
6 shiitake mushrooms (page 174), softened in hot water, stems removed and cut in large dice
2 tablespoons minced garlic
4 teaspoons minced ginger
Juice of 1 lime
3 1/2 tablespoons soy sauce
1 tablespoon molasses
1/2 teaspoon white pepper
1/4 cup English peas (may use frozen)
3 tablespoons minced scallions
1 small red bell pepper, minced
1/2 teaspoon toasted sesame oil
1/3 cup minced cilantro
Chili paste with garlic (page 157) (optional)

An exceptionally flavorful and satisfying soup that is thick, almost like a stew. Individual ingredients retain their integrity so that each bite is a complex balance of textures and tastes. For a spicy variation, you may stir in chili paste with garlic—available at Asian markets—at the end (though I prefer it without). But be careful—about as much chili paste as you can hold on the tip of one chopstick is all each bowl needs.

1. Rinse the barley then combine it with half of the stock and the salt in a 2-quart saucepan and bring to a boil. Reduce to a simmer, cover and cook, stirring occasionally, for 10 minutes. Add the burdock and continue to cook until the barley is tender, about 20 minutes.

2. Trim top stems and tough outer leaves from each piece of lemon grass, leaving stalks 5 to 6 inches long. To prepare, place a stalk on the counter and lay the flat side of a cleaver or large knife over the end of the lemon grass. Slap the cleaver with the heel of your hand to smash open and flatten the stalk, then roll the stalk over, move the cleaver up the stalk and slap it again. Slice the stalk into 3-inch pieces. Repeat with the remaining lemon grass. Set it aside.

3. Meanwhile, heat the oil in a large skillet until hot but not smoking. Add the onion, then stir and reduce heat to medium. Cook, stirring often, until the onions begin to wilt, about 5 minutes. Add the mushrooms, garlic and ginger and lime juice. Continue to cook, stirring frequently, until the button mushrooms are tender, about 10 minutes. Add this to the cooked barley. Stir in the remaining stock, lemon grass, soy sauce, molasses and pepper. Simmer gently, stirring occasionally, until the barley is very tender, about 25 minutes.

4. Remove and discard the lemon grass and burdock. Stir the peas into the soup and cook until tender, about 5 minutes. Add the scallions, red pepper, sesame oil and cilantro. Taste and adjust the seasonings (add the chili paste, if desired). Serve immediately. The soup may be prepared up to 5 days in advance if stored in an airtight container. It may be frozen for 2 months.

Baked Beet and Jalapeño Soup

Yield: 6 servings • Prep Time: 15 minutes • Cooking Time: 1 1/2 hours

3 pounds beets
1 head garlic
1 large yellow onion
1 pound russet potatoes
4 jalapeño peppers
1 tablespoon olive oil
3 cups hearty vegetable stock (page 39)
3/4 teaspoon salt
1/4 teaspoon black pepper

YOGURT CHEESE:
Cooked jalapeños (above)
1/2 cup nonfat yogurt

This is an intensely flavorful soup. The sweetness of beets is contrasted by jalapeño's bite and rounded out with a hint of butter. Baking the ingredients makes the recipe exceedingly simple to prepare.

1. Preheat the oven to 400°F. Wash the beets, garlic, onion and potatoes under cold water, scrubbing well to remove all dirt. Place the jalapeños on a small baking sheet and arrange the other vegetables 1 inch apart, in a shallow baking dish. Brush the beets and garlic with olive oil. Cover the baking pan with a lid or foil and place it in the oven on the middle rack. Place the jalapeños alongside, uncovered. Reduce the heat to 375°F. Bake until the vegetables are very soft when squeezed, turning them several times and checking for doneness as they cook. The peppers will be ready after about 20 minutes. Remove them from the oven and transfer them immediately to a brown paper bag to cool. (This will make them easier to peel.) Continue to cook the other vegetables until done. The onion and garlic will require about 50 minutes; the beets and potatoes will take about 1 1/2 hours. Remove each vegetable to a wire rack and cool after it is cooked. The vegetables may be baked and refrigerated, loosely covered, up to 4 days before proceeding with the recipe.

2. Once the peppers are cool enough to handle, carefully peel them and remove and discard the seeds and stems. Finely chop the peppers, then stir them into the yogurt. Line a small strainer with several layers of cheesecloth. Scrape the yogurt mixture into the strainer and place it over a bowl to drain. Cover it with a plate and refrigerate overnight. Transfer the drained yogurt "cheese" into a container. It may be prepared up to 2 days in advance if refrigerated in an airtight container.

3. To finish preparing the soup, remove the skin from the onion and chop it roughly. Place it in the processor and squeeze each clove of garlic from the skin into the chopping bowl. Purée the onion and garlic for about a minute, or until they are smooth. Cut each beet open and peel off the skin. Add it to the processor. Halve the potatoes and scrape them from their skins into the bowl as well. Purée the soup mixture until very smooth. You may need to work in two batches, depending on the size of your processor.

4. Scrape the puréed vegetables into a large soup pot. Whisk in the stock, then place the soup over medium heat and warm thoroughly. Mix a small amount of the jalapeño "cheese" into the soup. Add the salt and pepper. Taste and adjust the seasonings.

Miso Noodle Soup

Yield 6 servings • Prep Time: 15 minutes • Cooking Time: 20 minutes

In Japan, miso, which is renowned for its healing qualities, is often eaten as part of the day's first meal. This filling soup is a shining example of miso's soothing character and versatile nature. Different types of miso will produce extremely different effects, so feel free to experiment with this basic broth, using other types of miso. You may also replace noodles with cooked rice and vary the vegetables according to what is in season.

8 cups water
2 teaspoons minced garlic
2 teaspoons minced ginger
1/4 pound udon noodles (page 176) or soba noodles (page 174)
1 large carrot, sliced
1 stem of broccoli, cut in flowerets
8 mushrooms, sliced
1/2 cup mung bean sprouts
1/3 cup mellow white miso (page 171)
1/4 cup natto miso (page 171)

GARNISH:
2 teaspoons toasted sesame oil
4 scallions, minced

1. Combine the water, garlic and ginger in a 3-quart saucepan. Cover, place over high heat and bring to a boil. Lower heat to medium-high and stir in the noodles. Allow them to cook, stirring frequently to prevent them from sticking to the pan, for 3 minutes.

2. Add the carrots to the soup and continue to cook for 5 minutes. Stir in the broccoli. When it has turned bright green and is just beginning to get tender, about 5 minutes, add the mushrooms. Continue to cook until the noodles and vegetables are tender, 1 to 2 minutes more.

3. Stir the bean sprouts into the soup and remove it from the heat. Combine the two types of miso in a small mixing bowl. Mix enough of the soup water into the miso to make a smooth paste, then stir the miso into the soup. You may warm the soup if it has cooled, but do not return it to a boil as this will kill the beneficial digestive enzyme contained in the miso. Transfer the soup to a serving bowl and top with a sprinkling of sesame oil and minced scallions. Serve hot.

Caribbean Banana Bisque

Yield: 6 servings • Prep Time: 20 minutes • Cooking Time: 50 minutes

3 green bananas
1 head garlic
2 small white onions
1 chipolte pepper, softened in
    hot water, then chopped
1/2 teaspoon dried oregano
1/4 teaspoon ground cinnamon
1/4 teaspoon ground cloves
2 tablespoons lime juice
1/2 teaspoon salt
Freshly ground black pepper
2 cups coconut milk
1 carrot, cut in small dice
4 cups spinach leaves, chopped
4 cups Swiss chard leaves,
    chopped
3 1/2 cups light vegetable stock
    (page 38)

Bananas are used throughout the tropics in all sorts of savory dishes and this bisque is a shining example of what a versatile ingredient the banana is. It gives a creamy texture and subtle, sweet backdrop of taste to the otherwise spicy bisque. Bananas discolor very quickly, so, in terms of appearance, this soup is best prepared and eaten immediately.

1. Preheat the oven to 350°F. Rinse the bananas well and pierce each several times through the skin with the tine of a fork, then place them on a baking sheet. Wrap the garlic and onion in foil and place them on the sheet as well. Bake, turning once or twice, until they are very soft when squeezed. The bananas will be ready in about 45 minutes, and the onions may take up to an hour. As each is ready, remove it from the oven to cool.

2. When the bananas are cool enough to handle, peel them and cut them into pieces then put them in a food processor or blender. Squeeze each clove of garlic into the processor or blender bowl. Peel the onion and chop it roughly and add it to the bowl. Drain the chipolte pepper. Remove and discard the stem and seeds. Add the pepper to the processor along with the oregano, cinnamon, cloves, lime juice, salt and pepper. Purée the mixture, scraping the bowl as necessary and adding up to 1/2 cup of coconut milk to obtain a smooth texture.

3. Heat 1 1/2 cups of coconut milk in a 2-quart saucepan over medium heat. Add the carrot, then simmer until it can be easily pierced with a knife, about 20 minutes. Stir in the spinach and chard, and continue to cook, stirring frequently, until the greens are tender, about 8 minutes.

4. Whisk the banana purée and stock into the soup. Cook for about 5 minutes. Taste and adjust the seasonings. Serve immediately.

Cabbage Potato Soup

Yield: 6 servings • Prep Time: 25 minutes • Cooking Time: 3 1/2 hours

1/3 cup rye berries
2 cups sliced yellow onions
1 cup sliced carrot
1 stalk celery, sliced
1 small parsnip, sliced
6 red potatoes, cut in large cubes
    (about 3 pounds)
10 cups water
3 cloves garlic, sliced
6 peppercorns
1 tablespoon caraway seeds,
    crushed
1 teaspoon salt
1 sprig fresh thyme or
    1 teaspoon dried
1 bay leaf

This soup is a simple caraway-flavored broth bountifully garnished with cabbage and potato.

1. In a 6-quart saucepan, combine the rye berries, half of the sliced onion, the carrot, celery, parsnip, one pound of potatoes and the water. Add the garlic and spices, and bring to a boil. After 3 minutes, cover, reduce to a simmer and cook for 3 hours.

2. Strain the soup into a large bowl and discard the cooked vegetables. Return the broth to the saucepan and cook on high heat, uncovered, until it is reduced to 7 cups.

3. Heat the butter in the saucepan until hot but not smoking. Add the remaining onions and sauté for 2 minutes. Reduce the heat and continue to cook, stirring often, until the onions are wilted, about 10 minutes. Add the remaining potatoes and the strained broth and bring to a simmer. Cook until the potatoes are just beginning to become tender, about 15 minutes. Stir in the cabbage and continue to cook until the potatoes and cabbage are tender, about 5 minutes. Serve immediately.

Variation

1. Toast 2 teaspoons caraway seeds then grind them with a mortar and pestle or in an electric coffee grinder. Combine them with 3 tablespoons of mellow miso, 1/4 cup minced parsley and 1/4 teaspoon black pepper. Whisk this into the soup just before serving.

4 stalks Italian parsley
2 tablespoons melted butter
1 small head cabbage
  (about 1 pound)

Creamy Broccoli Soup

Yield: 6 servings • Prep Time: 25 minutes • Cooking Time: 50 minutes

This is a very simple and elegant creamed soup that can be served as part of an elaborate meal or as the main course for a light lunch. It may be puréed and served as is, with a slight texture from the broccoli, or passed through a fine mesh strainer for a smoother effect.

1. Combine the carrot, onion, garlic and stock in a 4-quart saucepan. Cover and bring to a boil. Stir in the salt, pepper, nutmeg and cayenne, then reduce the heat and simmer the soup until the vegetables are tender, about 25 minutes.

2. Cut the stems from the broccoli and trim the tough outer layer from the stems. Cut them into 1/2-inch pieces. Trim off and discard the tough outer layer, then cut the stems roughly into 1-inch pieces. Add the broccoli to the soup and continue to cook until the broccoli is tender, but still very green, about 10 minutes. Add the spinach and continue to cook for just two minutes, until the leaves are tender. Remove the soup immediately from the heat and strain it through a strainer into a large mixing bowl. This will insure that it remains a vibrant green.

3. Finely purée the vegetables in a food processor or blender. Stir them back into the broth and return the soup to a clean saucepan. Combine the arrowroot and water and whisk this mixture into the soup. Warm just to the boil so that it thickens. Do not overcook it or cover it once the broccoli and spinach have been added or it will turn an unappealing army green. Stir in the cream enrichment if desired. Taste and adjust the seasonings. Serve immediately garnished with the pieces of broccoli and carrot.

1 cup diced carrot
1/2 cup diced red onion
2 teaspoons minced garlic
8 cups hearty vegetable stock
  (page 39)
1/2 teaspoon salt
1/4 teaspoon pepper
1/4 cup nutmeg
Pinch of cayenne
8 cups chopped broccoli
4 cups fresh spinach leaves,
  chopped
2 tablespoons arrowroot
3 tablespoons water
1/4 cup crème fraîche (page 34)
  or soy cream (page 36)
  (optional)

GARNISH:
1/4 cup carrot cut into matchstick
  pieces, steamed until tender
12 small broccoli flowerets,
  steamed until tender

Fennel Root and Apple Soup with Basmati Rice

Yield: 6 servings • Prep Time: 25 minutes • Cooking Time: 1 hour

The delicate flavor of cooked fennel root, combined with basmati rice, serves as the backdrop for raw fennel's crisp bite and delicate anise flavor.

3 pounds fennel root
2 cups diced red onion
4 whole cloves garlic, peeled
8 cups light vegetable stock
    (page 38), made with 1 table-
    spoon fennel seeds
1/4 cup basmati rice
1/2 teaspoon salt
1/4 teaspoon ground nutmeg
1/4 teaspoon red pepper flakes
Freshly ground black pepper
1/4 cup walnut halves
2 red crisp red-skinned apples
1/2 cup buttermilk or
    plain nonfat yogurt (optional)

1. Trim the fennel tops from the bulbs. Remove the feathery leaf from the stalks and set it aside for a garnish. Halve each fennel bulb and, with the tip of a paring knife, trim the triangular-shaped core from each root half. Cut the bulbs into dice. You should have about 7 cups. Set 3 cups aside for garnish.

2. Combine 4 cups of the fennel root, the onion, garlic, stock, rice, salt, nutmeg and peppers in a 3-quart saucepan. Bring the soup to a boil, stirring frequently. Reduce heat to low and simmer, partially covered, for about 1 hour. Stir the soup occasionally as it cooks, and check to be certain it remains at a simmer.

3. As the soup cooks, toast the walnuts. Preheat the oven to 350°F. Place the nuts on a baking sheet and bake, stirring several times, until they are golden brown in the center when broken in half, about 12 minutes. Transfer the nuts to a clean kitchen towel and rub to remove the skins. Place the nuts in a bowl and set aside. Discard the skins.

4. Remove the cooked soup from the heat and cool briefly. Strain the vegetables from the broth, reserving the liquid. Purée the vegetables in a food processor or blender until very smooth. Stir the purée back into the broth and warm thoroughly.

5. Quarter, core and dice the apples. Stir them into the soup along with the reserved fennel root. Simmer for 5 minutes. Remove the soup from the heat and stir in the buttermilk. Taste and adjust the seasonings. Serve each bowl garnished with a few sprigs of fennel top and toasted walnuts.

Variation

1. Serve as is topped with paper-thin slices of Leyden (caraway spiced) cheese.

Curried Mushroom Bake

Yield: 6 servings • Prep Time: 20 minutes • Cooking Time: 1 3/4 hours

The delicate curry flavors blossom and merge with the mushrooms as the soup, which is extraordinarily simple to make, is slow-baked.

12 scallions, minced
1 tablespoon minced garlic
1/2 tablespoon minced ginger
2 tablespoons butter
    or vegetable oil
3/4 cup plain, nonfat yogurt
1 teaspoon ground cinnamon
2 teaspoons garam masala
    (page 169)
1/2 teaspoon ground cardamom
1/2 teaspoon turmeric

1. Preheat the oven to 350°F. Sauté the scallions, garlic and ginger in the butter over low heat until the onions are wilted, about 8 minutes. Transfer them to a 2-quart baking dish.

2. In a small mixing bowl, combine the yogurt with the cinnamon, garam masala, cardamom, turmeric, cayenne, salt and molasses. Slice the mushrooms and add them to the baking dish. Sprinkle them with lemon juice, then pour the yogurt mixture over them and stir to blend. Bake, covered, in the center of the oven until the mushrooms are very tender, about 1 3/4 hours. Stir the mixture several times as it cooks.

3. Remove the soup from the oven. It may be puréed in a food processor or blender at this point, or left as is with the vegetables whole. In either case, stir in the stock, then return to the oven to warm thoroughly. Just before serving, stir in the cilantro. Serve Cumin Scented Croutons. The soup is best prepared and eaten immediately.

1/4 teaspoon cayenne pepper
1 teaspoon salt
1 tablespoon molasses
3 pounds mushrooms, sliced
5 cups mushroom stock
2 tablespoons lemon juice
1/4 cup minced cilantro

GARNISH:
Cumin Scented Croutons
(page 150)

Sweet and Sour Cabbage Soup

Yield: 6 servings • Prep Time: 20 minutes • Cooking Time: 2 hours

This sweet, slightly sour soup is accented with fresh mint.

1. In a 6-quart saucepan, combine the prunes, half of the sliced onion, the carrot, celery, potatoes and one of each type of apple. Cover with the stock. Add the garlic, peppercorns, anise seed, salt, thyme, bay leaf, mint sprigs and parsley. Bring the soup to a boil. After 3 minutes, cover, reduce to a simmer and cook for 2 hours.

2. Strain the soup into a large bowl and discard the cooked vegetables. Heat the butter in the saucepan until hot but not smoking. Add the remaining onions and sauté for 2 minutes. Reduce the heat and continue to cook, stirring often, until the onions are wilted, about 10 minutes. Add the remaining apples, apple juice and the strained broth. Bring to a simmer. Cook until the apples are just beginning to become tender, about 10 minutes. Stir in the cabbage and continue to cook until the apples are tender and the cabbage is tender, but still vibrant in color, about 8 minutes.

3. Combine the honey, miso, mustard, vinegar and minced mint in a small bowl. Whisk enough soup broth into the miso mixture so that it is very smooth and pourable. Stir this into the soup. Taste and adjust the seasonings, then serve immediately. The soup is best prepared and eaten immediately.

1/3 cup prunes
2 cups sliced yellow onion
3/4 cup sliced carrot
1 stalk celery, sliced
2 cups cubed red potato
3 Granny Smith apples, peeled, cored and cubed
3 Winesap apples, peeled, cored and cubed
8 cups light vegetable stock (page 38)
3 cloves garlic
6 peppercorns
1 1/2 teaspoons anise seed
1 teaspoon salt
1 sprig fresh thyme or 1 teaspoon dried
1 bay leaf
4 sprigs fresh mint
4 stalks Italian parsley
1 tablespoon butter
1 cup unfiltered apple juice
1 small head cabbage (about 2 pounds)
2 teaspoons honey
3 tablespoons light miso (page 171)
1 teaspoon Dijon-style mustard
1 to 2 tablespoons rice vinegar
1/4 cup minced fresh mint leaves

Sweet Corn Chowder

Yield: 8 servings • Prep Time: 20 minutes • Cooking Time: 45 minutes

2 cups diced yellow onion
1 tablespoon butter
1 1/2 cups minced carrot
10 ears sweet corn
6 cups milk or soy milk
3 cups water
1 teaspoon salt
1/4 teaspoon black pepper
Pinch of cayenne

GARNISH:
10 fresh chive stems
4 tablespoons Jalapeño Butter
   prepared with chives
   (page 156) (optional)

Starch from the corn serves as the primary thickener and gives this soup the gustatory illusion of being rich and creamy. In late summer when local sweet corn is at its peak, make a large batch to freeze.

1. In a 3-quart saucepan, sauté the onion in the butter over medium heat, stirring frequently, until it has softened and is beginning to brown, about 15 minutes. Do not allow it to burn. Add the carrots and continue to cook, stirring often, for 5 minutes.

2. As the onion and carrot cook, prepare the corn. Shuck each ear, break in half and remove the kernels from the cobs by standing each ear on the cutting surface, broken side down, and shaving off the kernels from the tip of the corn down. You should have 4 1/2 cups of kernels. Set aside 3/4 cup of kernels for garnish.

3. Add the remaining corn to the onion and carrot and cook, stirring constantly, for 1 minute. Stir in the milk, water, salt, pepper and cayenne. Cover halfway and simmer for 20 minutes, or until the carrots are tender.

4. Remove the soup from the heat and strain, reserving the broth. In a food processor or blender, purée about 3/4 of the cooked vegetables. Stir the purée and the remaining cooked vegetables back into the soup and return it to the cooking pot. Add the reserved 3/4 cup of corn and snip the chives into the soup. Heat for 2 minutes to warm the corn and infuse the soup with a delicate scent of chives. Taste and adjust the seasonings. The soup may be prepared up to 3 days in advance if refrigerated in an airtight container. It may be frozen for 3 months.

Cream of Cauliflower Soup with Tomatoes and Parmesan

Yield: 6 servings • Prep Time: 25 minutes • Cooking Time: 45 minutes

2 tablespoons lemon juice
1 large head cauliflower
4 leeks, white part only,
   trimmed, washed and
   chopped
1 cup diced sweet onion
   (Vidalia, if possible)
1 russet potato, peeled and
   cubed
1 tablespoon minced garlic
1/2 cup dry white wine
8 cups hearty vegetable stock
   (page 39)
1/2 teaspoon salt
1/4 teaspoon pepper
Pinch of cayenne

Each serving of this classic-tasting, creamy cauliflower soup is topped with chopped tomatoes and a sprinkling of Parmesan for a striking presentation.

1. Fill a medium-sized mixing bowl with water and add the lemon juice. Trim and discard the leaves and tough stems from the cauliflower. Cut the rest into flowerets, trimming any tough skin from the stems of the flowerets. As you cut up the cauliflower, drop it immediately into the bowl of water and set aside as you prepare the rest of the vegetables. This step helps to retain the white color of cauliflower.

2. Combine the leeks, onion, potato, garlic, wine and stock in a 4-quart saucepan. Cover and bring to a boil. Stir in the salt, pepper, cayenne, nutmeg and parsley, then reduce the heat and simmer the soup for 15 minutes. Add the cauliflower and continue to cook until it is very tender, about 20 minutes. Re-

move from the heat and strain the soup into a large mixing bowl. Remove the parsley.

3. When the vegetables have cooled, purée them finely in a food mill or processor. Stir them back into the broth and return the soup to a clean saucepan. Combine the arrowroot and water, then add this mixture to the soup. Warm the soup just to the boil so that it thickens. Stir in the cream, taste and adjust the seasonings. Keep the soup warm as you prepare the garnish.

4. With the tip of a paring knife make a shallow cross, just through the skin, in the blossom end of each tomato. Trim around the stem and cut out a cone shape about an inch deep in the core of each tomato. Bring 1 1/2 quarts of water to a boil. Plunge the tomatoes into the water and cook until the cut cross of skin is easily peeled from the tomato, about 30 seconds. Remove the tomatoes from the water with a slotted spoon and place them in a strainer, over the sink and under cold running water, to stop their cooking. When they are cool enough to handle, peel them. Cut each in half widthwise and squeeze the seeds out of the tomatoes. Place them on a cutting board and chop.

5. Garnish each bowl of soup with a mound of chopped tomatoes in the center and a sprinkling of Parmesan, minced basil and mint.

1/4 teaspoon nutmeg
4 sprigs parsley
2 tablespoons arrowroot dissolved in 3 tablespoons cold water
1/2 cup cream or milk

GARNISH:
2 tomatoes
1/4 cup grated Parmesan
2 tablespoons minced basil
2 tablespoons minced mint

Potato Soup with Lemon Zest and Tarragon

Yield: 6 servings • Prep Time: 15 minutes • Cooking Time: 1 hour

This recipe was inspired by a luscious lemon- and tarragon-flavored potato salad served to me by my friend and colleague, Diane Farris.

1. Combine the potatoes, onion, stock, 1 tablespoon tarragon, salt and pepper in a 4-quart saucepan. Bring the soup to a boil, stirring often. Reduce to a simmer and cook, covered, until the onions are very tender, about 1 hour. Remove from the heat.

2. Strain the soup, saving the broth. Purée about 1/2 of the soup solids in a food mill or processor until smooth. Return all of the solids to the soup and return it to the cooking pot. Grate the zest from the lemons and add it to the soup. Stir in the tarragon and warm the soup briefly. Slice the lemons into rounds as a garnish for each serving. The soup may be prepared up to 5 days in advance if refrigerated in an airtight container. It may be frozen for up to 3 months.

6 russet potatoes, peeled and cubed (about 3 3/4 pounds)
1 1/2 cups white onion, diced
8 cups light vegetable stock (page 38)
1/4 cup fresh tarragon leaves, chopped (or 4 teaspoons dried)
1 1/2 teaspoons salt
1/4 teaspoon white pepper
2 lemons

Variation

1. Substitute orange for the lemon and 3 tablespoons of snipped chives for the tarragon.

Three Potato Chowder

Yield: 4 servings • Prep Time: 20 minutes • Cooking Time: 50 minutes

The crisp texture of broiled potato pancakes—served as the topping—makes this soup irresistible.

1 1/2 cup minced shallots
1 tablespoon butter or olive oil
1 cup diced onion
1 cup diced celery
1 tablespoon garlic
3 1/2 cups diced red potato
6 cups light vegetable stock
    (page 38) or water
7 allspice berries
1/4 teaspoon oregano
1/4 teaspoon salt
1 bay leaf
1 1/2 cups diced yam or sweet
    potato

GARNISH:
1 red skinned potato, grated
2 tablespoons butter

1. Sauté the shallots in the butter over medium heat for 10 minutes. Stir in the onions and celery and continue to cook, stirring often, for 20 minutes, or until the onions are very soft. Add the garlic and continue to cook for 5 minutes, then stir in the red-skinned potatoes, stock, allspice berries (wrapped in cheesecloth), oregano, salt and bay leaf.

2. Bring the soup to a boil, then cover and reduce to a simmer. Cook, stirring often, for 10 minutes. Stir in the sweet potato and continue to cook until all of the potatoes are tender.

3. As the soup cooks, prepare the garnish. Preheat the oven to 425°F. Form the grated potato into 16 small patties. Brush a baking sheet with melted butter and place the patties on the sheet. Brush them with butter and bake for 15 minutes. Turn once as they bake to brown each side evenly. (Alternatively, the patties may be fried on top of the stove in a skillet. They are crispier than oven-baked but require more butter.)

4. Once the soup is cooked, remove the bay leaf and allspice berries. Serve each bowl garnished with 4 potato cakes.

Sweet Potato Soup with Orange

Yield: 6 servings • Prep Time: 20 minutes • Cooking Time: 1 hour

This soup has an interesting combination of flavors; the addition of rosemary unites the tartness from orange rind with sweet potato.

2 1/2 pounds sweet potatoes,
    diced
1 1/2 cups diced yellow onion
1/2 cup sliced shallots
6 cups light vegetable stock
    (page 38)
1 tablespoon minced garlic
1 teaspoon salt
1/4 teaspoon black pepper
Pinch of cayenne
1 tablespoon fresh rosemary or
    1 teaspoon dried
6 peppercorns
2 navel oranges, sliced

1. Peel and cube the potatoes. Place them in a 4-quart saucepan with the onions and shallots. Add the stock, garlic, salt, pepper, and cayenne. Place the rosemary and peppercorns on a small square of cheesecloth. Bring the edges of the cloth together and tie the "bouquet garni" closed with a piece of kitchen twine. (Or place the rosemary and peppercorns in a stainless steel tea ball.) Add this to the soup with the sliced oranges.

2. Bring the soup to a boil, then reduce to a simmer. Cook, covered and stirring occasionally, until the potatoes are very tender, about 1 hour. Remove the soup from the heat and discard the rosemary and orange slices.

3. Mash about 1/3 of the potatoes against the side of the pan with the back of a cooking spoon. Taste and adjust the seasonings. Serve warm or at room temperature. The soup may be prepared up to 5 days in advance if refrigerated in an airtight container. It may be frozen for 3 months.

6 • Sweet Temptations

Apple Soup with Calvados and Toasted Pecans

Yield: 4 servings • Prep Time: 20 minutes • Cooking Time: 1 hour

The marriage of apples and pecans is perfectly harmonious. When calvados is added—as in this soup—the result is sublime.

1. Preheat the oven to 400°F. Wash the apples and prick each several times with the tine of a fork. Place the fruit on a baking sheet and bake in the center of the oven until soft when squeezed, about 45 minutes. Remove the apples from the oven and cool to room temperature. They may be baked up to 4 days in advance if refrigerated in a loosely folded plastic bag.

2. Quarter, core and peel each apple. Place the meat in a food processor or blender and purée until smooth. Crush the kuzu with a fork and mix it with the lemon juice and 2 tablespoons water in a small saucepan. Warm gently to dissolve the kuzu. Remove from the heat and stir in the calvados. Add this to the apples along with the milk. Blend again. Transfer the soup to an airtight container and refrigerate until chilled. It may be prepared 4 days in advance.

3. In a food processor or blender, grind the pecans until they are a finely ground, even-textured paste. Add the cinnamon, nutmeg, maple syrup and enough water to make the mixture a pourable consistency. Ladle chilled soup into individual bowls and garnish each with a generous swirl of pecan sauce.

2 Granny Smith apples
6 golden delicious apples
3 tablespoons kuzu (page 170)
2 tablespoons lemon juice
4 tablespoons water
3 tablespoons calvados or cognac (or to taste)
1 1/2 cups milk or soy milk mixed with 2 tablespoons soy milk powder (page 174)
3/4 cup pecans, toasted
1 teaspoon cinnamon
1/4 teaspoon nutmeg
3 to 5 tablespoons maple syrup
2 to 3 tablespoons water

Variations

1. Use only 1 1/4 cups milk and whisk in 1/4 cup crème fraîche (page 34) or soy cream (page 36) along with the milk.

2. Warm the soup to just below the boil and whisk the pecan sauce into the soup. Serve garnished with lemon wedges and sweet Lace Spice Cookies (page 159).

Caramelized Pear and Fudge Swirl Soup

Yield: 4 servings • Prep Time: 15 minutes • Cooking Time: 45 minutes

4 d'anjou pears
2 bosc pears
2 tablespoons lemon juice
3 tablespoons Eau de Vie de
　Poire or 2 teaspoons vanilla
1 cup milk or light cream

FUDGE SAUCE:
1/2 cup Dutch cocoa
2 tablespoons boiling water
4 tablespoons maple syrup

This heavenly concoction is light and delicate in flavor—a stunning example of the classic combination of pears and chocolate. Serve it as is or garnished with thin Ginger Snaps (page 159). The length of time it will take the pears to cook depends on their ripeness. For best results pick d'anjou pears that have a mild scent and are just beginning to soften. The bosc pears should have slight shriveling at the stem end and have just a little give in softness.

1. Preheat the oven to 400°F. Wash the pears and prick each several times with the tine of a fork. Place the fruit on a baking sheet and bake in the center of the oven until soft when squeezed, 35 to 40 minutes or until they are soft when squeezed. Remove the pears from the oven and cool to room temperature. The pears may be baked up to 5 days in advance if refrigerated in a loosely folded plastic bag.

2. Quarter, core and peel each pear. Place the fruit in a food processor or blender. Add the lemon juice, Eau de Vie or vanilla and blend the pear mixture until very smooth. Transfer it to a mixing bowl and chill for at least 2 hours. The soup may be prepared ahead to this point and refrigerated in an airtight container for up to 5 days. Before serving, whisk the milk or cream into the soup and blend thoroughly.

3. Place the cocoa in a small mixing bowl. Pour the boiling water over it and blend until smooth. Stir in the maple syrup. Serve the soup in individual serving bowls or goblets. Spoon about a tablespoon of the syrup into the center of each bowl of soup. If you wish, swirl strands of the chocolate into the soup by using the tip of a paring knife to draw the chocolate from the center of the spoonful out into the soup.

Banana Rum Soup with Fudge Swirl

Yield: 6 servings • Prep Time: 20 minutes • Cooking Time: 30 minutes

6 bananas
2 tablespoons lemon juice
2 tablespoons date sugar or
　barley malt powder (page 167)
2 teaspoons vanilla or
　1/4 cup dark Jamaican Rum
1/4 cup plain nonfat yogurt
　or soy milk
1 1/2 cups orange juice

FUDGE SAUCE:
1/2 cup Dutch cocoa
2 tablespoons boiling water
1/4 cup maple syrup

The tartness of orange balances banana's thick, rich flavor in this creamy soup. A swirl of fudge sauce complements both banana and orange. Use bananas that are not green but have no black spots.

1. Preheat the oven to 400°F. Wash the bananas and prick each several times with the tine of a fork, then place them on a baking sheet. Bake in the center of the oven until soft when squeezed, 20 to 25 minutes. Remove the bananas from the oven and cool to room temperature.

2. When the bananas are cool enough to handle, peel them and place the fruit in a food processor or blender. Add the lemon juice, date sugar, vanilla and yogurt, then blend until very smooth. Transfer the mixture to a mixing bowl,

whisk in the orange juice and blend thoroughly. The soup is best eaten within 8 hours as it begins to darken in color as it sits.

3. Place the cocoa in a small mixing bowl, then pour the boiling water over it and blend until smooth. Stir in the maple syrup. Ladle the soup into individual serving bowls or goblets. Spoon about a tablespoon of the syrup into the center of each bowl of soup. If you wish, swirl strands of the chocolate into the soup by using the tip of a paring knife to draw the chocolate from the center of the spoonful out into the soup.

Variation

1. Replace the orange juice with coconut milk and the rum with Grand Marnier.

The Big Chill

Yield: 6 servings • Prep Time: 10 minutes

Frozen bananas give a creamy, smooth consistency to this simple soup. Any soft ripened fruit (or combination of fruits) may be substituted for the strawberries.

2 pints strawberries
3 ripe bananas
3 medjool dates (or 6 other)
3 cups fruit juice (apple, orange, cherry, for example)
1/4 cup lime juice
2 1/2 cups nonfat yogurt
3 tablespoons minced mint
2 teaspoons vanilla
1/4 cup date sugar (page 168) or 3 tablespoons maple syrup (optional)

1. Set aside 6 unblemished strawberries for a garnish, then hull and slice the rest (you should have 2 cups of sliced fruit). Place the strawberries in an airtight container. Peel the bananas, cut them into 1-inch pieces and place them in a separate container. Freeze both until solid, at least 24 hours. Pit and quarter the dates. Set aside.

2. Thaw the fruit at room temperature for 10 minutes then place the bananas, strawberries, dates and 1/2 cup of the juice in a blender or food processor. Purée until smooth, scraping down the sides of the beaker as necessary. Add the remaining juice, yogurt, mint and vanilla. Blend, then taste and add sweetener, if desired. Pour into individual goblets or serving bowls. Garnish each serving with a whole strawberry placed in the center of the soup or on the plate beside the bowl. Serve immediately.

Variations

1. Serve with Chocolate Fudge Sauce (page 31) swirled into each serving.
2. Replace the yogurt with soy milk or fruit juice.

Chunky Apple Soup

Yield: 6 servings • Prep Time: 25 minutes • Cooking Time: 1 3/4 hours

6 cups unfiltered apple juice or apple cider
4 sweet oranges or honey tangerines
1/2 cup raisins
4 3-inch sticks cinnamon
1 1-inch piece ginger, sliced and smashed
1 teaspoon allspice berries
1/2 teaspoon cloves
1 1/2 cups water
6 sweet apples quartered, peeled, cored, and cut into large pieces
1/2 cup dried apples, chopped
3 tablespoons maple syrup (optional)

This rustic soup can be served warm or cold. Juicy pieces of apple are bathed in a spiced, syrupy broth for a most satisfying effect.

1. Pour the apple juice into a 4-quart saucepan. Rinse the tangerines very well, then slice one and add it to the saucepan. Juice the remaining tangerines; you should have 1 1/4 cups juice (add water to equal this volume if necessary). Add the tangerine juice to the soup. Stir in the raisins, cinnamon, ginger, allspice, cloves and water. Bring the soup to a boil, then reduce to a simmer and cook, stirring occasionally, for 1 hour. Remove from the heat and refrigerate overnight. This step may be eliminated, but the flavors will mellow if allowed to cool in this way.

2. Strain the soup into a large bowl. Discard the soup solids. Return the broth to the saucepan and add the chopped fresh and dried apples. Simmer until the fruit is very tender, about 40 minutes. Remove from the heat and serve warm or refrigerate. Before serving, taste and add maple syrup if desired. Serve with Cinnamon Croutons (page 150).

Mixed Fruit Soup

Yield: 6 servings • Prep Time: 25 minutes • Cooking Time: 1 1/2 hours

2 golden delicious apples, peeled, quartered and cored
1 Granny Smith apple, peeled, quartered and cored
2 bosc pears, peeled, quartered and cored
2 carrots, sliced
1 orange, peeled and sliced
1 3-inch cinnamon stick
4 whole cloves
1 star anise
1 1/4 cup Thompson raisins
8 cups water
1/2 teaspoon ground nutmeg
2 tablespoons agar flakes (page 167)
1/4 cup orange juice
5 cups sliced and/or diced fruit
1/4 cup maple syrup (optional)

I have not specified the type of fruit to use for the final garnish in this soup; you may suit your own tastes and budget. It is best to select three to six different types of fruit that complement one another in flavor, texture, color and shape.

1. Combine the apples, pears, carrots, oranges, cinnamon, cloves, anise, raisins and water in a 4-quart saucepan. Cover and bring to a boil, stirring often. Reduce the soup to a simmer and cook, stirring occasionally, for 1 1/2 hours. Remove from the heat, stir in the nutmeg and cool to room temperature. Strain the soup, reserving the broth and discarding the cooked fruit. The soup may be prepared to this point up to 3 days ahead if refrigerated in an airtight container. It may also be frozen for 3 months.

2. Combine the agar and orange juice in a small saucepan. Warm, stirring often, until the agar is completely dissolved, about 10 minutes. Stir this into the broth and chill for at least 20 minutes or up to 3 days.

3. Cut up the fresh fruit and add it to the soup broth. Refrigerate for at least 2 hours. Taste the soup for sweetness and add up to 1/4 cup maple syrup if needed. With a slotted spoon lift the sliced fruit out of the broth and arrange it in shallow serving bowls. Ladle the soup over and serve at once.

Creamy Apricot Soup

Yield: 8 servings • Prep Time: 25 minutes • Cooking Time: 20 minutes

This refreshing fruit soup may be served as the brisk starter to a summer lunch or a sooth-ing finish to a more substantial meal. It may be served cold or slightly warmed and, for variation, it can be garnished with a scattering of raspberries and freshly picked sprigs of mint.

4 pounds fresh, ripe apricots
6 1/2 cups water
4 cardamom pods, crushed
1 stick cinnamon
1/2 cup maple syrup
3 oranges
1/2 cup nonfat yogurt

1. Rinse the apricots, then cut each in half and discard the pits. Place the fruit in a 2-quart saucepan and cover with 6 cups of water. Wrap the cardamom in cheesecloth or place it in a tea ball. Add it to the apricots along with the cinna-mon and 1/4 cup of maple syrup. Place the pan over high heat, cover and bring to a boil, stirring frequently. Reduce to a simmer and cook, stirring often, for 10 minutes. Remove the soup from the heat and cool.

2. Strain the cooking liquid into a bowl. Remove the cardamom and cinna-mon from the soup solids. Purée the fruit through the fine blade of a food mill, then whisk it into the cooking liquids. Alternatively, you may purée the fruit in a food processor or blender, but before adding it to the soup, you must force the purée through a fine mesh strainer to remove the skins.

3. Using a very sharp paring knife, cut strips of skin from the oranges, top to bottom. If white pith remains attached to the underside of the strips, lay the piece of peel, pith side up, on the cutting board and shave off the pith. Stack the strips of peel and shred lengthwise into very thin strips. Juice each of the or-anges and strain the juice into a small saucepan. Add the strips of orange peel, remaining water and 1/4 cup maple syrup. Place the saucepan over high heat and bring to a boil. Reduce heat slightly and boil, stirring frequently, for about 15 minutes or until the strips of peel are soft and candied. Add the strips and their cooking liquid to the apricot mixture, cover and chill thoroughly.

4. Combine the yogurt with the remaining 2 tablespoons of maple syrup. Ladle the soup into individual serving bowls. Gently place just over a tablespoon of yogurt in the center of each bowl so that as much of the yogurt as possible floats. Draw the blade of a paring knife from the center of the yogurt into the soup, the back side of the blade leading the motion, so that swirls of the yogurt are created in the soup. Serve immediately.

Variations

1. Replace the 6 cups of water, above, with almond milk (page 34). Stir 1 tablespoon Amaretto into the finished soup and sprinkle toasted sliced almonds over each serving.

2. Stir 2 cups sliced and peeled apricots, peaches or nectarines into the fin-ished soup just before serving.

Brandied Cherry Soup

Yield: 8 servings • Prep Time: 25 minutes • Cooking Time: 20 minutes

6 cups Rainer cherries
2 cups bing cherries
2 cups fresh orange juice
2/3 cup maple sugar (page 171)
1/2 teaspoon nutmeg
1 cup milk
3 egg yolks
1/4 cup maple syrup
1 teaspoon vanilla
3 tablespoons brandy or
 cognac

The combination in this soup—cherry purée, blended with brandy and a sweet maple cream—is difficult to resist. The soup is then spooned over more sweet fresh cherries for a rich and elegant finish to a meal. Rainer cherries are a yellow sweet variety that are similar, but more subtle in taste, than bings. If they are unavailable, you may use all bings for this soup. You may also use frozen sweet cherries instead.

1. Pick over the cherries (keeping the two varieties separate) to remove all stems, debris and any that are overly soft. Rinse the cherries well and pit them. Place the Rainer cherries in a 4-quart saucepan. Add the orange juice, sugar and nutmeg. Stir and bring to a boil. Reduce heat to low and simmer, stirring occasionally, for 5 minutes. Cover, remove from heat, and cool to room temperature. Slice the bing cherries in half then cover and refrigerate until ready to serve.

2. Pour the cooked cherries into a blender or food processor and blend until smooth, about 1 minute. Rub the purée through a fine mesh strainer into a large mixing bowl. Stir in the bing cherries and set this aside while preparing the cream.

3. Rinse out a 1-quart heavy-bottomed saucepan with cold water, but do not dry it. Add the milk to the pan and scald. (Rinsing the pan before scalding helps to prevent a film from forming on the pan as the milk cooks.) Meanwhile, in a small mixing bowl, beat the eggs with the syrup and vanilla until frothy. Pour the scalded milk into the eggs, whisking constantly.

4. Pour this mixture back into the saucepan. Using a wooden spoon, stir the cream constantly over low heat as it cooks. Scrape the edges and the entire surface of the bottom of the pan as the cream cooks, but do not cause bubbles to form or it will become difficult to judge the thickness of the cream. Watch carefully as you stir; the moment the cream coats the back of the spoon—when you lift the spoon from the pan and draw a line with your finger through the cream, the line will remain—strain the cream through a fine mesh strainer into the puréed cherries. (If the cream overcooks, the eggs will curdle and have a separated, textured appearance.) Stir the brandy into the cherry mixture.

5. Place the soup in the refrigerator and chill thoroughly, stirring occasionally as it cools. The soup may be refrigerated in an airtight container for up to 3 days before serving. It cannot be frozen. Just before serving, stir the reserved bing cherries into the soup. Ladle the chilled soup into goblets or shallow bowls.

Pineapple Coconut Soup

Yield: 6 servings • Prep Time: 20 minutes • Cooking Time: 1 hour

The communion of pineapple and coconut with a splash of rum has been a favorite in cakes and drinks for years. This soup seems the logical next step for this favorite combination. Serve each bowl topped with Coconut Croutons (page 150) or toasted coconut.

1/4 cup sweet rice
4 cups water
1/2 cup chopped dried pineapple
1 lemon
1 fresh pineapple
3 cups coconut milk
1/4 cup orange blossom honey
1/4 cup dark Jamaican rum

GARNISH:
3 tablespoons toasted fresh
  coconut

1. Rinse the rice. In a 4-quart saucepan, combine the rice with the water and dried pineapple. Zest the lemon and stir this into the soup. Bring the soup to a boil, then reduce to a simmer and cook, stirring occasionally, until the rice is soft, about 50 minutes.

2. Peel, core and dice the pineapple. In a food processor or blender, purée half of the fruit finely, then pass it through a fine strainer. Add this to the soup, then stir in the remaining whole pieces of fruit. Stir in the coconut milk, honey and rum. Continue to cook for 5 minutes or until the pineapple has softened. Remove from the heat and serve immediately or at room temperature. Garnish each serving with Coconut Croutons (page 150) or a sprinkling of toasted coconut.

Grandma's Cinnamon Milk Toast Soup

Yield: 4 servings • Prep Time: 15 minutes • Cooking Time: 20 minutes

Not that I had a grandmother who made this for me, but it's the kind of nurturing food I always imagined a grandmother would produce. The quality of the soup rests in the quality of the bread you choose.

4 large slices bread
  (whole wheat, sourdough,
  multi-grain)
4 tablespoons butter, melted
2 teaspoons cinnamon
1/4 teaspoon ground ginger
1/2 cup maple sugar (page 171)
5 cups milk or soy milk
1/3 cup raisins
1 teaspoon minced candied
  ginger
1 1/2 teaspoons vanilla extract
4 teaspoons cornstarch
2 tablespoons cold water

1. Preheat the oven to 375°F. Place the bread on a baking sheet and bake it until very lightly toasted on both sides. Remove from the oven and brush both sides of the toast with butter. Combine the cinnamon, ground ginger and 1/4 cup of sugar, then sprinkle this evenly over one side of each piece of toast. Return to the oven and bake until the underside of the toast is a deep golden brown. Transfer the toast to a cake rack to cool. The toast may be prepared several hours in advance and stored, at room temperature, in an airtight container.

2. Rinse out a 2-quart saucepan with cold water. Drain, but do not dry it, then pour the milk into the pan. (This helps to prevent a film from forming on the bottom of the pan as the milk cooks.) Add the remaining sugar, raisins and candied ginger. Bring to a boil, then reduce to a simmer and cook for 2 minutes. Remove from the heat and stir in the vanilla. Cover and set aside for at least 30 minutes. The soup may be prepared to this point up to 2 days in advance if refrigerated in an airtight container.

3. Just before serving, combine the cornstarch and water. Warm the soup in a saucepan, then stir in the cornstarch. Bring just to a boil so that the soup thickens, stirring constantly. Place a slice of toast in each serving bowl and ladle the soup, raisins and ginger over. Serve immediately.

Cardamom Cashew Toast Soup

Yield: 4 servings • Prep Time: 15 minutes • Cooking Time: ?

4 large slices bread
  (whole wheat, sourdough,
  multi-grain)
4 tablespoons butter, melted
1 teaspoon ground cardamom
1/2 teaspoon ground cinnamon
1/4 teaspoon ground ginger
1/2 cup maple sugar (page 171)
2/3 cup raw cashews
2 1/2 cups soy milk or milk
1/3 cup currants
1 cup water
1 tablespoon rose flower water
  (page 169)
4 teaspoons cornstarch
2 tablespoons cold water

This warm, spicy soup makes a comforting start or finish to a cold winter's day. It is rich but not filling and fortified in protein with the addition of cashews and soy milk.

1. Preheat the oven to 375°F. Place the bread on a baking sheet and bake it until very lightly toasted on both sides. Remove the baking sheet from the oven and brush both sides of the toast with butter. Combine the cardamom, cinnamon, ginger and 1/4 cup sugar. Sprinkle this powder evenly over one side of each piece of toast. Return to the oven and bake until the underside of the toast is a deep golden brown. Transfer the toast to a cake rack to cool. The toast may be prepared several days in advance if stored, at room temperature, in an airtight container.

2. In a blender, combine the cashews and 1/2 cup of water. Blend for about 2 minutes. Check the consistency—it should be fine and evenly ground. Continue to blend until this cashew milk is very smooth, 5 to 8 minutes. Add additional water, if needed, to maintain the consistency. Blend in all remaining water and transfer the cashew milk to a 2-quart saucepan.

3. Rinse a 2-quart saucepan with cold water. Drain, but do not dry it, then pour the milk into the pan. (This helps to prevent a film from forming on the bottom of the pan as the milk cooks.) Add the remaining sugar and currants, then bring to a boil. Reduce to a simmer and cook for 2 minutes. Pour the milk into the cashew milk, then stir in the rose water. Cover and set aside for at least 30 minutes. The soup may be prepared to this point up to 2 days in advance, if refrigerated in an airtight container.

4. Just before serving, combine the cornstarch and water. Warm the soup in a saucepan, then stir in the cornstarch. Bring the soup just to a boil, stirring constantly, so that it thickens. Place a slice of toast in each serving bowl and ladle the soup and raisins over each. Serve immediately.

Chocolate Milk Toast Soup

Yield: 4 servings • Prep Time: 20 minutes • Cooking Time: 15 minutes

1 sweet orange
4 tablespoons butter
1/4 cup date sugar
4 large slices bread
  (whole wheat, sourdough,
  multi-grain)
4 cups coconut milk (page 37)
2 tablespoons maple syrup
2/3 cup chopped dark chocolate
  (may use date-sweetened
  carob chips)

Orange and chocolate combine beautifully in this simple variation of a milk toast soup. This soup may be made with coconut milk or soy milk and either chocolate or carob.

1. Grate 2 tablespoons zest from the orange. Combine it with the butter in a small saucepan. Melt the butter, then remove it from the heat and stir in the date sugar. Set this aside.

2. Preheat the oven to 375°F. Place the bread on a baking sheet and bake it until very lightly toasted on both sides. Remove the baking sheet from the oven and brush both sides of the toast with the melted butter mixture. Return the toast to the oven and bake it until the underside is a deep golden brown. Transfer the toast to a cake rack to cool. The toast may be prepared several hours in advance and stored, at room temperature, in an airtight container.

3. Squeeze the juice from the orange and combine it with the coconut milk maple syrup and chocolate chips in a 2-quart saucepan. Cook, stirring constantly, until the chocolate is melted. Remove from the heat and stir in the Grand Marnier. The soup may be prepared 24 hours in advance if refrigerated in an airtight container.

4. Just before serving, combine the arrowroot and water. Warm the soup in a saucepan, then stir in the arrowroot. Bring the soup just to the boil so that it thickens, stirring constantly. Place a slice of toast in each serving bowl and ladle the soup over this and sprinkle 1/4 cup raspberries and 1 tablespoon grated chocolate on top. Serve immediately.

Variations

1. Use slices of pound cake instead of bread for the toast.
2. Substitute strawberries, sliced apricots or bananas for the raspberries.

2 tablespoons Grand Marnier
   (optional)
1 tablespoon arrowroot
1 tablespoon cold water
1 cup raspberries

Mixed Fruit Compote

Yield: 6 servings • Prep Time: 15 minutes • Cooking Time: 35 minutes

The mellow, sweet taste of Chinese licorice root (available in natural foods stores) penetrates the rich broth in this soup and provides an interesting contrast to the crisp bite of fresh apples.

1. Scrub the oranges well under cold water. Slice 2 of the oranges into 1/2-inch-thick rounds and place them in a 3-quart saucepan. Squeeze and strain the juice from the remaining oranges. Measure the juice and add enough water to equal 8 cups, then add this to the saucepan with lemon juice. Stir in the dried fruit, rice syrup, licorice root and ginger.

2. Bring the soup to a boil, stirring often. Cover and reduce to a simmer, then cook, stirring occasionally, for 35 minutes. Remove the soup from the heat and stir in the calvados. Refrigerate, covered, for at least 24 hours. The soup may be prepared up to 5 days in advance to this point. Just before serving, dice the apple and stir it into the soup, then ladle into individual serving bowls.

Variation

1. Serve each portion garnished with a dollop of mascarpone cheese or crème fraîche (page 34) and sprinkle freshly grated nutmeg on top.

6 seedless oranges
2 tablespoons lemon juice
10 dried figs (calamyrna or
   Turkish, if available)
2/3 cup Thompson raisins
4 prunes, pitted and quartered
1/2 cup dried Turkish apricots
1/2 cup dried apple slices,
   chopped
1/2 cup golden raisins
1/2 cup rice syrup (page 172)
1 3-inch piece Chinese licorice
   root (or substitute 1 1/2
   tablespoons chopped licorice
   root, tied in a square of cheese
   cloth)
1 tablespoon minced ginger
1/3 cup calvados or Jamaican rum

GARNISH:
2 fresh apples, cut in small dice

Grand Marnier Surprise

Yield: 6 servings • Prep Time: 25 minutes • Cooking Time: 1 hour

1/3 cup hulled millet
2 1/2 cups water
1 1/2 cups orange juice
1 1/2 teaspoons minced ginger
1/2 cup chopped dried
    calamyrna figs
1/3 cup maple syrup
2 tablespoons Grand Marnier
    (optional)

GARNISH:
1 orange
18 whole dried calamyrna figs
2 1/4-inch slices ginger root
3 cups water
2 cups orange juice
1/2 cup maple syrup
2 tablespoons Grand Marnier
    (optional)

A creamy, pale yellow soup made from millet which is simmered in orange juice. Poached figs are arranged in each bowl over the soup with candied orange peel sprinkled over top.

1. Rinse the millet well. In a 2-quart saucepan, bring 2 1/2 cups of water and 1 1/2 cups of orange juice to a boil. Stir in the millet, minced ginger, chopped figs and 1/3 cup maple syrup. Reduce to a simmer and cook, covered and stirring occasionally, until the millet is very tender, about 55 minutes. Cool.

2. Purée the soup in a food processor or blender, then press the purée through a fine-mesh strainer. Reserve the thick liquid in a mixing bowl and discard the grainy bits of fig and millet that remain in the strainer. Add 2 tablespoons Grand Marnier. The soup may be prepared ahead and refrigerated in an airtight container for up to 5 days. Gently rewarm before serving.

3. To finish preparing the soup, wash and dry the garnish orange. With a swivel-bladed peeler, peel very thin strips from the orange. Stack the strips on top of each other, orange side up, and shred them finely. Place the shredded orange and whole figs in a 2-quart saucepan. Squeeze the juice from the orange and strain it into the saucepan. Add the water and maple syrup. Bring this to a boil, then reduce to a simmer and cook, stirring occasionally, until the liquid is syrupy and the strips of peel are tender, about 25 to 30 minutes. Remove from the heat and stir in the remaining Grand Marnier. Strain the syrup into the warm soup and whisk to combine. Divide the soup among serving bowls, arrange figs in the bowls and sprinkle shredded orange over the figs. The syrup may also be prepared and refrigerated in an airtight container for up to 5 days, but the figs and peel must be kept in the syrup, so do not strain the syrup and add it to the soup until just before serving.

Papaya Lime Soup

Yield: 4 servings • Prep Time: 15 minutes • Cooking Time: 20 minutes

1/2 cup dried rose petals
4 cups water
2 teaspoons lime zest
3 tablespoons maple sugar
    (page 171)
1 1/4 cups chopped dried papaya
1/4 cup lime juice
1 1/2 pounds ripe papaya
    (about 5 cups meat)
2 tablespoons rose flower water
    (page 169)

GARNISH:
1 to 2 limes
Maple Lime Pastry Cups
    (page 158)

Lime's tartness tempers the rich, sometimes overpowering, taste of papaya. Dried rose petals, used in teas and other culinary concoctions, add an interesting dimension to this smooth soup. Dried petals are available in most natural foods stores. If you find them from another source, check to be certain that the fresh flowers were not sprayed with pesticides.

1. In a 2-quart saucepan, combine the rose petals, water, lime zest, maple sugar and dried papaya. Bring to a boil, then reduce to a simmer and cover. Cook, stirring occasionally, for 20 minutes. Stir in the lime juice and transfer to a storage container. Cool to room temperature, then cover and refrigerate overnight or up to 2 days.

2. Halve the fresh papaya. Scrape out and discard the seeds, then peel the fruit and cut it into small cubes. Place 4 cups of fruit in a food processor or blender and refrigerate the rest in a small airtight container. Purée the fruit, scraping down the sides of the bowl as necessary until the papaya is absolutely smooth. Transfer the purée to a mixing bowl.

3. Strain the soup broth and discard the solids. Whisk the liquid into the purée, then stir in the reserved papaya and rose flower water. Taste the soup and add additional lime juice or maple syrup if necessary.

4. Wash the garnish lime well and dry it. With a zester or sharp paring knife, peel thin and narrow strips from the lime and form them into twists. Cut the lime into wedges. Serve the soup in individual serving bowls (or Maple Lime Pastry Cups) with a twist and wedge of lime floating in the center.

Peaches and Cream

Yield: 6 servings • Prep Time: 25 minutes • Cooking Time: 8 minutes

This rich, velvety soup can be eaten as is in small quantities or used as a soup base in which fresh fruit are floated just before serving.

1. Peel and slice the peaches. Place them in a bowl and sprinkle with the lemon juice and 3 tablespoons of maple sugar. Toss to coat, cover and set aside while preparing the soup.

2. In a medium-sized mixing bowl, whisk together the egg yolks and remaining maple sugar. Rinse out, but do not dry, a heavy-bottomed, 2-quart saucepan. (This will help prevent a film from forming on the inside of the pan as the milk cooks.) Add the vanilla bean, then scald the milk. Immediately pour the milk into the egg yolks, whisking constantly. (Leave the vanilla in the pan.) Return the egg mixture to the saucepan and cook it over low heat, stirring constantly with a wooden spoon, until it lightly coats the back of the spoon. (When you draw your finger across the back of the spoon, the line should remain visible.) As you stir the soup, be careful to use a gentle motion so as not to cause bubbles to form on the surface, which will make it difficult to judge the consistency of the soup. Do not allow the soup to boil or the egg yolks will curdle. When the soup thickens, immediately pour it through a fine-mesh strainer into a mixing bowl. Scrape the seeds from the vanilla bean into the soup, then stir in the rum and allow the soup to cool to room temperature, stirring occasionally.

3. Finely purée half of the peaches in a food mill or processor. Whisk the purée and orange juice into the soup. Stir in the remaining sliced peaches, saving a few to garnish each bowl. Chill the soup, covered, until ready to serve. The soup may be prepared to this point up to 2 days in advance if refrigerated in an airtight container. Serve the soup garnished with a dollop of crème fraîche and slices of peaches in the center. Sprinkle date sugar and pine nuts over the cream and serve.

2 pounds fresh peaches
2 tablespoons lemon juice
2/3 cup maple sugar (page 171)
3 egg yolks
1 vanilla bean
3 cups milk
1 tablespoon Jamaican dark rum (optional)
1 cup orange or unfiltered apple juice

GARNISH:
1/4 cup crème fraîche (page 34) or plain nonfat yogurt
2 tablespoons date sugar (page 168) or maple sugar (page 171)
2 tablespoons toasted pine nuts (optional)

Variations

1. Replace the peaches with nectarines or apricots.
2. For a dairy-free version, omit the eggs and replace the milk with soy milk. To make the cream base, combine the soy milk, maple sugar and vanilla bean in a small saucepan. Dissolve 1 tablespoon cornstarch in 2 tablespoons cold water and stir this into the soy milk. Bring just to a boil, whisking constantly, then strain into a mixing bowl. Scrape in the vanilla seeds, add the rum and continue with the recipe as above.

Satsuma Squeeze

Yield: 8 servings • Prep Time: 25 minutes • Cooking Time: 25 minutes

The intense flavor of tangerines balances like magic with the unusual combination of tastes found in this soup. It was inspired by a tangerine-based hors d'oeuvre I once ran across in Memphis, Tennessee.

5 honey tangerines
6 satsuma tangerines or
    clementines (or other small,
    sweet tangerines)
1/2 cup honey
1 teaspoon minced ginger
2/3 cup water
2 tablespoons rosemary,
    crushed
1/4 cup Jamaican dark rum
2 tablespoons cider vinegar
2 teaspoons soy sauce

GARNISH:
1 small sprig rosemary

1. Wash the honey tangerines well and dry them. Using a swivel-bladed peeler, remove thin strips of the zest, avoiding the white pith as much as possible. Stack the pieces of peel and shred them into matchstick-sized strips. Place them in a saucepan.

2. Halve the honey tangerines and juice them. Measure the juice and add water if necessary to equal 4 cups. Strain the juice into the pan with the zest. Add the honey, ginger and water, then bring the soup to a boil. Wrap the rosemary in a small square of cheesecloth and tie the bundle shut with a piece of kitchen twine. Add this to the soup, then reduce to a simmer and cook, uncovered, stirring occasionally, until the zest is very tender, about 25 minutes.

3. Meanwhile, peel and section the satsumas. (It is more elegant, but not necessary, to remove the membrane from around the sections.) Place them in a large mixing bowl.

4. When the zest is tender, stir the rum, vinegar and soy sauce into the soup. Pour this over the sectioned tangerines and refrigerate 24 to 48 hours, turning occasionally. Just before serving, remove the rosemary from the soup. Ladle broth and fruit into serving bowls and garnish with a tiny sprig of rosemary.

Raspberry Banana Soup

Yield: 6 servings • Prep Time: 15 minutes

A simple and refreshing soup that serves equally well as a sweet first course or a dessert. You may use frozen, unsweetened raspberries for this soup. They are available year-round and are often less expensive than fresh.

5 cups raspberries
2 large, ripe bananas
1 cup apple juice
6 tablespoons rice syrup
    (page 172)
3 cups nonfat yogurt
3 tablespoons kirsch
2 tablespoons lime juice
1/2 cup crème fraîche (page 34)
    or additional yogurt

1. Rinse the raspberries, then place them in a plastic bag. Seal the bag shut, then freeze. Peel the bananas and place them in a separate plastic bag, and freeze. When all of the fruit is frozen solid, proceed with the recipe. This step may be executed up to 10 days in advance of continuing with the recipe.

2. Thaw the fruit for 10 minutes at room temperature. Place the raspberries in a blender or food processor with half of the apple juice and purée until smooth. Add 1/4 cup of rice syrup, the yogurt and kirsch. Blend thoroughly and transfer to a bowl. Rinse out the blender beaker.

3. Cut the bananas into 1-inch pieces and place them in the blender with the remaining rice syrup and apple juice, the lime juice and crème fraîche or additional yogurt. Blend until smooth. Taste each purée and adjust the sweetness if necessary.

4. To serve, hold the raspberry mixture over the top edge of the serving bowl and the banana mixture over the bottom edge of the bowl. Begin pouring both raspberry and banana mixtures into the bowl simultaneously, and as you do so, move the banana mixture up to the top of the bowl on the right-hand side of the bowl, and the strawberry mixture down to the bottom of the bowl on the left-hand side. A sort of "Yin Yang" pattern will occur in the bowl. To complete the design you may wish to place a raspberry in the top and bottom "eyes" of the pattern. Serve immediately. The soup is best prepared and eaten immediately.

Midnight Sun

Yield: 6 servings • Prep Time: 20 minutes • Cooking Time: 7 minutes

Star anise and almonds combine for a subtle undertone to complement the penetrating taste of blueberries. The soup is ideal in midsummer when fresh blueberries are at their peak.

2 pints blueberries (4 cups)
2 cups fresh orange juice
2/3 cup date sugar (page 168)
4 pieces star anise
1/4 cup sliced almonds
1/2 cup water, milk or soy milk

GARNISH:
1 apple, peeled and sliced

1. Pick over the blueberries to remove all stems, debris and any berries that are overly soft. Transfer the rest of the blueberries to a strainer and rinse well. Place them in a 4-quart saucepan. Add the orange juice, sugar and star anise. Stir and bring to a boil. Reduce heat to low and simmer, stirring occasionally, for 5 minutes. Cover, remove from heat, and cool to room temperature.

2. Place the almonds and 1/4 cup of water (milk or soy milk) in a blender. Blend for about 30 seconds. Gradually add the remaining liquid and continue to blend until the nuts are very finely ground, about 8 minutes. Scrape down the sides of the blender beaker several times so the mixture is evenly blended. Pour this "nut milk" into a large bowl and set aside.

3. Remove the star anise from the saucepan and pour the blueberries into the blender and blend until smooth, about 1 minute. Rub the fruit purée through a fine-mesh strainer into the almond milk. (This step may be omitted, resulting in a slightly less smooth-textured soup.)

4. Chill the soup thoroughly before tasting for sweetness. Depending on the rest of the menu and your personal taste, you may wish to add up to 3 tablespoons more date sugar to the finished soup. If this is the case, warm 1/2 cup of soup with the additional sugar until the sugar is completely dissolved. Return this to the remaining soup and chill. Ladle into small individual serving bowls and garnish with a slice of apple.

Cherry Sunrise

Yield: 6 servings • Prep Time: 20 minutes • Cooking Time: 15 minutes

6 cups bing cherries
2 cups fresh orange juice
2/3 cup maple sugar (page 171)
1/2 teaspoon nutmeg
1 1/4 cups hazelnuts
1 1/4 cups water
6 ripe pears

GARNISH:
6 sprigs fresh mint

Two rich ingredients, cherries and hazelnuts, team up for a deliciously memorable effect. Slices of pear, arranged as a fan on the surface of the soup, accent the light purple hue of this cherry purée.

1. Pick over the cherries to remove all stems, debris and any that are overly soft. Transfer the rest of the cherries to a strainer and rinse well, then pit them (or use frozen sweet cherries). Place them in a 4-quart saucepan. Add the orange juice, sugar and nutmeg. Stir and bring to a boil. Reduce heat to low and simmer, stirring occasionally, for 10 minutes. Cover, remove from heat, and cool to room temperature.

2. Preheat the oven to 375°F. Place the hazelnuts on a baking sheet and toast until brown to the core, about 12 minutes. Transfer them immediately to a clean kitchen towel and rub with the towel to remove the skins. Place the nuts and 1/2 cup of water in a blender. Blend for about 30 seconds. Gradually add the remaining water and continue to blend until the nuts are very finely ground, about 8 minutes. Scrape down the sides of the blender beaker several times so the mixture is evenly blended. Pour this "nut milk" into a large bowl and set aside.

3. When the cherries have cooled, pour them into the blender. Blend until smooth, about 1 minute. Rub the cherries through a fine-mesh strainer into the hazelnut milk. Mix well and refrigerate, covered, for at least 2 hours or up to 5 days.

4. Just before serving, quarter, core and peel the pears. Cut the quarters lengthwise into thin slices, keeping the slices nestled together in quarters. Ladle the soup into shallow serving bowls and fan the pear slices over the soup. Garnish each bowl with a sprig of mint.

Tapioca Sweet Corn Soup

Yield: 6 servings • Prep Time: 25 minutes • Cooking Time: 20 minutes

1/3 cup instant tapioca
3 cups water
1/4 teaspoon salt
1/2 cup golden raisins
3 cups coconut milk (page 37)
1/3 cup maple syrup
    or 1/2 cup rice syrup (page 172)
2 ears fresh sweet corn
1 1/2 cups pitted sweet cherries

GARNISH:
1/4 cup grated fresh coconut,
    toasted
1/4 cup slivered almonds
    (page 33), toasted

This is a takeoff on the traditional Thai soup made with corn and sago, a tapioca-like root starch. Though frozen corn may be used, I think it is best to save this unusual soup for a hot summer's evening when fresh sweet corn, cut straight from the cob, is available. You may serve it as a light first course (in which case use rice syrup as the sweetener and reduce the amount to 1/4 cup).

1. Combine the tapioca, water, salt and raisins in a 2-quart saucepan. Bring this to a boil, then reduce to a simmer and cook, stirring occasionally, until the tapioca is soft, about 20 minutes. Stir in the coconut milk, maple syrup and corn. Continue to cook for 3 minutes or until the corn has just had time to plump.

2. Remove the soup from the heat and cool to room temperature. Halve the cherries and divide them among serving bowls. Ladle soup into each bowl and garnish with a sprinkling of toasted coconut and almonds.

Carrot Date Soup

Yield: 6 servings • Prep Time: 25 minutes • Cooking Time: 1 hour

Carrots, which are often used as a sweet in India, are the base for this thick, cardamom spiked soup. It may be served warm or at room temperature and, for dessert, is nice garnished with Maple Lime Snaps (page 158).

1. Peel and grate the carrots. In a 2-quart saucepan, combine the milk, ginger, cinnamon and dates. Wrap the cardamom pods in a square of cheesecloth and tie the bundle shut. Add it to the pan and bring the liquid to a boil. Stir in the carrots and reduce to a simmer. Stir in the molasses and maple syrup, then cook, stirring occasionally, until the carrots are very tender, about 1 1/2 hours.

2. Remove the soup from the heat. Stir in the vanilla, lime zest and juice, then cover and set aside for 20 minutes. Remove and discard the cardamom. Transfer the soup to a food processor or blender and purée it until it is very smooth. Press the purée through a fine-mesh strainer. Discard the 1/4 to 1/3 cup of solids that will not go through the strainer. In a small mixing bowl combine the yogurt and maple syrup for the garnish. Serve the soup in individual bowls with a dollop of sweetened yogurt in the center.

1 pound carrots
4 cups milk or rice milk
   (page 172)
1/2 teaspoon minced ginger root
1/4 teaspoon ground cinnamon
1/3 cup chopped pitted dates
1 teaspoon cardamom pods,
   crushed
3 tablespoons molasses
4 tablespoons maple syrup
2 teaspoons vanilla
1 teaspoon grated lime zest
1 tablespoon lime juice

GARNISH:
1/2 cup plain nonfat yogurt
1 tablespoon maple syrup

Variations

1. Substitute 2 cups milk and 2 cups cashew milk (page 34) for the milk in the recipe above. Replace the lime zest and juice with orange and serve the soup warm, topped with chopped toasted cashews.

2. For a savory version, replace the milk called for above with 2 cups of light vegetable stock and 2 cups of milk. Add 1/2 teaspoon of salt to the carrots as they cook. Proceed with the recipe as above, and serve topped with Corn Bread squares (page 148).

Spiced Yam Soup

Yield: 4 servings • Prep Time: 20 minutes • Cooking Time: 2 hours

1 1/2 pounds garnet yams
1/3 cup dried apples, chopped
1/2 cup unfiltered apple juice
1 teaspoon ground cinnamon
1/2 teaspoon minced ginger root
1/4 teaspoon ground nutmeg
1/8 teaspoon ground allspice
1/8 teaspoon ground cloves
1 lemon
3 cups milk or soy milk
3 to 4 tablespoons maple syrup

GARNISH:
1/3 cup pecans, toasted (page 33)
    and chopped

Garnet yams, which are high in natural sugar, become extremely sweet—caramelized—when baked until very soft. Here they serve as the base for a spicy dessert soup.

1. Preheat the oven to 450ºF. Wash the yams under cold water, scrubbing them well with a vegetable brush to remove all dirt. Place them on a baking sheet in the center of the oven. After 30 minutes, reduce the heat to 375ºF and continue to bake until the yams are extremely soft when squeezed, about 1 1/4 hours. Remove the yams from the oven and cool. They may be prepared up to 5 days in advance if refrigerated in a loosely folded plastic bag.

2. As the yams cook, combine the dried apples and the apple juice. Set this aside until the apples are very tender. Drain the apples, reserving the juice. Place them in a food processor or blender with the cinnamon, ginger, nutmeg, allspice and cloves. Grate the zest from the lemon and add this to the processor along with the juice from the lemon. Peel the cooked yams and place their meat in the processor as well. Purée this mixture, scraping the sides of the bowl down until it is very smooth.

3. Transfer the purée to a large mixing bowl and whisk in the reserved apple juice, milk and maple syrup. Taste and add more lemon juice or syrup if desired. Serve cold or at room temperature sprinkled with pecans.

Variations

1. Grind 3/4 cup toasted pecans in a blender into an even-textured nut butter. Just before serving, whisk 1/4 cup of warm soup into the nut butter, then stir this back into the soup and serve warm.

2. Poke a slightly green banana several times with the tines of a fork. Place it on the baking sheet next to the yams and bake until very soft, about 40 minutes. Remove the banana from the oven to cool. Peel the banana and purée it with the yam. Proceed with the recipe as above.

Butternut Squash Soup

Yield: 6 servings • Prep Time: 25 minutes • Cooking Time: 1 hour

1 2-pound butternut or
    delicata squash (about 4
    cups, grated)
3 tablespoons butter
6 tablespoons maple syrup
2 tablespoons finely minced
    candied ginger
1 1/2 teaspoon ground cinnamon
1/4 teaspoon ground nutmeg

This filling soup is somewhere between a thick porridge and a soup. It can be served as an end to a light meal in midwinter, or as a side dish, prepared with half the maple syrup.

1. Halve the squash, then scrape out and discard all seeds and stringy membrane. Peel the squash and grate it on a large-holed surface of a grater. You should have about 4 cups. Heat the butter in a 2-quart saucepan over moderate heat. Add the squash, 2 tablespoons maple syrup, ginger, cinnamon, nutmeg and cloves. Cook gently, stirring frequently, until the squash begins to soften, about 12 minutes. Stir in the raisins and water. Cover and simmer for 1 hour, stirring often.

2. After the soup has been cooking for 45 minutes prepare the remaining ingredients. In a small mixing bowl, combine 1/4 cup of the milk and the crushed kuzu. Mix to blend and set aside. In a small saucepan, combine the remaining milk and maple syrup with the vanilla bean. Simmer gently, stirring occasionally, for 15 minutes. Stir the kuzu mixture and add it to the milk. Bring just to a boil, then remove it from the heat. When the vanilla bean is cool enough to handle, scrape the seeds into the milk and discard the pod.

3. When the soup is cooked, remove it from the heat and mix in the milk mixture. Allow the soup to cool and serve it lukewarm or at room temperature, garnished with a dollop of yogurt if desired.

1/8 teaspoon ground cloves
3/4 cup raisins
2 1/2 cups water
1 1/2 cups milk or soy milk
2 1/2 tablespoons kuzu (page 170)
1/2 vanilla bean, split
1 cup nonfat yogurt or low-fat sour cream (optional)

Hidden Jewel Cardamom Soup

Yield: 6 servings • Prep Time: 20 minutes • Cooking Time: 50 minutes

Sweet rice is a short-grain, sticky rice that is available both brown and white. Both are nice and work well in this recipe. The first is sweeter, but more "rustic" in texture and appearance. The soup may be served as a smooth purée, or you may omit Step 3 and serve it as a thick pudding. In either case, it is a soothing and filling dessert.

1. Rinse the rice well. In a 2-quart saucepan, bring the water to a boil. Stir in the rice, ginger, cardamom and cinnamon. Reduce the soup to a simmer and cook, covered, stirring occasionally, until the rice is very tender, about 50 minutes.

2. Add the milk, chopped dates, rice syrup and vanilla bean to the rice and continue to simmer, stirring often, for 40 minutes. Remove from the heat and cool. Lift the vanilla bean from the soup and scrape the seeds into the rice. Discard the pod.

3. Purée the soup to a medium-fine texture in a food processor or blender. Taste and adjust the seasonings. The soup may be prepared up to 3 days in advance if refrigerated in an airtight container.

4. Using the tip of a paring knife, make a short, lengthwise slice along the side of each whole date. Remove and discard the pits. Cream the mascarpone or cream cheese and stir in the rum. Stuff the dates with the cheese filling, then squeeze the slit edges of each date together to seal. Place the dates in a 2-quart saucepan and cover with the soup. Simmer for 5 minutes, occasionally stirring gently to prevent the dates from sticking to the bottom of the pan. Spoon one date into each soup bowl, then top with soup. Sprinkle a small amount of cinnamon in the center of each bowl. Serve warm or at room temperature.

1/3 cup sweet brown rice
4 cups water
1 teaspoon minced ginger
2 teaspoons ground cardamom
1/2 teaspoon cinnamon
3 cups milk or rice milk (page 172)
1/2 cup chopped pitted dates (medjool, if available)
1/2 cup rice syrup
1 vanilla bean, split

GARNISH:
6 whole dates (medjool, if available)
4 tablespoons mascarpone cheese or cream cheese
2 tablespoons rum (optional)

Creamy Lemon and Barley Soup

Yield: 6 servings • Prep Time: 10 minutes • Cooking Time: 1 1/4 hours

1/2 cup pearl barley
4 3/4 cups water
2 lemons
3/4 to 1 cup maple sugar
(page 171)
1/2 cup dried cranberries or
cherries
3 tablespoons orange flower
water (page 169)

This sweet barley soup has a tangy lemon undertone that is sweetened with maple sugar. Dried cranberries or cherries give an accent of color and flavor to this naturally thick soup.

1. Rinse the barley in several changes of cold water. In a 3-quart saucepan, bring 4 cups of water to a boil. Stir in the barley and reduce to a simmer. Cook, covered, stirring occasionally, until the barley is tender, about 45 minutes.

2. Wash and dry the lemons. Grate the zest from both lemons, using a grating surface that gives tiny, delicate strands, if possible. Squeeze the juice from the lemons and strain it into the cooked barley. Stir in the zest, maple sugar, dried cranberries and remaining water. Continue to simmer, stirring often, for 10 minutes. Remove from the heat and stir in the orange water. Transfer to a storage container and refrigerate, covered, until cold. The soup may be prepared up to 5 days in advance if refrigerated in an airtight container.

Plum Passion

Yield: 6 servings • Prep Time: 20 minutes • Cooking Time: 20 minutes

3/4 cup pitted prunes
1/4 cup Armagnac brandy
4 cups pitted blood or elephant
plums
2 cups fresh apple juice
1/2 cup maple sugar (page 171)
1/2 cup raw cashews
2/3 cup water, milk or soy milk
1/2 to 3/4 cup milk or amasake
(page 167) (optional)

The classic combination of prunes and Armagnac are lightened with the addition of blood plums and cashew milk.

1. Chop the prunes roughly and combine them with the Armagnac in a small bowl. Set this aside for at least 24 hours to soak in the flavor. Before continuing with the recipe, drain the prunes, saving their soaking juices.

2. Place the prunes and plums in a 4-quart saucepan. Add the apple juice and sugar. Stir and bring to a boil. Reduce heat to low and simmer, stirring occasionally, for 20 minutes. Cover, remove from heat, and cool to room temperature.

3. Place the cashews with the 2/3 cup water in a blender and blend until very smooth, about 5 minutes. Add the plum mixture and continue to purée until very smooth, about 3 minutes. Stir the reserved soaking liquid into the soup and chill the soup thoroughly, tasting for sweetness. If you wish to add more maple sugar, warm 1/2 cup of soup with the additional sugar until the sugar is completely dissolved. Return this to the remaining soup and chill. Just before serving stir in the milk enrichment if desired.

Raspberry Cream Cordial

Yield: 6 servings • Prep Time: 20 minutes

You may use frozen, unsweetened raspberries for this soup. They are available year-round and are often less expensive than fresh. In the peak of summer, though, when raspberries are readily available, it is well worth the splurge to use fresh berries.

1. Place the raspberries in a strainer and rinse very quickly and gently under cold running water. Pick out about 1/2 cup of the best berries for a garnish and set them aside on a clean kitchen towel, in one layer, to dry. Place the rest of the berries in a blender or food processor and purée thoroughly. Rub the puréed berries through a fine-mesh strainer into a mixing bowl and set this aside.

2. Place the sliced almonds in the blender with 3/4 cup of milk. Blend for about 5 minutes, adding additional milk if necessary to make a very smooth consistency. As the nut milk blends, you will need to scrape down the sides of the blender beaker from time to time, to insure that the nuts grind evenly. Transfer to a storage container, stir in the fruit purée, 3 tablespoons rice syrup, almond extract, 1 tablespoon Eau de Vie (optional) and the remaining milk. Cover and refrigerate.

3. In a small saucepan, combine the agar and water. Bring this to a boil, then simmer, stirring often until the agar is dissolved, about 10 minutes. Stir this into the soup and chill for at least 2 hours or up to 2 days.

4. To serve the soup, place the reserved raspberries in a small bowl and sprinkle them with 2 tablespoons of Eau de Vie (optional). Refrigerate for 30 minutes. Just before serving, beat the cream until slightly thickened. Add the remaining rice syrup and continue to beat until thick enough to hold a soft peak. Ladle the soup into individual bowls and garnish with whole berries, toasted almonds and rosettes of cream. Serve immediately.

4 cups raspberries
1/2 cup sliced almonds
3 cups soy milk or milk
5 tablespoons rice syrup
  (page 172)
2 teaspoons almond extract
1 to 3 tablespoons Eau de Vie de
  Framboise (optional)
1 1/2 tablespoons agar flakes
  (page 167)
1/4 cup water
1/3 cup heavy cream or yogurt

GARNISH:
2 tablespoons slivered almonds,
  toasted
Cream

Orzo Almond Soup with Raspberries

Yield: 6 servings • Prep Time: 5 minutes • Cooking Time: 20 minutes

This light pasta soup is bursting with the complementary flavors and aromas of almonds and raspberries.

1. In a 3-quart saucepan bring the water to a boil. Add the salt, maple syrup and orzo. Return to a boil and cook, stirring occasionally, until the pasta is soft, about 15 minutes.

2. Meanwhile, place the almonds in a blender with 1 cup of milk. Blend until very smooth, then gradually add the remaining milk and continue to blend until very finely ground, about 8 minutes. Pour the almond milk into a mixing bowl.

3. When the orzo is cooked, stir in the almond milk. Remove from the heat and stir in the amasaki and Amaretto, then cool to room temperature or refrigerate, covered, for up to 5 days.

4. Just before serving, stir the raspberries into the soup. Taste for sweetness and adjust with the addition of maple syrup if necessary. Ladle the soup into serving bowls and garnish with a sprinkling of toasted almonds.

4 cups water
1/2 teaspoon salt
3 tablespoons maple syrup
1/3 cup orzo (Greek rice-shaped
  pasta)
2 cups sliced almonds
1 3/4 cups milk
1 1/4 cups plain amasake
  (page 167)
2 tablespoons Amaretto
1 pint fresh raspberries

GARNISH:
1/4 cup slivered almonds, toasted
  (page 33)

Sangria Soup

Yield: 6 servings • Prep Time: 25 minutes • Cooking Time: 25 minutes

6 seedless oranges
3 cups water
2/3 cup honey
2 teaspoons anise seeds, crushed
3 blood oranges or honey
   tangerines
2 teaspoons vanilla
4 cups orange juice
1 cup dry red wine
2 tablespoons lime juice
3 tablespoons Grand Marnier
3 peaches, sliced
2 apricots, sliced
1 cup sliced strawberries

On a hot summer's evening this is the perfect finish to a Mediterranean-style meal. The soup is only reminiscent of a true sangria. The type and quality of wine used will alter the flavor notably, so choose one that suits your taste and does not conflict with other foods served in the menu.

1. Wash the oranges well, scrubbing their skins thoroughly. Slice 2 of them into 1/2-inch-thick rounds. Place them in a 4-quart saucepan and cover with water. Add the honey and anise seed, cover and bring to a boil. Reduce to a simmer, cover and cook, stirring occasionally, until the orange skins are tender, about 20 minutes. Remove from the heat.

2. Peel the blood oranges and the remaining seedless oranges. Section each and, if desired, peel the membrane from each section. Add all of these to the soup. Stir in the vanilla, orange juice, wine, lime juice, Grand Marnier, peaches and apricots. Transfer the soup to a storage container, cover and refrigerate overnight. Two hours before serving, stir in the strawberries. Serve in chilled goblets.

7 • Finishing Touches

Pear Biscuits

Yield: 24 biscuits • Prep Time: 15 minutes • Cooking Time: 18 minutes

These flaky biscuits are made rich and moist with the addition of pear butter. They are equally good with savory soups as they are with desserts.

1 cup + 1 tablespoon whole wheat flour
1 cup + 1 tablespoon unbleached white flour
2 teaspoons non-aluminum baking powder
1/2 teaspoon salt
6 tablespoons butter, chilled
2/3 cup pear butter
2 to 3 tablespoons soy milk

1. Preheat the oven to 400°F. In a small mixing bowl, combine the flours, baking powder and salt. Cut the butter into small pieces and, with your finger tips or using two knives, work it into the flour until the mixture resembles coarse meal.

2. Make a well in the center of the flour. Place the pear butter and 3 tablespoons of milk in the well. Quickly stir in the flour, working just until the dough forms a sticky ball. If necessary add an additional tablespoon of milk.

3. Immediately turn the dough out onto a lightly floured work surface. Sprinkle flour on top, then pat the dough out to about 1/2 inch thickness. Fold it in half, then rotate the dough 90 degrees. Repeat this patting, rolling and turning step 3 more times, dusting with flour as needed.

4. Pat out the dough so that it is about 1 inch thick. Cut it into 1 1/2-inch rounds. Reform the scraps into one piece and cut them as well. To shape, rotate each biscuit in a circle between the thumb and pointing finger of one hand. Stabilize the biscuit by holding the top and bottom with your other hand. The shaped biscuit should be about 1 inch high with a small depression in the center. Place the biscuits almost touching in a shallow baking pan. Bake until slightly puffed, lightly browned around the edges, and cooked through, about 15 minutes. Turn out upside down onto a cake rack and serve immediately. The biscuits may be prepared ahead and refrigerated in an airtight container for 24 hours. Rewarm before serving.

Variation

1. For a sweet potato biscuit, substitute 1 cup puréed sweet potato for the pear butter and reduce the flour by 2 tablespoons.

Corn Bread

Yield: 16 large or 36 small pieces • Prep Time: 10 minutes • Cooking Time: 12 to 20 minutes (depending on size)

1 cup yellow cornmeal
1/2 cup unbleached white flour
1/2 cup whole wheat flour
1/2 teaspoon salt
1/2 teaspoon non-aluminum
  baking powder (optional)
4 tablespoons butter
1 to 2 eggs
3 tablespoons maple syrup
1 cup milk or buttermilk

Corn bread makes an ideal accompaniment to many soups because of its light interesting texture and slightly sweet taste. It may be baked in a shallow baking dish then cut into diamonds or other shapes, or it may be baked in miniature or large muffin tins. You may use various different flours (see the variations) and may make the corn bread dairy-free by substituting tofu for the eggs and soy or rice milk for the milk.

1. Preheat the oven to 400°F. In a large mixing bowl, combine the cornmeal, flour, salt and baking powder. Stir well and set aside.

2. Place the butter in a 9-inch square or 9- x 13-inch baking pan and put this in the oven to melt. In a small mixing bowl beat together the eggs, maple syrup and milk until very frothy. Pour as much of the melted butter from the baking pan as comes out, without scraping the pan, into the egg mixture. Spread the remaining butter over the bottom and sides of the pan.

3. Stir the egg mixture into the dry ingredients and mix until they are just combined. Pour this into the prepared pan and bake in the center of the oven until the corn bread is lightly browned and has begun to pull away from the edges of the pan (12 to 20 minutes, depending on the size of the pan). A toothpick inserted in the center will come out clean. Remove from the oven and cool for at least 5 minutes before cutting. Cut the corn bread into squares, triangles, diamonds or other shapes. The corn bread may be baked ahead and refrigerated in a plastic bag up to 24 hours before using. It does not freeze well. Rewarm before serving.

Variations

1. Substitute 1 1/2 cups spelt flour for the whole wheat and 3/4 cup rice flour for the white flour.

2. For a dairy-free version, substitute 8 ounces puréed tofu for the eggs and 3 tablespoons vegetable oil for the butter. (The oil need not be heated in the oven before adding to the recipe.)

3. Sprinkle sesame seeds on the bottom and sides of the baking pan before pouring in the batter. Top the unbaked batter with sesame seeds.

4. Stir 2/3 cup freshly cut corn kernels and 1 to 3 tablespoons chopped canned chili peppers into the batter just before baking.

Garlic Croutons

Yield: About 4 cups • Prep Time: 5 minutes • Cooking Time: 15 minutes

As a child one of the few foods I relished was tomato soup—not so much for the taste of the soup itself as for the croutons my father would sprinkle on top. To this day I find good croutons irresistible. Variations on this basic recipe are limitless, incorporating spices and breads that complement virtually any soup.

10 1/2-inch-thick pieces bread
6 tablespoons butter or olive oil
2 cloves garlic
2 tablespoons minced parsley

1. Preheat the oven to 375°F. Place the bread on a clean work surface. Melt the butter in a small saucepan, then press the garlic through a garlic press into the butter. Reduce the heat to low and cook for 5 minutes to impregnate the butter with the garlic. Do not allow the garlic to turn brown and burn or it will become bitter. Remove the butter from the heat and stir in the parsley.

2. Using a pastry brush, paint the bread with the butter mixture then flip each slice and paint the other side. Stack the bread and cut it into cubes using a wavy-edged bread knife. Scatter the croutons in one layer on a baking sheet and place it in the oven. Bake, tossing the croutons once or twice as they cook, until lightly browned around the edges. Cool on the baking sheets and store in an airtight container until ready to use. The croutons may be prepared up to 10 days ahead.

Variations

1. Virtually any combination of seasonings and most breads or crackers can replace the ingredients called for here. For instance, croutons made from triangles of whole wheat tortilla brushed with melted butter and sprinkled with ground cumin and salt complement Black Bean Soup. Rice cakes brushed with garlic butter and sprinkled with Five-Spice Powder are a good complement to Onion Arame Soup, and sourdough bread sprinkled with grated Parmesan cheese and sesame seeds is good with Porcini Bouillon. Different breads and crackers cook more or less quickly, so check as you bake them to prevent burning.

2. You may also reduce the amount of fat used by half. If you do so, you must decrease the oven temperature to 300°F and increase the baking time to 35 minutes. These croutons do not have the same melt-in-the-mouth quality and may be less intensely flavored due to less butter, so stronger spices, such as cayenne or cinnamon, make good additions.

Cumin Scented Croutons

Yield: About 4 cups • Prep Time: 10 minutes • Cooking Time: 15 minutes

10 1/2-inch-thick slices bread
2 egg whites
3 tablespoons olive oil or
    melted butter
1 teaspoon minced garlic
2 teaspoons ground cumin
1/2 teaspoon salt
3 tablespoons minced cilantro
    or oregano

In this reduced fat version of the original, egg white replaces much of the fat used in traditional croutons. As with the previous recipe, most seasonings and spices can be added to these croutons so that they complement virtually any soup. Likewise, the variations suggested below can be used with the traditional crouton.

1. Preheat the oven to 375°F. Place the bread on a clean work surface. Beat the egg whites until frothy. Add the remaining ingredients and beat again to blend.

2. Using a pastry brush, paint the bread with the egg mixture then flip each slice and paint the other side. Stack the bread and cut it into cubes using a wavy-edged bread knife. Scatter the croutons in one layer on a lightly oiled baking sheet, then place it in the oven. Bake, tossing the croutons several times as they cook, until lightly browned around the edges, about 15 minutes. Immediately transfer the croutons to a cake rack to cool. Store in an airtight container, at room temperature, until ready to use. The croutons may be prepared up to 10 days ahead.

Variations

1. For sweet croutons to top dessert soups, beat together 2 egg whites, 1/4 cup maple sugar or 3 tablespoons barley malt powder, a pinch of salt and 2 tablespoons melted butter.

2. For a spicy sweet crouton, add 1 1/2 teaspoons of cinnamon to the previous variation. You may also add a combination of spices such as 1 teaspoon cinnamon, 1/4 teaspoon allspice and 1/8 teaspoon each of ground ginger and cloves.

3. Coconut croutons may be made either sweet or savory. For a dessert topping, add 3 tablespoons grated dried coconut, 3 tablespoons maple sugar, 1/2 teaspoon vanilla and 2 tablespoons melted butter to the egg whites before brushing the bread. For a savory version, use 3 tablespoons grated coconut, 2 teaspoons ground cumin, 1 teaspoon minced garlic, 1/2 teaspoon salt, 3 tablespoons of minced mint and 2 tablespoons melted butter.

Parmesan Cups

Yield: 24 small or 6 large cups • Prep Time: 15 minutes • Cooking Time: 15 to 20 minutes

6 slices bread
3 tablespoons butter, melted
3 tablespoons grated Parmesan

These cups, which make a simple and versatile bread garnish, are actually just shaped croutons. A miniature cup may be floated in the center of a soup as a crust to hold another garnish. Large cups can be used as serving bowls. The recipe requires two matching muffin tins so that the cups may be molded into one by the bottom of the other.

1. Preheat the oven to 375°F. Trim crusts from the bread. Using a rolling pin, slightly flatten the bread, then brush both sides of each slice with melted butter. Sprinkle Parmesan on one side.

2. For large cups, press each square of bread into a large muffin tin, Parmesan side down. The edges will stick up above the tip of the mold. Place another muffin tin on top and press to mold to the tin. Depending on the quality of the bread you use, you may need to begin pressing the cups in place with your fingers to be certain they do not tear. For miniature cups, quarter each slice of bread and press into miniature muffin tins. Again, press into place with a second set of tins (work in batches of 12, if necessary).

3. Leave the tins stacked and place them in the preheated oven. Bake for 8 minutes, or until the cups have firmed in shape. Remove the top tin and continue to bake until the cups are a golden brown, about 5 minutes.

Variation

1. Omit the Parmesan and add spices such as minced garlic, cinnamon and maple sugar, or cumin and salt to the butter before brushing on the bread.

Sweet Onion Crisps

Yield: About 2 cups • Prep Time: 5 minutes • Cooking Time: 35 minutes

Finely shredded onions tossed in oil then crisped in the oven make a delightful topping for almost any savory soup. I first saw the traditional Indian method of preparing these crisps—slow-cooked in deep fat—in a memorable cooking demonstration by Julie Sahni. Then, while living in India, I saw a woman prepare a similar recipe by partially sun-drying the onions. Here a slow oven and a small amount of oil results in a reduced-fat version of the original idea.

1 large sweet onion (Vidalia or
   Maui, if possible)
3 tablespoons light vegetable oil

1. Peel the onion, leaving it whole, but removing the papery skin as well as all tough outer layers of the meat. Using a very sharp cleaver or chef's knife, slice the onion paper-thin. Separate the slices into rings and place on a clean kitchen towel. Pat the rings to remove excess moisture, then spread them out into a thin layer and allow to rest at room temperature for 30 minutes.

2. Preheat the oven to 300°F. Lightly brush a baking sheet with oil, then transfer the onion rings to a mixing bowl and toss with the remaining oil. Place the baking sheet in the center of the oven and cook until the onions are evenly browned, about 35 minutes. As the onions cook, stir and toss them frequently so that they cook evenly. During the last 15 minutes of cooking this is particularly critical, as depending on the thickness, they may take slightly less or more time to cook. They will appear to be cooking at a rather slow pace, then suddenly they will burn if they are not watched carefully. Once browned, transfer them immediately to a cake rack to cool. If they brown unevenly, and some begin to burn before others are cooked (this will happen if they are not evenly sliced), remove those that are cooked, and allow the others to continue cooking. Cool the rings to room temperature. When they are crisp, use them immediately or store in an airtight container at room temperature for up to 3 days.

Spiced Sesame Crackers

Yield: 24 crackers • Prep Time: 20 minutes • Cooking Time: 20 minutes

2 tablespoons anise seed,
  crushed
6 tablespoons boiling water
1/3 cup rice flour
1/2 cup unbleached white flour
1/2 cup whole pastry wheat flour
1 teaspoon garlic powder
  (optional)
1/2 teaspoon salt
6 tablespoons butter, chilled
1 egg white
1/3 cup sesame seeds

These flaky, anise-scented crackers are quick and simple to prepare. Use them as a topping for chowders and light soups, or on the side with more substantial bean soups. The seed used may be varied to suit virtually any soup.

1. Place the anise seeds in a small bowl and pour the boiling water over them. Cover and allow them to steep until cooled to room temperature. Preheat the oven to 400°F.

2. In a mixing bowl, combine the rice and wheat flours with the garlic powder and salt. Stir to blend. Cut the butter into the flour and, with your fingertips or two knives, work the butter into the flour mixture until it is the texture of oatmeal. Strain the anise water and mix it into the flour, tossing until the mixture holds together. Form the dough into a ball and wrap it in wax paper and refrigerate for at least 20 minutes or up to 24 hours.

3. Beat the egg white until frothy. On a lightly floured work surface, roll the dough to about 1/4 inch thickness. Brush the dough with a thin coating of egg glaze and sprinkle sesame seeds on top. Cut the dough into rounds or other shapes and place them on the prepared baking sheet. Bake in the center of the preheated oven until they begin to brown around the edges, about 10 minutes. Alternatively, you may roll the dough into 1-inch balls, roll in sesame seeds, then place on the baking sheet and flatten with a fork before baking.

Variations

1. Omit the garlic powder and add 2 tablespoons maple sugar to the dry ingredients before working in the butter. Sprinkle with a combination of anise and sesame seeds.

2. Use whole cinnamon, cloves, and/or allspice in place of the anise to flavor the water.

3. With a flavored or plain dough, sprinkle cheese or freshly cracked black pepper on top before baking.

Toasted Corn Tortillas

Yield: 32 tortillas • Prep Time: 10 minutes • Cooking Time: 12 minutes

4 corn tortillas
4 tablespoons melted butter
1 teaspoon garlic powder
  (optional)
1 teaspoon date sugar (page 168)
  or maple sugar (page 171)
1/4 teaspoon salt

This simple recipe is essentially a crouton made from flat bread. It is a good solution if you are looking for a crisp garnish to complement a spicy soup—regardless of whether or not it has Southwestern or Mexican influence.

1. Preheat the oven to 375°F. Place the tortillas on a clean work surface. Combine the butter, garlic powder, sugar and salt. Brush the tortillas on both sides with the butter mixture. Stack the tortillas and cut each evenly into 8 pie-shaped wedges. Place the tortillas on a lightly oiled baking sheet.

2. Bake the tortillas until lightly browned around the edges, about 12 minutes. Remove them to a cake rack to cool. When completely cool, store them at room temperature in an airtight container. The tortillas may be prepared up to 5 days in advance. Warm them very briefly, for about 3 minutes, in a moderate oven before serving.

Variations

1. Use wheat tortillas instead of corn. Depending on the size of the wheat tortilla, you may need more of the butter mixture.

2. Select very thin whole wheat tortillas and simply bake them without any brushing. These are light and crisp, with very little fat.

3. Replace the tortillas with whole wheat chapatis. Use 5 tablespoons of butter and 1 tablespoon curry powder in addition to the garlic, sugar and salt listed above. (Most store-bought varieties are more like oil-free or low-fat tortillas rather than authentic fresh, puffy Indian chapatis. Nonetheless, they make a good accompaniment to soups as they are and can be used in this recipe quite effectively.)

Spinach Dumplings

Yield: 20 dumplings • Prep Time: 25 minutes • Cooking Time: 8 minutes

Light and slightly chewy, with a hint of walnut flavor, these dumplings are a very nice accompaniment to many simple puréed vegetable soups.

1/2 cup minced shallots or onion
1 tablespoon minced garlic
2 teaspoons butter or oil
1 egg or 5 ounces soft tofu
5 ounces frozen chopped spinach, thawed
1/4 cup toasted walnuts (see page 33)
Salt and pepper to taste
Pinch of nutmeg
1/2 cup flour

1. Sauté the shallots and garlic in the butter, stirring constantly, over medium-low heat until they are wilted, about 10 minutes. Remove them from the heat and set aside to cool.

2. Beat the egg lightly and set it aside (or drain the tofu thoroughly by gently squeezing it in a clean kitchen towel). Place the spinach on a clean kitchen towel, draw the corners of the towel together and twist the towel to extract as much liquid from the spinach as possible. Place the walnuts in a food processor or blender and chop them until fine. Add the spinach and shallots. Mix in the salt, pepper, nutmeg and egg or tofu. Process until smooth. Add enough flour to form a light but firm dough. The dough is best prepared and used immediately.

3. To form a dumpling, scoop out a heaping teaspoon of the dough. With a second teaspoon, smooth the top of the dough and shape the dumpling into a small egg-shaped oval. Drop each dumpling, as it is formed, into the simmering soup. Do not boil the soup. Cook the dumplings about 3 minutes. Transfer them to a bowl of warm salt water for just a few minutes as you finish cooking the soup. Place 4 to 6 dumplings in each serving bowl and top with the finished soup. Serve immediately.

Sun-Dried Tomato and Parmesan Dumplings

Yield: 16 to 20 dumplings • Prep Time: 10 minutes • Cooking Time: 10 minutes

1 cup whole wheat or
unbleached white flour
1 teaspoon non-aluminum
baking powder
2 eggs
2/3 to 3/4 cup milk
3 tablespoons minced fresh
basil
3 tablespoons diced sun dried
tomatoes
1/3 cup grated Parmesan

Dumplings make filling additions to bouillons and other light broth-based soups. The procedure for all is the same, though ingredients vary.

1. In a small mixing bowl, combine the flour and baking powder. Stir to blend. In another bowl, whisk together the eggs and 2/3 cup of milk. Stir the two together, working quickly to blend. If necessary, add the remaining milk to form a firm but soft batter. Mix in the basil, sun-dried tomatoes and Parmesan. Do not over beat, as this toughens the batter.

2. Have soup broth or salted water at a simmer in a covered pot. Shape the dumplings using 2 teaspoons. Scoop a heaping teaspoon of batter into one spoon. With the other, smooth over the top of the batter to form a small egg shape. Remove the second spoon and slip the original spoon into the simmering water; the dumpling should slide off the spoon. (If the first one does not, give it a nudge—the second one will.) Continue to shape all of the dumplings in the same manner.

3. Cover the pot and keep the broth just at a simmer. Do not allow it to boil or the dumplings will begin to disintegrate. After 10 minutes, remove the lid and serve the soup immediately.

Variations

1. For a wheat-free dumpling, use 2/3 cup rice flour, 1/4 cup soy flour, 1 teaspoon baking powder, 2 beaten eggs, 2/3 cup milk and 1/4 cup grated cheese.

2. For a rye and Leyden (spiced cheese) dumpling, use 1/2 cup each of rye and unbleached white flours, 1 teaspoon baking powder, 2 beaten eggs, 2/3 cup milk and 1/3 cup grated Leyden cheese.

Gorgonzola Won Tons

Yield: 32 won tons • Prep Time: 20 minutes • Cooking Time: 8 minutes

8 egg roll wrappers
8 ounces Gorgonzola cheese
Freshly ground black pepper

Steamed won tons make an elegant garnish for otherwise simple, clear soups. In this recipe I list several fillings that are called for in the soup recipes. But do not hesitate to experiment with your own creations. The best cheeses to use are either inherently soft or they have something added to them (such as a creamy cheese or yogurt) that will help them to bind. Select a filling for the won tons that will complement the character of the soup.

1. Stack the egg roll wrappers on a cutting board and quarter them to form 4 squares from each wrapper. Cover with a very lightly dampened kitchen towel so the wrappers do not dry out as you are shaping the won tons. Place the Gorgonzola in a small bowl and season lightly with pepper. Cream until smooth.

2. To form a won ton, place one wrapper square on a clean, dry work surface with one tip pointing to the edge of the counter so that it looks like a diamond from above. Put a teaspoon of cheese in the center of the bottom half of the won ton, then brush a thin strip of water around the edges of the bottom half of the wrapper. Fold the top half of the wrapper over the cheese to form a triangle. Tuck the wrapper snugly around the mound of cheese as you fold, and press the outer edges of the triangle together to seal.

3. Rotate the won ton 180 degrees so that the tip that was pointing down now points up, and the other two tips (now on the bottom half of the triangle) point to the sides of the cutting surface. Dampen one of the bottom half tips, then pull the two bottom half tips together, placing the undampened one on top of the other and squeezing to seal the tips together. The won ton should have a sort of tortellini shape. Set the won ton aside on a lightly floured plate while you prepare the rest. The won tons may be prepared ahead and refrigerated for several hours or frozen for up to 2 weeks, if stored in one layer on a lightly floured surface and in an airtight container.

4. To cook the won tons, bring 2 quarts of lightly salted water to a boil. Reduce to a simmer and drop the won tons into the water. Stir the water often as they cook to prevent sticking. Cook until the skins are just tender but not overly soft, about 6 minutes if refrigerated, 8 minutes if frozen. Remove from the water and drain briefly on a clean kitchen towel. Serve immediately as a garnish.

Variations

1. For curried potato won tons, sauté 1/2 cup diced onions in 1 teaspoon peanut oil until beginning to soften, about 8 minutes. Add 1 tablespoon curry powder and 1 cup cooked potatoes cut in small dice. Continue to cook for 5 minutes. Remove from the heat and stir in 1 teaspoon of brown mustard seeds that have been cooked until they pop in 1 teaspoon of peanut oil. Cool the filling before using it to fill the won tons.

2. Combine 3/4 cup low-fat ricotta cheese with 2 teaspoons minced garlic and 1/2 cup chopped basil leaves. Season to taste with salt and freshly ground black pepper.

Minted Yogurt Cheese

Yield: 1 scant cup • Prep Time: 5 minutes

This is a light nonfat cheese made from yogurt. The flavors below may be varied to suit your taste or the soup into which the cheese is mixed.

1 cup nonfat yogurt
1/2 cup chopped mint
1/2 teaspoon salt
1/4 teaspoon ground cinnamon

1. Line a strainer with two layers of cheesecloth. Place the yogurt in the cheesecloth and fold the cloth around the yogurt. Place the strainer over a bowl and refrigerate overnight.

2. When the cheese has drained for at least 6 hours, squeeze the cheesecloth gently to remove as much remaining liquid as possible. Transfer the cheese to a bowl and stir in the mint, salt and cinnamon. Use immediately or refrigerate in an airtight container for up to 2 days.

Jalapeño Butter

Yield: 1/2 pound • Prep Time: 10 minutes

2 sticks unsalted butter,
    at room temperature
1/2 teaspoon salt
1/4 cup minced jalapeño
    peppers
2 tablespoons minced garlic
1/3 cup minced fresh cilantro,
    chives or mint

This is a classic composed butter—butter to which other ingredients are added. Composed butters may be used as enrichments, stirred in just before serving a soup. Other fresh herbs or spices may be added instead of those listed below.

1. Cream the butter by hand or in a food processor. Mix in the remaining ingredients and blend thoroughly. Place the butter on a piece of wax paper and roll into a 1-inch-thick log. Chill completely, then slice into rounds before using. Composed butter will keep for 10 days in the refrigerator or may be frozen for up to 3 months.

Variations

1. Omit the jalapeños. Add 1/4 to 1/2 cup of any soft-leaved herb in place of the cilantro. Tarragon, chervil, basil, parsley and mint are particularly good. More exotic ingredients such as sorrel, nasturtium flowers, violet flowers or fennel may also be added. The garlic may be eliminated.

2. Omit the jalapeños and add 1 to 3 tablespoons of dried herbs and spices and/or a small amount of sweetener such as rice syrup. Cardamom, cumin, cinnamon and nutmeg work well.

Apple Chutney

Yield: About 2 cups • Prep Time: 10 minutes • Cooking Time: 35 minutes

1 large Granny Smith apple,
    peeled, cored and cut in
    small dice
1/3 cup diced onion
1/2 cup water
1 teaspoon minced garlic
1/2 teaspoon ginger root
5 tablespoons orange juice
1/3 cup golden raisins
1/2 teaspoon salt
1/8 teaspoon cayenne (or to taste)
1/4 cup minced cilantro

Indian chutneys can be found in a broad range of spiciness, flavors, textures and consistencies. They are used as a condiment, and though in India it is not traditional to add them to soups, they—like a pesto—work well by adding a concentrated punch of flavor.

1. In a 2-quart saucepan, combine the apple, onion, water, garlic, ginger and orange juice. Place over moderate heat and cook, stirring often, for 10 minutes. Add the raisins, salt and cayenne and continue to cook over low heat, stirring frequently, until the apples are very soft, about 25 minutes.

2. Remove the chutney from the heat and mash the apples slightly with the back of a fork. Stir in the cilantro. Transfer the chutney to an airtight container and refrigerate until ready to use. The chutney may be prepared up to a week in advance.

Pesto

Yield: 1 to 1 1/4 cups • Prep Time: 20 minutes

One of the most popular classic concoctions to hit American tables in the last ten years or so is pesto. The garlicky Parmesan and basil paste is a standard in Italian cooking used to adorn pasta and enrich various other dishes. Pistou is a similar French paste (known as a rouillé) which is stirred into a Provençal bean soup by that name. I include this recipe for pesto which may be stirred into soups as a finishing touch. Variations include a cilantro pesto as well as a dairy-free version. In all cases I give a range of ingredients you may use, depending on how strongly you want the presto to taste of garlic, cheese (or miso) and basil.

2 to 6 cloves garlic, halved with
   germinating center removed
2 tablespoons pine nuts
   (optional)
3 to 4 cups lightly packed basil
   leaves
1/2 to 1 cup freshly grated Italian
   Reggiano Parmesan
3 tablespoons room olive oil

1. Have all ingredients prepared and measured before you begin. Fit the processor with the metal chopping blade. Lock the lid in place and turn on the motor. Drop the garlic through the feed tube with the motor running. Process until it is very finely ground, scraping the sides of the bowl once or twice, if necessary.

2. Add the pine nuts and process with an on-off motion until they are evenly ground. Add the basil leaves and continue to process, using an on-off motion and scraping the sides of the bowl occasionally, until it is coarsely ground. Add the Parmesan and process to blend. With the motor running slowly add the oil. Blend until smooth. Transfer the pesto to an airtight container and refrigerate for up to 10 days, or freeze for 3 months.

Variations

1. Replace the pine nuts with toasted pumpkin seeds and the basil with cilantro.

2. Use either the original recipe or the cilantro version, replacing the Parmesan with 4 tablespoons of mellow white miso. Omit the oil. This version is very salty, which should be taken into account when using it as a flavoring. It yields about 3/4 of a cup.

Chili Paste

Yield: 1 1/2 cups • Prep Time: 20 minutes

Use this fiery paste as a condiment, served at the table, for guests to spike soups as they wish.

1 ancho pepper (page 167),
   softened in 1/4 cup hot water
1 small onion, quartered
1 jalapeño pepper, diced
2 cloves garlic, minced
1 small tomato, quartered with
   stem end trimmed
2 1/2 tablespoons cider vinegar
1/2 teaspoon salt
1 teaspoon tomato paste
1/4 cup minced cilantro or mint
1 tablespoon honey

1. Drain the ancho pepper, saving the soaking liquid. Remove and discard the stem and seeds from the pepper, then chop it and set aside.

2. In a food processor fitted with the metal chopping blade, chop the onion, using an on-off action. Add the ancho, jalapeño and garlic and pulse again to blend. Then add the remaining ingredients and mix thoroughly. If you wish to have a slightly thinner paste, mix in the reserved soaking liquid. Taste and add more salt if desired. The paste may be prepared up to a week in advance if refrigerated in an airtight container. It may be frozen for 2 months.

Maple Lime Snaps

Yield: 12 large or 36 small cookies • Prep Time: 25 minutes • Cooking Time: 10 to 15 minutes

3 egg whites
1/2 cup maple sugar (page 171)
1 lime
1 teaspoon vanilla (optional)
1/2 cup slivered almonds
6 tablespoons whole wheat
    flour
6 tablespoons melted butter
Flour for dusting

Crisp and delicate wafers perfumed with lime serve as an attractive and tasty serving bowl for a number of sweet soups. You may also shape the cookies into small rounds that may be served as a garnish alongside the soup. In this version of the classic French Tuille cookie, whole wheat flour replaces white and maple sugar is used instead of white sugar. A note of caution: forming this sort of cookie takes patience and practice, but once you get the feel for it, it is very easy.

1. Preheat the oven to 375°F. In a small mixing bowl, beat the egg whites with the maple sugar, using a fork, until the mixture is frothy. Rinse the lime well and dry it, then finely grate the zest and add this to the egg mixture. Juice the lime and stir the juice, along with the vanilla, into the eggs.

2. Fit the processor with the metal chopping blade. Add the almonds and flour and grind to a fine powder. (You may also use a blender.) Whip the nut mixture into the eggs and blend. Stir in 4 tablespoons of the melted butter, mix well and set the batter aside. The batter may be prepared up to 5 days in advance if refrigerated in an airtight container.

3. Evenly brush a large cookie sheet with melted butter, then dust it with flour, knocking off extra flour by tapping the baking sheet on the edge of the sink. For large pastry cups, trace 6 to 8 7-inch rounds on the baking sheet, using a small plate as the outline and the tip of a paring knife to mark the circumference.

4. In the center of each circle, place 1 tablespoon of batter. For each cookie, using the back of a teaspoon, spread the batter into a round the size of the outline. To do so, hold the back of the spoon parallel to the baking sheet, about 1/4 inch from the surface of the sheet. Start in the center of the circle. Making small circular strokes and working your way out from the center to the edges, shape the batter into a 7-inch round. Forming these cookies takes practice. There are several tricks to keep in mind: work quickly and trust an even circular stroke and the consistency of the batter to help in the shaping. Do not press down too hard with the spoon because tiny pieces of almond will drag on the back of the spoon and cause holes to form in the batter. Rotate the baking sheet beneath the spoon as you work. The batter should be evenly thin and transparent, without holes. To form individual cookies, use one teaspoon of batter per cookie and spread them out to about 3 inches each.

5. Place the baking sheet in the center of the oven and bake until the cookies are very lightly browned around the edges. Watch the cookies as they bake to avoid burning. Once cooked, remove them from the baking sheet and shape one by one. Using a rounded metal spatula or pancake turner, loosen the cookie from the sheet. For the large cups, invert the cookie into a rice bowl and gently press it into the bowl, allowing the edges to ripple, but forming a flat bottom. For small cookies, invert them into French bread pans or place them, baking sheet side down, over a rolling pin. Work quickly, and, if necessary, return the baking sheet to the oven between shaping each cookie so that the cookies remain soft. As soon as the molded cookies are cool and crisp, transfer them to a cake rack to cool completely. Store at room temperature in an airtight container for up to 10 days.

6. Use large cups as individual serving bowls or smaller tile-shaped cookies as a garnish for virtually any sweet soup.

Variations

1. Omit the lime flavoring.
2. Substitute 10 tablespoons of rice flour for the wheat flour.
3. Substitute pecans or other nuts for the almonds.

Ginger Snaps

Yield: 2 dozen cookies • Prep Time: 10 minutes • Cooking Time: 12 minutes

These snaps are light and crisp and make a good accompaniment to many fruit-based soups.

1. In a small saucepan, combine the butter, maple sugar, molasses, ginger, cinnamon and salt. Warm gently until the butter is melted. Combine the rice flour, baking soda and lemon zest. Stir this into the butter mixture along with the lemon juice and orange flower water. Set the batter aside at room temperature for 20 minutes.

2. Preheat the oven to 350ºF. Drop teaspoons of the batter onto a buttered cookie sheet, spacing them about 1 1/2 inches apart. Bake for 8 minutes. Remove from the oven and cool for 3 minutes on the baking sheet. Transfer to a cake rack to cool completely. Store in an airtight container at room temperature. The cookies may be prepared up to 10 days in advance.

4 tablespoons butter
1/3 cup maple sugar
5 tablespoons molasses
1 3/4 teaspoons ground ginger
1/4 teaspoon cinnamon
1/8 teaspoon salt
1 1/3 cups rice flour
1 teaspoon baking soda
1 tablespoon grated lemon zest
2 tablespoons lemon juice
1 teaspoon orange flower water (page 169) or 1 teaspoon vanilla

Lace Spice Crisps

Yield: 24 cookies • Prep Time: 10 minutes • Cooking Time: 10 minutes

These light and delicate cookie crisps can be made hot and spicy and used as an accompaniment to savory soups or made sweet and used as a complement for dessert soups.

1. Preheat the oven to 350ºF. In a small mixing bowl, combine the flour, baking powder, sugar and spices. Add the remaining ingredients and mix well. Use a 1 teaspoon measure to drop the batter on an ungreased cookie sheet about 2 inches apart, then press lightly with a fork to flatten.

2. Bake the cookies until they have lightly browned around the edges, about 15 minutes. Remove the cookie sheet from the oven. With a metal spatula, carefully remove the cookies from the sheet and transfer them to a cake rack to cool. If the cookies harden on the baking sheet before they are removed, warm them briefly in the oven to soften. Store the cookies in an airtight container at room temperature for up to 1 week.

1/2 cup whole wheat flour
1/4 teaspoon non-aluminum baking powder (optional)
1/2 cup maple sugar
1/2 teaspoon salt
1/2 teaspoon garlic powder
1/2 teaspoon cinnamon
1/4 teaspoon cloves
1/8 teaspoon cayenne pepper
6 tablespoons melted butter
3/4 cup rolled oats
2 tablespoons nonfat yogurt
2 tablespoons rice syrup (page 172)

Variation

1. Omit the salt, garlic and cayenne pepper from the dry mixture. Increase the cinnamon to 1 teaspoon and add 1/2 teaspoon dried ginger and 1/4 teaspoon allspice.

Chocolate Leaves

Yield: 24 medium-sized leaves • Prep Time: 30 minutes • Cooking Time: 10 minutes

24 fresh 1-inch leaves
12 ounces semi-sweet chocolate

Chocolate leaves make a beautiful garnish for dessert soups, strategically nestled in around fresh fruit on top of the soup or alongside the bowl. When selecting leaves to coat with chocolate, be certain they are non-toxic.

1. Line a large baking sheet with parchment or wax paper. Clean the leaves by rinsing each to remove all dust and dirt. Carefully pat the leaves dry, then lay them on a clean kitchen towel to air-dry for at least 30 minutes. The leaves may be cleaned up to 2 hours before proceeding with the recipe.

2. Chop the chocolate into rough pieces and place it in the top of a small, clean and dry double boiler (or use a small saucepan placed in a larger one, being certain that no water from the bottom pan can get into the top). Place water in the bottom of the double boiler so that it comes to the bottom of the top pan. Bring the water to a simmer with both pans in place. As the chocolate begins to melt, stir it occasionally. Do not allow drops of water to get into the chocolate at any time, or the chocolate will "seize" and become unworkable.

3. When the chocolate is thoroughly melted and has reached 115°F, remove the top pan from the heat. Wipe all water from the bottom of the pan so that it will not get into the chocolate. Stir the chocolate to cool briefly and allow it to thicken slightly.

4. Immediately coat the leaves with chocolate. To do this, hold a leaf by the stem and carefully brush the underside with chocolate. Alternatively, dip the leaf into the chocolate. In either case, do not allow the chocolate to go over the edge of the leaf or it will be difficult to unmold. Place the leaf top side down on the parchment and coat the remaining leaves. Place the baking sheet in the re-frigerator until the leaves are completely firm.

5. Peel off and discard the real leaves from the chocolate. The chocolate leaves may be refrigerated, placed in a single layer in an airtight container, for several months.

Variation

1. For carob leaves, use date-sweetened carob chips and proceed with the directions as above.

Appendix

Substitutions and Alternatives

Throughout the text I make reference to recipe substitutions and alterations that may be made if you wish to avoid certain foods in your diet.

Most often dairy products (because they are animal products and/or high in fat and cholesterol), wheat flour (because of allergies) and white sugar (because it is highly refined) are the ingredients people wish to eliminate from their diet. Below I briefly explore the function of these ingredients in cooking and how you may alter recipes to avoid them.

Eggs

Eggs serve various functions. In soups, they may serve as a high protein garnish or a thickener. Eggs may also be used to bind ingredients or as a leavening agent in baked goods. In this book when eggs are called for as a garnish or finishing touch—as in Hot and Sour Soup—they may be omitted with no problem. (Egg Drop Soup should, of course, be avoided as eggs are the primary ingredient.) When used to thicken a soup—as in Brandied Cherry Soup—they produce an extremely velvety effect. You may approximate this thickened texture by using a combination of arrowroot and kudzu. (For each cup of liquid, add 1 teaspoon arrowroot and 2 tablespoons kudzu, dissolved together in 2 tablespoons cold water, then added to the liquid. Bring the liquid to a boil and remove from the heat immediately.) When whole eggs are used as a binder—as in Spinach Walnut Dumplings—they may be replaced by drained puréed tofu mixed with flour (4 ounces tofu and 1 tablespoon flour per egg). When whole eggs are used to leaven baked goods—as in Corn Bread—2 egg whites plus 1 teaspoon of oil may replace 1 whole egg. Alternatively, for each egg you may use 4 ounces of drained tofu, puréed until smooth, or 1/4 cup of yogurt mixed with 1 teaspoon baking soda. I have not found a satisfactory substitute when egg whites are used as a binder or for clarifying soups.

Butter

Oil or margarine may be substituted, 1 to 1, for butter. I always prefer oil, except in the few instances (like a composed butter or in some baked goods) when the texture of butter is required to make the recipe work. I do not recommend margarine as enthusiastically because it is a hydrogenated fat. If, however, you are on a dairy-free diet, margarine can be an important substitute.

Milk, Cream, Yogurt, Cheese

These ingredients mellow the taste and texture of soups and make them richer in character. In baked goods milk produces a softer grain than other liquids.

Depending on the taste of the recipe, soy or rice milk may be substituted for dairy milk, 1 to 1. You may also substitute nut milk, coconut milk or soy milk fortified with dry soy milk powder for a richer effect. When cream is called for, soy cream (page 37) can be substituted, though it should not be boiled. Soy yogurt can replace yogurt and soy cheese may be substituted for cow cheese, 1 to 1. Long boiling and high heat may cause the soy milk and other soy products to separate. Fortifying the soy milk with dry soy milk powder gives it a richer quality.

Thickeners

Allergic reactions to wheat and corn are common. When flour or cornstarch is used as thickeners, alternative flours may be used to thicken, substituting 1 to 1 (page 163). Be aware of flavor and color differences that alternative flours may produce.

Grain Thickening Chart

The following is a list of common grains and starches that can be used to thicken soups. Thickness will depend both on the quantity and type of thickener used in addition to the composition of the soup. (Starchy ingredients, such as potatoes, found in the main body of the soup will increase thickness and watery ingredients, such as mushrooms, may decrease a soup's thickness.) All flours I tested thickened to approximately the same degree as wheat flour, and powdered starches were approximately the same as cornstarch. For this reason I have included only these two in the following list.

Name of Thickener	Amount of Liquid	Amount of Thickener	Comments
Wheat Flour	6 cups	1/4 cup	Unbleached white recommended
Other Flours	6 cups	5 tablespoons	May be strong or discolor soup
Cornstarch	6 cups	2 tablespoons	Breaks down if overcooked
Rice (raw)	6 cups	2 tablespoons	All types of rice thicken equally
Rice Bran	6 cups	1/4 cup	Other brans tend to separate out
Oat Bran	6 cups	3 tablespoons	More pasty than rice bran
Wheat Germ	6 cups	5 tablespoons	Heavy effect
Barley	6 cups	2 tablespoons	Pearled barley is best
Oatmeal	6 cups	2 tablespoons	Leaves lumps
Triticale	6 cups	3 tablespoons	Leaves lumps
Rye Flakes	6 cups	2 tablespoons	Strong flavor
White Potato	6 cups	1 cup (grated)	Baking type is best
Yam or Sweet Potato	6 cups	1 1/4 cups (grated)	Yams may be slightly watery
Bread	6 cups	1 1/2 cups (soft, crumbled)	Flavor of bread may intensify

Weights and Measures of Common Ingredients

Ingredient	Weight	Measure
Apple (1 average)	8 ounces	1 1/2 cups, diced
Beans (1 cup raw)		
Split peas	7 ounces	2 1/2 cups, cooked
Kidney Beans	6 1/2 ounces	2 cups, cooked
Garbanzos	6 ounces	2 cups cooked
Carrot (1 average)	3 ounces	1/2 cup, diced 2/3 cup grated
Celery (1 stalk)	3 ounces	1/2 cup, diced
Cheese	4 ounces	3/4-1 cup, grated 3/4 cup, crumbled
Garlic	1 clove	1 teaspoon, minced
Ginger	1/4-inch	1 teaspoon, minced
Kale/Greens	4 ounces	4 1/2 cups, chopped 2 cups, chopped & packed
Leeks (1 average)		
Green and white	8 ounces	2 cups, chopped
White only	8 ounces	3/4 cup, chopped
Mushrooms	1/2 pound	3 cups, sliced
Onion (1 average)	1/2 pound	1 cup, diced
Potato (1 average)	10 ounces	2 cups, diced
Scallions (2 average)	1 ounce	1/4 cup, minced
Tomato (1 average)	1/2 pound	1 cup, diced
Parsley (1 small bunch)	2 ounces	1/4 cup, minced

Definition of Terms

Acidulated Water. Water to which lemon juice or vinegar is added. Light-colored fruit and vegetables may be stored in acidulated water to retard discoloration.

Bouquet Garni. Herbs tied together with string or wrapped in cheesecloth and tied into a sachet.

Caramelize. To cook slowly, either in the oven or on top of the stove, until natural sugars contained in an ingredient are released and begin to brown, adding a rich, sweet quality to the ingredient.

Chop. To cut into pieces that are roughly square shaped. To chop most vegetables, first slice them into 1/4- to 1/2-inch-wide pieces. Stack the pieces and cut, lengthwise, into "logs," then cut crosswise into cubes. To chop herbs and other leaf vegetables, simply hold the leaves in a bunch and slice through the leaves, then cut through the pile of leaves in the opposite direction until all are evenly chopped. Small ingredients, such as cilantro, are usually chopped into smaller pieces than are large ingredients, such as tomatoes.

Cube. To cut into large pieces, usually about 1- to 1 1/2-inch square.

Dice. To cut into small cubes that are about 1/4- to 1/2-inch square. This is the same procedure as chopping, but you cut smaller pieces.

Julienne. To cut into squared strips, about the width of a small matchstick. The strips may vary in length (usually between 2 to 5 inches) depending on the requirements of the recipe. To julienne a zucchini, for instance, trim off and discard the ends. Then slice the zucchini lengthwise into 1/8-inch-wide pieces. Stack these pieces and cut them lengthwise into very thin, long pieces.

Mince. To chop very evenly and finely, as in minced garlic, parsley or ginger.

Non-reactive pan. Cookware in which foods may be cooked without discoloring. Some metals, most notably copper, aluminum and iron, "react" with foods such as eggs or ingredients with a high acid content. The result is usually that the food discolors and/or becomes metallic smelling or tasting.

Pinch. Less than 1/8 of a teaspoon. Roughly speaking, it is the amount you can hold on the tip of a paring knife.

Reduce. To boil a broth or soup without a cover in order to reduce its volume through evaporation.

Roll cut. An attractive cut, used often in Chinese cooking, for cutting carrots and some other long vegetables. To make a roll cut, slice the end off a carrot, holding the knife perpendicular to the counter and cutting straight down through the carrot so that the end cut is at about a 45 degree slant. Roll the carrot over 90 degrees (so that the side that was on top is on the counter) and move it under the knife to the length of the cut you desire. Again cut the carrot at a 45 degree slant. Repeat the rolling and cutting.

Sauté. The French word *sauté* means to jump and that is what is intended when foods are sautéed. To sauté, heat a small amount of oil or butter over medium-high to high heat until it is hot but not smoking. Add the ingredient(s) and toss to coat with the fat. There should be a sizzling sound when the ingredient hits the fat. You may sauté quickly, with the heat remaining on the original setting, or, after about a minute, reduce the heat slightly. In either case the ingredients are stirred and tossed constantly (or the pan may be shaken so that ingredients roll into the side of the pan and gently "toss" themselves).

Scald. To bring to a point just below the boil. The entire surface of a liquid seems to expand slightly and tiny bubbles are visible around the edge of the pan.

Shred. To cut into very thin strips, much like grating except the shredded pieces are usually long and paper-thin. To shred leaves, such as basil or sorrel, clean and dry the leaves, remove the stems, then stack the leaves in a neat pile. With a chef's knife or cleaver cut very thin strips, lengthwise, through the leaves. Cabbage, onions and other "layered" vegetables may be halved then shredded into fine pieces by cutting through the layers across the grain. Other vegetables may be cut into thin strips (unless they are already thin, like snow peas) and then stacked and shredded like leaves.

Simmer. Cook a liquid at a very low boil. Gentle bubbles will be visible.

Skim. To remove something (usually scum that rises to the surface when a broth or soup is first cooking) from the surface of a soup. Skimming removes impurities which sometimes leave a slightly undesired flavor in the soup and/or may affect the clarity of the broth. The best utensil for skimming is a flat, small-hole slotted spoon.

Slice. To cut in even, thin pieces. Average slice should be about 1/4 inch thick.

Steam. To place in a steaming rack, over (not touching) rapidly boiling water, then to cook, covered tightly, until tender. Vegetables cooked in this manner should be served immediately. If they are not to be eaten right away, immediately transfer them to a strainer in the sink and run cold tap water over them to stop their cooking and retain their color. Once cold to the touch, stop the rinsing and shake the strainer to remove as much water as possible. Then place the vegetables in one layer on a clean kitchen towel to drain. Prepared in this way, they may be refrigerated in an airtight container for up to 3 days before being used.

Taste and adjust the seasonings. To taste a dish just before serving after all ingredients are added. The dish should be at the temperature it will be served. Small amounts of additional seasonings—those that have already been added to the soup—are then added if desired. The best choice is often salt, pepper, cream (or a cream-like enrichment), or a freshly chopped fresh herb.

Glossary of Ingredients

Agar Agar. Red seaweed which is processed into translucent bars, flakes or powder. It has a very mild taste and is used as a vegetarian gelatin (as most commercial gelatin is derived from animal sources). Agar differs from traditional gelatin in that it must be dissolved in water, then simmered for 10 minutes. It will gel at room temperature. A small amount added to a soup which is to be served cold will give the soup a pleasant viscous quality.

Amasake. Amasake is a sweetener/beverage produced by incubating cooked sweet rice with cultured brown rice (koji). The result is a thick, very sweet liquid that may be used as an enrichment or leavener. A small amount of amasake (used as is or diluted with water) added to soups contributes creaminess and a delicately sweet taste. It is available in the dairy and/or frozen case of most natural foods stores and some supermarkets. Honey or sugar may be substituted to taste.

Ancho Pepper. Dried poblano peppers, ancho peppers are large, flat and deep red to black in color. They are mildly hot with a wholesome aftertaste.

Arame. A brown alga which is shredded into long delicate strands. It has a light flavor and texture that many people who "don't eat seaweed" enjoy. It should be quickly soaked before adding to a recipe, but should never be cooked too long, or it will begin to dissolve.

Barley Malt Powder. Dehydrated syrup which is made from sprouted barley. It is less sweet than sugar and has a strong characteristic flavor. Barley malt syrup or half the amount of molasses may be substituted.

Burdock Root. Burdock root is a long, thin, stick-like root, available in most natural foods stores and some Asian markets. Select roots that are no more than 1 inch in diameter and those that are firm, never flaccid. Burdock should be washed and scrubbed with a brush or scrubbie before use. It is usually not peeled as it discolors very quickly when exposed to the air. It lends a powerful wholesome undertone to stocks and soups and may be eaten or removed before the soup is served. Refrigerate in a loosely folded plastic bag.

Butter. I recommend using only unsalted butter in all recipes. My preference is based on two factors. First, salt is added partly as a preservative, so salted butter may be less fresh than unsalted, and the "rancid" taste is obscured by the salt. Second, if you use salted butter, you do not fully control for salt, thereby making it more difficult to get the taste you want in the finished soup. If you do not include butter in your diet, an equal measure of vegetable oil may be substituted in most soups. Depending on other ingredients found in the soup, olive, peanut or non-toasted sesame oil are good choices. You may also substitute margarine, though because it is hydrogenated, I recommend oil if it physically works in a recipe. (For some baked goods, oil does not have the desired effect.)

Chanterelle Mushrooms. Also known as girolles, chanterelles are a beautiful, light orange, trumpet-shaped mushroom. Their taste is mild and buttery, but rich. When unavailable, Hedgehog mushrooms may be substituted.

Chili Paste with Garlic. A spicy seasoning/condiment which is often used in Chinese cooking. It is made from ground chilies, garlic, oil and salt and is sold in Asian markets and many fine supermarkets. A very small amount will contribute quite a lot of heat to a dish. After opening, it will keep indefinitely if refrigerated.

Chili Peppers. Very hot small peppers, available dried and fresh in most supermarkets. The dried variety is best browned before being added to a dish, to release its strong flavor.

Chipotle Pepper. Smoked and dried jalapeño pepper. Lends heat and a smoky aftertaste to dishes. Available in Latin American markets.

Cloud Ear Mushrooms. Also called Tree Ear and Wood Ear mushrooms and are large, dark brown to black and flat. They are used for texture in many Asian dishes.

Date Sugar. This is made from ground, dehydrated dates. It is very sweet and can be substituted in equal amounts for sugar in many recipes. When stored it may clump, and it should be crushed before being measured. Date sugar tends to burn easily, so for baking it is best to mix it with a small amount of water to form a syrup, then use the syrup as you would maple syrup. Date sugar is available in most natural foods stores.

Daikon. Daikon or Japanese radish is a white root vegetable that resembles a carrot in shape. It can range in size anywhere from 8 inches to 2 feet. The root should be light in color and firm, never shriveled or bendable. The interior flesh is extremely pearly and white and makes a stunning garnish when carved into shapes or shredded. Its mild taste has a slight bite, making it an excellent last-minute addition to soups. Refrigerate in a loosely folded plastic bag.

Dulse. A purplish-red, flat-leaf sea vegetable that has been a common ingredient in the West for centuries. It may be eaten raw or quickly rinsed before being added to a dish. It also adds deep tone in taste and aroma to soups if cooked as part of the broth.

Enoki Mushrooms. Generally sold in small packages or bunches, enoki mushrooms have delicate, long white stems with tiny button caps. The root end should be trimmed and discarded, but the mushroom need not be rinsed. Their taste is mild with a distinctive fresh quality. They may be stirred into a soup, raw, at the very end. Cooked, they may become slightly "squeaky" when bitten—a quality you may or may not enjoy.

Epazote. This is an herb which grows wild throughout western United States and Mexico. It has a strong and distinctive flavor, so it should be used in moderation. When added to the cooking water of dried beans, it is said to aid in digestion.

Fermented Black Beans. Typical of Chinese cuisine, fermented black beans are beans that have been preserved in a salty brine, then dried and fermented. They are used as a flavoring in many dishes. By themselves they are overpoweringly salty and forceful. They are sold in Asian markets and many fine grocery stores.

Five-Spice Powder. A seasoning mixture, used in Chinese cuisine, made from five fragrant spices, typically star anise, Szechwan peppercorns, cinnamon, cloves and licorice root. Five-spice powder is available in Asian markets and many fine grocery stores.

Flower Water. Water perfumed by the essence of a flower, commonly rose or orange. These are often used in middle and far eastern cuisines and add a lingering aroma to a dish. They are readily available in Middle Eastern markets and many natural foods stores.

Galangal. A ginger-like root that is used commonly in Southwest Asian cooking. It is hotter but less pungent than ginger and is usually added to dishes as a smashed round, rather than minced (as ginger). It is available in Asian markets. Ginger root may be substituted.

Garam Masala. A fragrant blend of a number of spices, such as cinnamon, cloves, cumin, dried peppers and cardamom, which is used frequently in Indian cooking. Every Indian cook has their own recipe, but several commercial brands are readily available in this country at Asian markets and fine grocery stores.

Garlic. You may use either purple or white garlic for any of the recipes in this book. Elephant garlic is much milder, which must be taken into account if it is substituted. Select heads of garlic in which all cloves are firm and fit snugly to the core. The papery skin should be full, never shriveled.

To peel garlic, remove a clove from the head, then lay it down on the cutting surface. Place the flat side of the blade of a large knife on the garlic and slap the blade gently to crack the skin. Do not hit the knife so hard that the garlic is flattened. The peel should come off the clove easily. Trim off any tough root end that remains attached, then slice the clove in half lengthwise. With the tip of a paring knife, lift out and discard the germinating center of the clove. The garlic is now ready to be used in any recipe.

Occasionally whole cloves of garlic are called for in the recipes. If they are not removed from the soup at the end of cooking, they should be peeled before adding to the soup. Whole heads of garlic may also be baked and used as a condiment. Rinse the head and place it on a baking sheet. Drizzle oil over the garlic and bake, uncovered, at 350°F. for 40 to 45 minutes. A sweet, creamy "garlic paste" (far milder than its raw counterpart) may then be squeezed from each clove.

Ghee. This Indian term is simply clarified butter. The simplest method for making ghee is to cut 1 pound of butter into small pieces and place them in a heavy-bottomed, 1-quart saucepan. Melt the butter over a very low flame. Skim and discard foam that rises to the surface, then set the pan aside to cool. The solids will sink to the bottom and the ghee may be poured off the top. Refrigerated in an airtight container, ghee will keep for up to 6 months.

Ginger. Ginger is readily available fresh, in root form, pickled, crystallized and as a dried powder. Fresh ginger root should be plump with tight, smooth skin. No moldy or soft spots should be visible. A small piece broken off the main root should be an even cream to pale golden color and the broken root should give off a fresh, appealing, gingery scent. Refrigerate ginger root loose, in the vegetable drawer, for up to 3 weeks. Cut off and discard tough, woody ends before using. Pickled ginger is used in Japan and China as a garnish and pickle. Thin slices of ginger root are pickled in a salty, rice vinegar brine. Avoid brands containing artificial colors (they will be very red or bright in color). Crystallized and powdered ginger are available in the spice section of most major grocery stores. The different types of ginger can not be used interchangeably.

Hing (Asafoetida). This powerful seasoning, used extensively throughout India, is a resin extracted from Ferula plants. When dried, its flavor and aroma have a strong sulfur-like quality, and it is used, in tiny quantities, to mirror the sulfuric effect of onion. Most often you will find hing in powdered form, having been mixed with rice starch and gum arabic to prevent clumping. It is available in Asian and Middle Eastern markets and most natural foods stores. Use hing with extreme caution, as it can be overpowering.

Jalapeño Pepper. A widely available chilie pepper that is cone shaped with a rounded tip. It is usually 2 to 3 inches long, has green to red to purple skin which may have rough brown lines on it. It is medium-hot but should be handled with caution to avoid burning sensitive skin.

Jicama. A light brown-skinned, rounded oval root vegetable, common to Mexican cooking. It must be peeled. Its white flesh is crisp, juicy and slightly sweet. It may be eaten raw or added for the final minutes of cooking to soups.

Kombu. Kombu is a sea vegetable which is sold in 8- to 12-inch strips. It resembles a stiff, grey-black piece of wood, and is used in stocks and when cooking beans both for flavor and to increase digestibility of beans.

Kuzu. Kuzu is a white powdery starch—used as a thickener—which is derived from the root of the kudzu plant. It has been used in the Orient for centuries, where it is believed to aid digestive disorders. For soup making, it serves as a thickener, much like arrowroot, but with a beautiful, translucent quality. When stored, it tends to clump and must be crushed with a fork before being mixed with cold water for use.

Leeks. Leeks are a fundamental ingredient in many soups. If they are unavailable, you may substitute a mixture of 3/4 white onions and 1/4 scallions. Recipes in which leeks predominate (vichyssoise, leek soup, etc.) should be avoided if leeks are not available.

Select leeks that are slender and firm, without slimy or tough outer leaves. Leeks often contain a great deal of dirt inside the leaves, so they must be cleaned thoroughly. To do so, slice off the root end, even with the bottom of the leek. With the tip of a paring knife, carve out and discard a cone-shaped piece from the tough root end core. Trim off tough pieces of the green top and remove all tough outer leaves. Place the leek on a cutting surface and cut it, lengthwise, beginning about 1 inch from the root end and slicing through the leek up to the top of the green part. Turn the leek over 90 degrees and cut again in the same manner. Rinse the leek under cold water, rubbing the leaves inside and out and making certain to rinse out the center of the leek.

Lemon Grass. Lemon grass is an ingredient often used in Thai and other southeast Asian cuisines. Stalks of lemon grass are available in Asian markets and should be selected for firm, light-colored bulbs with fresh looking stem tops. It adds a very pleasant lemony aroma to dishes and, though large pieces of the stalk may be served in a dish, only finely sliced, very fresh bulb ends are eatable. To prepare lemon grass, trim top stems and tough outer leaves from each piece of lemon grass, leaving stalks 5 to 6 inches long. Place a stalk on the counter and lay the flat side of a cleaver or large knife over the end of the lemon grass. Slap the cleaver with the heel of your hand to flatten the stalk, then roll the stalk over, move the cleaver up the stalk and slap it again. To release optimal flavor, the lemon grass must be flattened by the blows. Refrigerate lemon grass stalks in a loosely folded plastic bag, or with the tips of the bulb ends immersed in a small amount of water.

Lemon (Lime or Orange) Zest. Citrus zest is obtained by grating—on the finest grating disk available—the outermost layer of skin from fresh citrus. The under layer of the skin and the pith should not be included in the gratings. As citrus is often highly sprayed with pesticides, it is advisable *always* to wash and dry the fruit well before zesting. When available, organic citrus is preferable.

Lily Buds. Lily buds may be purchased, dried, in Asian markets and many fine supermarkets. They are the' buds from a particular type of Tiger Lily flower and add an interesting texture and subtle tang in flavor to a soup.

Lime Leaves. Fresh lime leaves are used in many Asian dishes for their slightly bitter, lime undertone. They are available in Asian markets. A small amount of grated lime zest may be substituted.

Maple Sugar. Maple sugar is crystallized maple syrup. It may be used interchangeably with sugar in most recipes, though it has a distinctively maple taste. It is available sold in bulk in many natural foods stores. Pre-bottled maple sugar is also available, but it tends to be far more costly.

Mirin. Mirin is a sweet Japanese cooking wine made from sweet rice. The best quality mirin is made from sweet rice, rice koji and water with no added sugar, alcohol or chemical fermenting agents.

Miso. A fermented soy bean paste which is made by mixing cooked beans with a mold (koji), salt and water. The mixture ferments for anywhere from 2 months to 5 years. Other beans or grains may also be mixed into the paste. The best misos are non-pasteurized. Different types of beans used and variations in storage time and place, results in misos that taste very different. All are notably salty, but they may be mild, light and mellow, or pungent and dark. In soup making, miso adds depth and slight body with quality reminiscent of meat broth. Miso contains an enzyme (lactobacillus bacteria) that aids in digestion. This enzyme is killed if the soup is boiled

When first tasting miso, many people prefer the lighter varieties or those, such as natto miso, that have other ingredients added to the paste (in this case ginger and barley). As with most ingredients, it is best, therefore, to experiment with various flavors and find which suit your personal preference. Miso will last indefinitely if refrigerated, tightly covered. If a small amount of mold forms on the surface, it should be scraped off and discarded, but the rest of the miso should be safe to eat.

Mochi. Mochi, a traditional feast food in Japan, is made from rice that is soaked, steamed and pounded. The paste is then rolled into an even thickness and is dried in slabs. A vacuum-packed variety is available, as are fresh, more perishable brands which need refrigeration. Texture varies from brand to brand. Mochi is available in most natural foods stores. Before eating, mochi must be baked or simmered.

Morel Mushrooms. These mushrooms are a distinctive brown to dark brown color for which there is no substitute. They have hollow, cone-shaped caps with a spongy look to them. Their rich, nutty flavor and meaty texture make them an excellent addition to dishes that contain a variety of mushrooms. Beware of false morels—sometimes found in the wild—if eaten raw they are deadly.

Non-aluminum Baking Powder. Baking powder to which no aluminum is added. Available in most natural food stores.

Nori. Most commonly known as the wrapping for nori rolls, nori sheets are made by finely chopping a sea vegetable, then drying it into a sheet by laying it on bamboo mat. Its flavor is enhanced by toasting it; passing it very quickly over the flame of a gas burner, or under a broiler until it darkens in color, curls and crisps slightly.

Pasilla Peppers. These peppers are sold both fresh and dried in Latin American markets. They are a moderately hot pepper that measure 5 to 6 inches in length and about 1 inch in width, with a blunt end. They are dark green when fresh and a dark red-brown when dried.

Poblano Pepper. A deep green, fresh pepper which matures to a dark red. It is usually 3 1/2 to 4 inches long, less rounded than a bell pepper and is wide at the stem end then tapers to a point. It is mildly hot and is available in Latin American markets and fine grocery stores.

Porcini Mushrooms. Also called cepes, porcini mushrooms have a rich aroma and wholesome, alluring quality. They have light brown, umbrella-shaped caps and thick, meaty stems. You are more likely to find them dried than fresh.

Rice Milk. This is sold commercially by one large company and locally by small producers. It is made by grinding cooked rice, then draining the liquid. It may have oil added to it for consistency.

Rice Noodles. Translucent noodles made from rice flour that, when cooked, have a delicate, slightly rubbery texture. They are available in thick and thin cut and require very little, if any cooking, beyond a brief soak in hot liquid. Rice noodles are available in Asian markets and many fine grocery stores.

Rice Syrup. Rice syrup and rice malt syrup are made from adding either an enzyme from sprouted barley, or the sprouted barley itself to cooked rice. The resulting thick syrup resembles honey in appearance but is thicker and less intensely sweet. Rice malt syrup has a distinctive barley taste to it, whereas the simple syrup has a gentle, mellow quality. Rice syrup may be substituted in equal amounts for honey, though the result will be less sweet. It is available in natural foods stores.

Scallions. Also called green onions, scallions are a fundamental flavor of Asian-style stocks and are used chopped or shredded in many soups. Select scallions that are moderate in size (those that are too large will be tough, and small scallions are more difficult to work with). They should be crisp and never slimy. To clean them, slice off the root ends and tough top section of leaves. Pull off all tough outer leaves, and pull off any slimy, transparent layer of leaf that remains. Rinse the scallions well and pat them dry on a clean kitchen towel. Cleaned scallions may be refrigerated in a loosely folded plastic bag for up to 4 days.

To mince, chop or shred scallions, line up about a hand's width of cleaned scallions on a chopping board so that they are parallel to the counter edge. Have all white ends facing in the same direction. Use the edge of the cleaver or chef's knife to even the ends into a neat row. Place the flat edge of the knife on the white end of the scallions, and slap the knife with your other hand to flatten the scallions. Move the knife to the top of the scallions and slap again. To mince or chop, carefully slice the row of scallions in half lengthwise. First, hold all of the scallions in place with one hand and, using a sawing motion, slide the knife from the white ends of the onions to the green tips. As you begin to work the knife through the scallions, you will have to hold the green ends in place. As you continue to move the knife towards the green ends, transfer your hold on the scallions to the sliced white ends and pull the knife through. If you are mincing, cut the strips crosswise into very small pieces. To shred the scallions, after slicing them in half lengthwise, cut them crosswise, in half. Place the two piles of scallions next to each other and cut them lengthwise into fine strips.

Seitan. Used extensively in Asia as a meat substitute, seitan is the gluten that remains when wheat flour is rinsed and kneaded in water. Whole wheat flour when soaked briefly, then gently rinsed and drained again and again, will yield an elastic, fibrous ball of seitan. It is a concentrated source of protein and, once simmered in a flavorful broth, becomes a very meat-like ingredient. Seitan may be made from scratch (a rather laborious endeavor), or from a convenient package mix made by Arrowhead Mills. It may also be bought ready cooked, but in this case has distinctive flavor that might not complement a recipe. In all forms it is sold in most natural foods stores. Cook raw seitan within 24 hours. Simmered seitan will keep, refrigerated in its cooking liquid, for up to 5 days. For more information about seitan and its uses I recommend reading *The Book of Seitan*, by Barbara and Leonard Jacobs.

Serrano Pepper. A small, slightly curved chili pepper that usually ranges in size from 1 to 2 inches and may be green, red or orange-brown. It is very hot and care should be exercised after touching to avoid burning the eyes or other sensitive skin. These peppers are sold fresh in the produce section of many fine grocery stores. Jalapeño pepper may be substituted.

Shallots. Shallots look like red-brown, skinned, large cloves of garlic and have a rich, onion-like flavor that has an edge of garlic. If they are unavailable, substitute a mixture of 3 1/2 tablespoons chopped onion and 1 teaspoon chopped garlic for each 1/4 cup of shallot called for in a recipe.

Shiitake Mushrooms. Known in Japan as the "perfumed" mushroom, shiitakes are commonly used in Chinese and other Asian cuisines. They have large, flat tawny brown caps with cream-colored undersides. They are slightly chewy with what is sometimes characterized as a "meaty" taste.

Szechwan Peppercorns. A seasoning commonly used in Chinese cooking, Szechwan peppercorns are an open-husked peppercorn with a penetrating aroma and taste. They are best toasted before being added to dishes.

Soba Noodles. These classic Japanese noodles have a narrow, flat shape and are traditionally made from 100% buckwheat. All soba noodles have a grey hue to them, some darker than others. Those made with additional flours may be lighter in color and less expensive. Soba noodles are available in Asian markets and most natural food stores.

Soy Cheese. A relatively new food found in some natural foods stores. Soy cheese comes in various flavors and, depending on the brand, may be very creamy (or even rubbery) to dry. It is made from soy milk to which caseinate and natural flavorings are added. It is an acquired taste, eaten raw, but may be considered a valuable cholesterol-free non-dairy addition to the diet. The creamier varieties melt more evenly when baked. Soy cheese may be substituted for dairy cheese in all recipes.

Soy Milk. The liquid resulting from ground soy beans which are cooked in water, then strained. It is available commercially in various flavors ("original" usually meaning plain). It may be sold fresh in the dairy case or unrefrigerated in aseptic packages. It has a slight chalky taste but should never smell or taste unpleasant. Soy milk may be substituted for dairy milk in all recipes, though it curdles easily when boiled, especially in the presence of acid. When substituting it in soups, it may need to be added towards the end of cooking, if long cooking is required.

Soy Milk Powder. Soy milk powder is dehydrated soy milk. It is sold in bulk in many natural foods stores and some Asian markets.

Soy Yogurt. Another newcomer to the market is yogurt made with yogurt culture but using soy milk instead of dairy milk. It may be substituted for dairy yogurt in all recipes.

Straw Mushrooms. Most commonly found canned, straw mushrooms are a small variety with dark brown-grey caps and creamy stems. They are mild in flavor and add good texture to soups.

Sun-Dried Tomatoes. Sun-dried tomatoes are available dry and packed in oil. The most delectable are those from Italy that have been packed in seasoned oil. They are also far higher in price and fat content than those that are simply dried. This variety must be soaked in hot water before using. (You may then drain them and soak them in good quality olive oil with garlic and other seasonings, if you wish—but they are then high in fat.) You may use either in these recipes, but be familiar with the brand and type you choose, as those that are packed in oil can have an intense, overpowering flavor and you may need to use fewer.

Tahini. Tahini is a peanut butter-like paste made from finely ground, hulled sesame seeds. It is available toasted or untoasted (which has a raw but milder flavor) in most large grocery stores and natural foods markets.

Tamari and Soy Sauce. Traditional seasonings used throughout Asia in many recipes for their salty taste and rich, caramel color. Soy sauce (known as shoyu) is traditionally made from soybeans, wheat and salt that are fermented in wooden kegs—much like wine—for at least 2 years. Traditional tamari is somewhat like soy sauce in taste, but it is the liquid which rises and is skimmed from the surface of miso. Traditionally, tamari contained no wheat and was more intensely flavored than soy sauce. Today both soy sauce and tamari have become so popular in the West that the names have not always remained true to traditional methods of preparation. There has been an attempt to clarify the confusion, so most companies now label the sauces: tamari shoyu or soy sauce (for that prepared with wheat) and tamari (for that prepared without wheat). More recently, low sodium soy sauce has become available. The best is made from a double fermentation process in which no salt is added to the second fermentation. Check the label when you buy any brand of tamari or soy sauce. The more information you can glean from this, the more likely you are to get a satisfactory sauce. Look to be certain that whole beans were used, whether or not the sauce contains wheat, how the reduction of sodium was achieved and that no colors or preservatives were added. Soy sauce sold in Asian markets—and some sauces—may not always have this kind of information on the label, so again, experimenting with brands until you find one that suits you is advisable.

Tamarind. Tamarind is the pod from a tall tamarind tree that grows in India and throughout Southeast Asia. The pods are peeled and seeded, then compacted into blocks before being sold. Tamarind has a very dark brown color and strong, lemon-like aroma. It must be softened in hot water and strained before being used.

Tempeh. A traditional food of Indonesia, tempeh is made from whole, cooked soy beans which are incubated with a mold culture (Rhizopus oligosporus). This causes the beans to bind together. It has a full flavor and meat-like texture. Other ingredients (sea vegetables, seeds, nuts, etc.) may be added to the tempeh before it ferments, resulting in variations of taste and texture. Tempeh may be found in the dairy or frozen cases of many natural foods stores. It may be stored frozen, for up to 3 months and will keep refrigerated, well wrapped, for up to a week. The mold on the tempeh continues to "ripen" when refrigerated and flavor will intensify. If the tempeh has a powerful smell or has a green tinge to it, do not eat it. Tempeh is best cooked for at least 20 minutes to aid digestibility.

Tofu. Soy milk which has a curdling agent added to it (usually nigari). It is then drained and pressed, like cheese. Depending on these factors, its texture may be soft or firm. Tofu has a very mild taste that makes it an ideal ingredient in soups to counter or absorb strong flavors.

That sold fresh, often found in Asian markets, should be eaten within a few days of purchase. Packaged, refrigerated tofu will have an expiration date clearly marked on it and should be consumed by that date. Aseptic packages of "silken" tofu—which is very smooth—may be stored at room temperature for months before being opened. All unused portions of tofu should be refrigerated in a glass or plastic container which should be filled with fresh water daily. When refrigerated tofu has become sour, the water surrounding it will be cloudy and the tofu will have a rancid, sour smell. It should not be used in this case.

All tofu, except silken varieties, may be frozen. To do so, drain the block of tofu, then slice it into 1-inch-thick blocks. Individually wrap these slices in plastic, then place them in an airtight container and freeze until solid. Tofu will keep frozen for up to 2 months. Before using, thaw the tofu in its wrapper, then place it, unwrapped, between two cutting boards. Press the boards together and place a heavy skillet on top. Drain for 30 minutes. The tofu may then be grated, chopped or diced. The texture of tofu changes radically when frozen; it is more firm, almost spongy and meat-like. Frozen tofu responds very well to long cooking.

Tree Oyster Mushrooms. These mushrooms are a light pearl grey to brown that look like a fan and may come in clusters. Their flavor is mild and, when cooked, their texture is reminiscent of true oysters. They are available canned in some Asian markets, but fresh tree oysters are far superior.

Udon Noodles. Udon noodles are a flat Japanese wheat noodle, about the width of fettucini. They are light in color, with a delightful, chewy texture. If unavailable fettucini may be substituted. Udon noodles are available in Asian markets and most natural food stores.

Wakame. A very tender, delicate-tasting sea vegetable. It cooks very quickly and gives delightful aroma and texture to soups. It is traditionally found in miso soup.

Index

About the Author

Mary F. Taylor received the Grande Diplome from L'Ecole des Trois Gormandes in Neuilly, France and trained at L'Ecole LeNotre. More recently, Taylor studied classic Indian cooking while living in Mysore, South India. She has many years' experience teaching, cooking and catering. She also spent six years working in various facets of the natural foods industry. She is passionate in her pursuit of well-being and peace of mind through good food, good eating, yoga and laughter. She lives in Boulder, Colorado.

The Crossing Press
publishes many cookbooks.
For a free catalog, call toll-free
800/ 777-1048
Please specify a cookbook catalog